Blockchain Prophecy

GARY MCALISTER

 Gary McAlister PO Box 1010 Maroochydore, Queensland 4558
www.BankcoinReserve.com

First Printing: 2017.

ISBN: 0648173704

ISBN-13: 978-0648173700

DEDICATION

This Guidebook is dedicated to my team who has never wavered in their conviction to support and work around the clock on this project with me. My wonderful lady Nina of 28 years; how lucky I am to have someone as supportive as her. When at times it seems all is for nothing, she picks me up and says, try another way. This book is one such "another way".

Ruthie and David, my partners in the U.S., especially Ruthie who worked with me day and night (my day-her night and my night-her day), for the last few years. Ruthie and her team have truly been amazing. My brothers and sisters, who have been there for me in finance and in faith, are sincerely appreciated.

My Uncle Ahi, including all the shareholders in AAABlockchain Ltd, for stepping up when everyone else thought I was crazy when I said we are going to transition our financial system, from interest to earnings, using Bankcoin and the Blockchain. He said when do we start? My brother Thomas for pulling the discovery apart, and formulating it into the most incredible wholesale retail model I have ever seen. Paul Birch and his team for their continued dedication and support. Betty, Geoff, Doug, and Barry for working tirelessly on Country, Treasury, and private placement trade programs. Rabbi Nathan (Nate) Segal and family for giving me their time in prayer and guidance. Gary Karena and team for their prayers. Ivan and team from DHealth who just keeps pushing those boundaries it's incredible.

To all those working on blockchain don't give up keep going people are going to say you are crazy and that it can't be done when you know somehow it can please keep going do not let anyone or anything stop you.

CONTENTS

Table of Contents

ACKNOWLEDGMENTS

I would like to acknowledge our forefathers who for many years tried to find a solution to the debt-based riba, usury, interest-bearing equation. Hon. Charles N. Fowler who I pay tribute to in this guidebook said it best, that the Central Bank model has fundamental defects. He tried for nine years to remedy them, to no avail. I also pay tribute to Sir Henry Fowler (later Viscount Fowler). His committee recommended that the official Indian rupee be based on the gold standard and was often referred to as the Fowler Committee.

Because of Blockchain technology which led to The Bankcoin Reserve (BCR) patented solutions, these defects can now be addressed by every Country, Bank, Credit Union, financial institution, monetary fund, and individual around the world.

Trained BCR engineering techs have developed solutions that Countries can use to regain their Sovereignty over time, with enough incentive to never go back to the system of borrowing at interest; meaning to take from Peter (the tax payer) to pay Paul (the multinational lender who types in the digits to make the loan).

Now, the "borrowing-at-interest" days are reaching an end. Leaders around the world have an opportunity to once and for all say enough of the old ways. Let's look to the future and put in place a parallel system that is pro-growth and pro-Sovereignty; a system that will help pay down debt and interest, and start to build the Countries' Sovereign Treasury reserves sustainably. That system is using this new AAABlockchain technology and Patented digital mining commodities/assets (Bankcoin's) from The Bankcoin Reserve (BCR) who sets the market price via its formula and rating

SOVEREIGN SOLUTION

Great leaders understand true Sovereignty. The issue has always been that there was no way to be truly sovereign when a Country borrows from multinational entities. With interest rates accruing, these entities hope that the Country will never be able to pay back the loan, thereby forcing the Country to give up its Sovereign wealth, land, water, fishing rights, votes, etc.

The Bankcoin Reserve (BCR) offers a truly Sovereign solution.

AAABlockchain Limited technology provides a set of rails called digital Blockchain; and on those rails the ability to transfer a digital commodity.

Blockchain is a self-calculating ledger with enormous capacity to maintain a continuously growing list of records (blocks), with a timestamp and link to a previous block. Once recorded, the data in any given block cannot be altered. The ledger itself can also be programmed to trigger transactions automatically.

The Australian Tax Office (ATO) has ruled Blockchain to be an asset; and the Commodities Futures Trading Commission (CFTC) in the USA has ruled Blockchain to be a commodity. As a truly Sovereign solution, by way of BCR Patented products and proprietary processes, The Bankcoin Reserve (BCR) provides digital mining and mined commodities to Countries by way of allocation at no cost.

Therefore, all Countries with smart leaders understand the benefits of putting in a set of rails (Blockchain) as a backup, alongside the Country's existing financial system. The use of The Bankcoin Reserve (BCR) Bankcoin and AAABlockchain solutions will pay down the interest and debt the Country owes externally, enabling the Country to regain and strengthen its Sovereign position.

The Bankcoin Reserve's (BCR) solution is to plug and play, meaning the technology simply sits on a computer tablet. No changes need to be made to Country's current operations. There is no interference or disruption of the existing financial institutions in the Country. BCR's Patented solution is developed and designed to transition the Country from a debt-based, interest-bearing system to a Sovereign reserve, revenue-earning system.

For example: Country's GDP is $40B (U.S. Dollars). The Bankcoin Reserve (BCR) allocates 10% of that amount in Bankcoin digital mining commodities, $4B, at no cost to the Country. The Bankcoin amount will be mined on the Blockchain for the Country's Treasury at 1% of its GDP, $400M per annum, debt and interest free, under contract for 25 years. (There is a one-time setup fee of 0.1% of $400k.)

The Bankcoin Reserve (BCR) can increase the allocation over time, with a number that is appropriate, as there is a 10% of GDP hard-coded cap.

Additional revenue to the Country will come from the match of $400M from the Bankcoins BCR monetizes, using the same process as for the Treasury.

The IMF, World Bank, ADB, UN and all those institutions that are in the business of buying Treasury bonds and/or making loans available to these Countries, can transition to Bankcoin under a license agreement that will enable them to generate more money, as well as more control. Bankcoin is a product and process they can work hand in hand with. Therefore, institutions that are in the lending business can engage with The Bankcoin Reserve (BCR), learn the product, understand it fully, acquire a license, and go/grow forward.

The Bankcoin Reserve (BCR) has multiple models available. BCR along with AAABlockchain "Blockchain" solutions provide an upgrade to Country's current way of doing business.

The benefits to Countries using BCR Bankcoin along with Blockchain are:

• To remove the need for the Country to borrow and be indebted to external entities.

• Since the Country no longer needs to borrow, the interest burden is no longer there for the tax payers to repay. Country no longer needs to sell new Treasury bonds to pay down the interest on old Treasury bonds.

• BCR Bankcoin is the only Sovereign product available that is asset/commodity-based with an earning/yield/revenue secondary mining product and process protected by its Patents.

• Governments (Countries) now have a new revenue-earning model to work with and can reduce taxes accordingly to offset this new gain.

• Treasury now has a new revenue model that is not coming from the people of the Country via increased taxes. With BCR Bankcoin, the Treasury can reduce and/or eliminate income tax all together.

• The Internal Revenue Department (IRD) now has several new revenue streams coming in which helps their budget and will minimize their deficits.

• The Central Bank has a new revenue model to cover its costs and make a profit, which is also good for private Banks.

• BCR Bankcoin is plug and play, simple to implement, with not much training required. Possible technical problems have been addressed.

• Anti-money laundering and know your customer (AML/KYC) compliance, auditing and insurance is covered. As BCR Bankcoin is private, all entities are known and is a closed loop, meaning no external entities can enter.

• The Bankcoin Reserve (BCR) is fully committed to the Countries it enters, therefore 10% of the BCR matched funds are left in the Country for job creation and infrastructure; and 10% is committed externally to bring in what it believes the Country needs: training, teachers, schools, hospitals, staff and machinery. The 10% committed funds will be used to fund these specialty items.

Notes:

2 QUESTIONS & ANSWERS

What is The Bankcoin Reserve (BCR) Bankcoin?

In 2014, The Bankcoin Reserve (BCR) started to mine its cryptocurrency Bankcoin on the Blockchain. Bankcoin, initially created as a Banking and financial product, fully adheres to the laws and regulations set by governments. In Australia, Bankcoin was ruled an asset. In the United States, Bankcoin was ruled a commodity. So, from that point forward, Bankcoin became an asset and/or a commodity.

BCR discovered and developed Bankcoin for Banks to address the flaws in the Banking system. After three years of development and testing, Bankcoin is ready for implementation along with AAABlockchain Ltd. Blockchain Patented products and processes.

• What is AAABlockchain Ltd.?

Registered as AAABlockchain Ltd., Belize (Commonwealth Country), Director Nina Taylor holds the patents for all AAABlockchain systems and projects.

• What is The Bankcoin Reserve (BCR)?

BCR was instituted to provide the Bankcoin community with security and a stable price and pricing mechanism (gold ounce price). Should any issues arise throughout the Bankcoin network, BCR has multiple Bankcoin holdings for a secure position. The Bankcoin Reserve is the authority over all Bankcoin discoveries. It is a self-regulated Reserve and complies with all national and international regulations, including know your customer and anti-money laundering (KYC/AML).

• How was The Bankcoin Reserve (BCR) Bankcoin Price Formula determined?

The Bankcoin Reserve (BCR) sets the price for Bankcoin using the International Standard for pricing. Bankcoin pricing is now set on the 1st of every month by taking the ceiling market price of 1 ounce gold over the previous month. That amount then becomes the floor price of Bankcoin for the next month. If the price in the gold market has not changed, only the date will be changed. If gold has gone over the current Bankcoin price, that change will be reflected on the website. The current price is announced as the 'Fixed' price for Bankcoin and all business is conducted based on that price. BCR is a market price-taker not a market price-maker, meaning the gold market determines the price. For market stability and confidence, BCR uses that price as the floor price for Bankcoin.

• What problems are solved by BCR Bankcoin?

BCR Bankcoin is a high value/low volume proposition; exactly what Banks, financial institutions, insurance, and monetary-funds require. The problem of being able to move large sums of asset commodity value around the world quickly at very low cost is solved by BCR Bankcoin. To move 1M Bankcoin's, fiat value $1.375B (U.S. Dollars) from one Country to the other, it takes a few seconds and a network fee cost of 52 cents.

Bankcoin's are geared to Banks and financial institutions. Therefore, the amount of Bankcoin's moved is not an issue. The built-in private exchange of Bankcoin's eliminates the need to engage multiple exchanges. It also eliminates, on the other side, the need to wait for "however long it takes" to unload the Bankcoin's; the liquidity would be there at any value.

The BCR Bankcoin and AAABlockchain system provides Governments, Banks, Family Offices, and individuals with a high net worth, a quick, viable method to move funds from Country to Country, at minimal cost.

The Bankcoin Reserve (BCR) does not buy low and sell high when the market embraces volatility. BCR Bankcoin is the complete opposite. Buy. Hold to mine up to 10% pa. Sell what you mine – at a stable price – with upside growth and minimal downside risk.

Two sets of gains include secondary mining up to 10% per annum, and the possibility of the gold price increasing.

• What opportunities do The Bankcoin Reserve (BCR) Bankcoin provide to Banks, financial institutions, etc.?

Bankcoin is an asset commodity. Banks that want to increase their loan book, can accept Bankcoin as collateral from BCR Bankcoin holders who want a loan to acquire a business, building, or anything that is income producing.

The technology involves either installing a Bankcoin wallet in the Bank's built-in, private exchange platform (website), or accepting the Bankcoin wallet on an 8" tablet. The Bankcoin "client" can then start mining for the Bank as part of the arrangement, if desired or required.

Is The Bankcoin Reserve (BCR) Bankcoin Scalable?

The Bankcoin Reserve (BCR) was granted Patents (registered in the Commonwealth of Australia Patents Office) and also on WIPO that allow BCR the ability to discover new Bankcoin's on the Blockchain. Each Country that comes onboard would have its own Bankcoin on the Blockchain. Each Country that comes onboard would have its own Blockchain; and a specific set of protocols.

• What are the Protocols?

Each Country has its own BCR Bankcoin, i.e., BankUS and BankAU. The Bankcoin Reserve (BCR) determines the amount of capacity that the Country's Bankcoin-mine needs. For example, 100M BankAU is discovered. From that, BCR determines value of the Bankcoin discovery using a formula based on GDP of Country. The Country's Bank must secondary mine.

For example, BCR Bankcoin "BANK" on the Blockchain, has a market valuation of $1,375.00 (determined by the 1 ounce price of gold). Whereas BCR Bankcoin "BANKA" on the Blockchain has a market valuation of $13,750.00. BANKA is a private Bankcoin and used as an insurance asset commodity. Once discovered, more fiat value cannot be added to it. (Similarly, a politician who maxes out his credit card cannot then vote to raise the debt ceiling to increase his credit card limit.) These are the protocols and discoveries BCR determines for each Country, each Bank, each financial institution, etc.

- Is The Bankcoin Reserve (BCR) Bankcoin scarcity real?

BCR Bankcoin is scarce because the price cannot go to zero. What this means is there will be a limited number of Bankcoin's in the marketplace to acquire. This may be expected to diminish over time as more and more Countries acquire Bankcoin for the specific purpose of staking what comes through the Bankcoin network, and to mint the transaction fees.

If a Country's Central Bank has 1,000 Bankcoin's valued at $1.375M and it is mining up to 10% per annum, 100 Bankcoin's over the year, in addition to the 1,000 Bankcoin's, at the end of the year the Bank will have 1,100. Divide 100 by 365 and you get 0.27397260 a day, $376.71. (These are approximate numbers because mining is not an exact science.)

- What makes The Bankcoin Reserve (BCR) Bankcoin unique?

BCR Bankcoin is unique because of its ability to cater to any, and all, sectors. BCR Patents explain Bankcoin's vast capabilities to change and improve a system when it comes to interest usury, riba. Fiat can be traded for Bankcoin which, when mined will add 10% per annum. Bankcoin can be used as security or collateral against loans. Bankcoin can be used to insure/underwrite. The ethical uses for Bankcoin are endless.

BCR discovered and developed Product innovations that blend delivery methods to suit the Banks and the specific needs of customers. Because of that, Banks will see a measurable improvement in the performance of their accounts, an instant return on investment, and the development of new markets.

• How much will The Bank Coin Reserve (BCR) Bankcoin investment cost a Country?

There is no direct cost to the Country or its citizens. All secondary mining operations, meaning the 10%, are what gets monetized by the Central Bank, including the Treasury and Central Bank and BCR's matched funds. There are no direct costs to the Country; the mining 10% covers everything.

• How long would it take to implement?

Because The Bankcoin Reserve (BCR) manages all the Bankcoin's, all contracts are dealt with by BCR and a third party professional International accounting/auditing firm. The only thing that needs to be done in the Country is the installation of a laptop/tablet to accept Bit messages. This is a closed loop system. Blockchain messaging systems are in play fast, are secure peer to peer, and is free.

• Can a Central Bank monetize?

Absolutely! Central Bank charters provide Banks with the license and ability to acquire assets/commodities. With The Bankcoin Reserve (BCR) Bankcoin, this is exactly what they would be doing.

Bankcoin's are Product assets/commodities. Processed on the Blockchain, Central Banks can monetize and hold those assets/commodities as Sovereign reserves for when natural disasters arise. Banks can leverage their Bankcoin's to deal with their Country's disasters, and other needs, as opposed to requesting aid packages from other Countries.

This process is not new; Countries were once on the gold standard and the Banks had gold reserves. This technological financial innovation could be equated to going back to the gold standard. The main difference is that this asset/commodity has a secondary mining component that increases, whereas gold fluctuates in price and is only a fraction of the fiat leant out against it.

To clarify this point; if you had one Bankcoin and held it for a year it would, by default, secondary-mine approximately 10% per annum. That 10% can be monetized and/or held as reserve. And that one Bankcoin will do it all over again the next year. In comparison, if the market price went up, to realize that gain from 1 ounce of gold with the same value, it would have to be sold, leaving .9.

• So, knowing this, how can The Bankcoin Reserve (BCR) Bankcoin bring the Country back onto a gold standard using the Blockchain innovation where there are no losers?

BCR Bankcoin provides new money and new wealth that is debt and interest free - allowing for a Sovereign Country where everyone prospers. Countries could also implement Bankcoin as a Sovereign option out of the Treasury, an option that may be quicker and may only require an executive order, especially if the Central Bank is privately owned. This option eliminates indebting the nation.

• What is the innovations' main purpose?

To transition the government/Country from a debt-based interest imposition to an asset/commodity earnings model that puts the Country into a positive and sustainable position - a position where the Country no longer needs to pay down debt and interest to outside external multinational entities.

Each Country is different. For example, a Country that owns $3T in US Treasury bonds is not sovereign. Sovereignty is a Country that owns $3T in surplus earning - enough per annum where there is no deficit. Sovereignty is a Country that exports or trades its surplus to other Countries.

Another innovative purpose is to strengthen the Country's Treasury's position, specifically Countries that must increase taxes as the only way to increase its revenues, taxes instituted primarily to pay the interest on loans.

The Bankcoin Reserve (BCR) Bankcoin innovation makes it possible for the Country's Treasury to grow with population growth when the numbers are worked out correctly as GDP per capita. For example, each new child that is born should have a Sovereign position within the Country. Monetization of a birth certificate is flawed as it does not directly signify the requirements of the child's needs in relation to public education, healthcare and all the things required and necessary before that child is old enough to contribute to the Country and/or society. The other issue is when that child does come of contributing age, such as sixteen and leaves the Country, leaving a sixteen-year debt burden on the public purse that the Treasury cannot make up.

Bankcoin innovation creates reserves in the positive for those sixteen years, whether the child contributes or not. Bankcoin continues to mine and/or discover new mines for the Treasury for the length of the contract.

Another beneficial purpose is the Country's Central Bank now has an income stream that it did not previously have. The Country therefore has the capacity to support the public and private sector via its tools and instruments in relation to retail commercial Bank connections which lend and borrow from the Central Bank and create the climate for growth among the business sector. By default, this leads to increased confidence minimizing the negative boom/bust cycles which create havoc on the economy.

- Why would an Islamic Country want to implement it?

The Bankcoin Reserve's (BCR) Islamic Banking Sharia Finance Innovation Patent provides the closest model to no-interest (meaning no riba) Banking, which is in line with Islamic principles and therefore Islamic Banking. Countries that implement this Treasury product will have in a sense, a monopoly for the following reasons:

It is written and has been said that if there is an option to not be engaged with riba then that option must be taken over all else. All backdoor riba deals/mark ups in the current marketplace are darura. BCR technology provides a genuine, open, honest, and fully transparent Islamic Banking solution.

As an example: A Bank finances an individual with $10K for a car, but the individual ends up re-paying the Bank with interest that can end up costing the individual $20k. That goes against islamic principles. BCR Bankcoin on the Blockchain are the first products that fully address the non-riba requirements, as set out in the Quran and sharia law.

• Why would a Country not want to implement The Bankcoin Reserve (BCR) Bankcoin and AAABlockchain?

Corruption would be number one. The biggest issue world leaders face is the corruption from top to bottom within its Central Bank. And Treasuries BCR Bankcoin and AAABlockchain, eliminates the possibility of kickbacks because BCR Bankcoin is fully accountable, with an International Accounting Firm overseeing and auditing the entire process through the blockexplorer.

So, no more kickbacks from the lenders to the corrupt politicians and those that work in the Central Bank Banking system when the Country's leader wants to build a road, bridge, school, hospital, or employ more police officers and fire-fighters, but have no money to do it without borrowing from external entities at interest. With BCR Bankcoin and AAABlockchain technology, the Country can transition from over time, and at the same time support the Banks by making positive changes to its current method of financing loans and deposits.

• What Positive change is incurred by the usage of BCR Bankcoin and AAABlockchain?

By transitioning cash reserves held at the Central Bank to BCR Bankcoin on AAABlockchain, instead of it costing retail and commercial Banks, Countries now have an option and solution where they receive earnings from the reserves – a good option where the Central Bank could share in those earnings.

• Will retail and commercial Banks welcome this innovation - as they are currently making money off the interest on the Treasury bonds?

If retail and commercial Banks are accustomed to corrupt practices, BCR Bankcoin will end this abusive business model. BCR Bankcoin provides the first Patented claim as a deposit product for retail and commercial Banks where they make more money than they had by extracting from the government and their customers.

• Is there a cap, as inflation is a cause for concern?

In relation to BCR Bankcoin as a Treasury product, there is cap of 10% of GDP unless the case can be made for an increase. BCR Bankcoin is not a fiat product where governments can endlessly raise their debt ceilings. On the earnings revenue yield side, BCR Bankcoin grows with population growth.

For example, inflation is a hidden tax geared to pay back debts and interest on external loans. New money must be brought into existence to cover the amount of debt outstanding which by default dilutes the value of money (fiat) in circulation. Prices in the economy are not going up; however, money is worth less.

BCR Bankcoin sits outside the current financial system so that governments have external options to still operate using their old method.

• How long would it take to set up and implement The Bankcoin Reserve (BCR) and AAABlockchain system in a Country's Bank?

Once the legal contract and licensing agreements are approved and the engagement fee is paid, the technology is installed in a tablet/laptop in the Central Bank and/or Treasury. The tablet/laptop may be connected to a wireless internet connection or tethered to a phone. Once a week (or as agreed upon), a message from BCR is sent to the responsible party (in Bank or Treasury) and they or their staff then processes it as they would any other internet financial transaction.

• What are the possible risks for a Country adopting BCR Bankcoin and AAABlockchain technology in their Banking system?

- Internet connection drops locally.
- Master node and node server disconnects from cloud.
- Main internets switch and/or hop breaks down and disconnects from physical locations.

Recognizing the possibility of these risks, The Bankcoin Reserve (BCR) manages all Bankcoin accounts in relation to the Treasury Product for the Countries that implement it until the time comes that the Country is capable of handling possible problems on its own, without the technical expertise of BCR staff.

To compensate for these possible problems, or other risks, BCR provides double insurance on the 10% earnings to guarantee that Country receives their 10%. In case of catastrophic failure, BCR would provide its legal and accounting professionals with stored backups for continuity of supply.

• What does The Bankcoin Reserve (BCR) Match mean?

The BCR Match is where whatever the Country mines and monetizes via the Central Bank/Treasury, so does BCR. For example, if a Country mines $137.5M per annum, the BCR would match that.

The purpose of the BCR Match is to strengthen the Country's internal revenue service via the 20-25% tax; as well as 10% left in Country by the BCR to invest in new jobs, pay wages, build schools, hospitals, roads etc. Another 10% external to the Country is for BCR to bring in goods and services, i.e., teachers, trade trainers, medical staff and equipment, machinery, etc.

PURPOSE FOR GUIDEBOOK

The main purpose for this guidebook is to inform Country Leaders that The Bankcoin Reserve (BCR) and AAABlockchain provides a new solution to the Banking system. Taking out loans and/or selling Treasury bonds is no longer the only option. BCR Bankcoin and AAABlockchain technology can be implemented immediately at no allocation cost to the Country. Countries such as Greece, Portugal, Puerto Rico, the Pacific Islands Countries, and Belize choose to incorporate this option into their Banking system would be working towards being out of the debt-based interest bearing downward spiral and could pay the bond holders out in full.

This guidebook is to enumerate the capabilities provided under The Bankcoin Reserve (BCR) and AAABlockchain Patented technology, and emphasize that Blockchain has zero tolerance for corruption. AAABlockchain ledger exposes back door dealings and/or kickbacks. This transparency enables a Country to move forward with strength.

This guidebook is to share information about the incredible AAABlockchain technology that processes and corrects major flaws and defects in the current Banking and financial system.

This guidebook is written to entice, engage and invite thoughtful leaders of Countries, and smart decision makers in charge of Banks, financial institutions and monetary funds, to be part of The Bankcoin Reserve (BCR) Bankcoin and AAABlockchain innovative technology.

This guidebook is about Sovereignty.

This guidebook proudly documents the many Patents granted to The Bankcoin Reserve and AAABlockchain Ltd. by the Commonwealth of Australia Patents Office. These Patents include:

1 2014101156 New method for Banks & Financial institutions using crypto currency for savings & deposit taking. example Bankcoin mines/mints interest, mines/mints transaction fees, proof of stake, pos. AAABlockchain Limited Taylor, Nina 2014-09-18 GRANTED

2 2014101277 New method for Banks, financial institutions and monetary funds to provide ethical loans finance including Islamic finance with no interest or usury. Banks, financial institutions and monetary funds can replace interest or usury using this new method which is an internal crypto currency block chain dependent process the minting of new coin and mining of transaction fees. AAABlockchain Limited Taylor, Nina 2014-10-20 GRANTED

3 2014101324 This new monetary innovation method/process using crypto currency applies to and for entities, which require an income/revenue producing asset using any form of named/renamed crypto currency, using any form of Blockchain/chain process using the wallet which mints/mines new coin assets. AAABlockchain Limited Taylor, Nina 2014-11-03 GRANTED

4 2016100394 Blockchain Digital Mining Asset/Commodity innovation for Private Placement, High Yield Investment, Tier 1,2,3, MTN buy/sell Structured Financial Trading Programs and Platforms. McAlister, Gary MR McAlister, Gary 2016-04-11 GRANTED

5 2016100178 New stock/share/bond innovation using principle mined cryptographic currency/digital mining assets/commodities which secondary mine for stock/share/bond holders on/using the Blockchain/any chain/shared ledger on a cryptographic currency/digital mining assets/commodities exchange. Terry, Gary McAlister MR Terry, Gary McAlister 2016-02-17 GRANTED

6 2017100375 New digital mine discovery franchise innovation for but not limited to Governments, treasuries, Central Banks, Banks, financial institutions, monetary funds, judicial entities, real estates, properties commercial, industrial, domestic, foreign, stock, bond and share markets, insurance captive underwriting

institutions, public, private, wholesale, retail and service sectors using the Blockchain to discover a master franchise and or for the discovery of franchises of the new digital mines. McAlister, Gary MR McAlister, Gary 2017-04-04 GRANTED

7 2017100426 New Islamic Banking Sharia Compliant Blockchain Innovation Patent that has no Riba, usury or interest component for but not limited to savings, deposit, ethical loans, finance, stock share bond, Private Placement Programs, Digitally discover new mine deposits to franchise & new monetary system using Blockchains POS proof of stake/secondary mining mine discovery process of assets and commodities for entities such as but not limited to Governments, treasuries, Central Banks, Banks, financial institutions, monetary funds, judicial entities, profit-sharing Blockchain franchise investments PSBFI's. McAlister, Gary MR; Taylor, Nina MISS McAlister, Gary; Taylor, Nina 2017-04-18 GRANTED

8 2017101206 New Blockchain Foreign Exchange Innovation Patent international funds transfers settled locally/nationally by our blockchain sender and receiver in but not limited to both countries matching algorithm and POS proof of stake secondary mining process.for entities such as but not limited to Governments, treasuries, central banks, banks, financial institutions, monetary funds, judicial entities, real estates, properties commercial, industrial, domestic, foreign, stock, bond, share and IT software markets, insurance captive Islamic banking sharia compliant blockchain foreign exchange innovation. Taylor, Nina; McAlister, Gary 2017-09-04 FILED Trademarks filed for AML FX First Blockchain Foreign Exchange

WHERE, WHY AND HOW

In 2009, a gentleman by the name of Satoshi Nakamoto invented a decentralized financial system that knew no borders; for the first time a truly global financial system that anyone, anywhere, could use and take advantage of. He put together some of the greatest minds in the world to match his own, and after the Global Financial Crisis (GFC) of 2008, Satoshi and his team of coders and cryptographers created a national currency that that had no boarders. The success of Bitcoin and the Blockchain (its rails) is a testament to their hard work and persistence, and the trigger that spurred me to develop The Bankcoin Reserve (BCR) Bankcoin.

With a clean and renewable invention background, the first Patent granted to The Bankcoin Reserve (Gary McAlister and/or Nina Taylor) by the Commonwealth of Australia Patents Office was in 2014. To date, Eight Patents have been granted, with others pending.

The premise of this guidebook is heavily weighted to the subject of government's Treasuries and Central Banks - where the generational debt, along with income tax, is generated. It seems obvious that these Countries and their Institutions are prime for education about new technology; a new Banking system to improve the lives of the people in these Countries!

The Patents granted for The Bankcoin Reserve (BCR) and AAABlockchain innovations, allows BCR to give a Country the mining rights to its Bankcoin Mines. The Country uses these rights and mines the Bankcoin. The Bankcoin commodity the Country then extracts from the mine belongs to the Country for them to monetize in the form of national currency. The Country has 100% Sovereign reserves which can be leveraged in time of need, i.e., natural disasters etc. The beauty of BCR Bankcoin is that it is a Government-allocated Digital Mining Commodity. BCR Bankcoin on AAABlockchain practices are ethical, non-interest, non-usury, non-riba Innovations invented for the Central Bank, Treasury bond and Commodities markets.

Mentioned earlier, Cryptocurrency has been ruled an asset by governments and other entities such as the Australian Taxation Office (ATO). Australia ruled it an asset, the Commodity Futures Trading Commission (CFTC) in the United States ruled it a commodity, and judges around the world ruled it as property.

BCR Bankcoin, which started out as a Cryptocurrency and converted by law to an asset and commodity property, is a stand-alone product and medium of exchange. It does not need to be backed by something nor is it a representation of something.

This is fundamental to the pricing of BCR Bankcoin products. BCR Bankcoin is a digital mining commodity on the Blockchain. It has a private value of $1,375 which was derived using the gold standard (before Brexit). If the gold price is over the current price, BCR would reflect that change accordingly and update the price of Bankcoin.

Starting in 2014, The Bank Coin Reserve (BCR) discovered, developed, and patented its Bankcoin on the AAABlockchain - transitioning from the debt-based system to an earnings revenue yield model.

In 2016, BCR discovered, developed and Patented Private Placement Programs – using digital asset commodity which earns, as opposed to fiat programs with gold being the requirement. And, Stock Shares Bonds – a new company/government structure and earnings model, with proof of stake secondary mining.

2017 BCR developed and Patented Digital Mine Franchise Discovery – the first Blockchain mine discovery franchise using AAABlockchain.

In 2017, BCR developed and patented the first new Islamic Banking, Sharia-Compliant Blockchain Innovation that has no riba, usury or interest component. It can be used for, but not limited to, savings, deposits, ethical loans, finance, stocks, bonds, Private Placement Programs, and more.

Its proof of stake/secondary mining discovery process benefits entities such as, but not limited to, Governments, treasuries, Central Banks, Banks, financial institutions, monetary funds, judicial entities, real estate properties, commercial, industrial, domestic, foreign, stocks, bonds and share markets, insurance-captive underwriting institutions, public, private, wholesale, retail and service sectors, profit-sharing Blockchain franchise investments, and those who want to be a part of the first sharia compliant Blockchain innovation.

THE BANKCOIN RESERVE (BCR) AAABLOCKCHAIN LTD. PATENTS

The Patents were applied for in this order and the inventive steps are the following proof of stake secondary mining, and mine discovery using the Blockchain.

2014

Deposit and Savings - transition from giving interest to earnings, using the Blockchain, with proof of stake secondary mining.

Loan and finance - transition from taking interest to earnings, using the Blockchain for proof of stake secondary mining.

New monetary system - transition from debt based system to earnings revenue yield model, using the Blockchain for proof of stake secondary mining.

2016

Private Placement Programs - using gold-standard backing, BCR Bankcoin, as a digital asset commodity, earns as opposed to fiat programs, using the Blockchain for proof of stake secondary mining.

Stock Shares Bonds - new company government structure and earnings model, using the Blockchain for proof of stake secondary mining.

2017

Digital Mine Franchise Discovery - first Blockchain mine discovery franchise, using the Blockchain for proof of stake secondary mining.

New Islamic Banking Sharia Compliant Blockchain Innovation Patent, the first Blockchain Islamic Banking sharia-compliant product that removes riba, interest usury, from the equation and replaces it with a true digital mining commodity earnings component.

With full sharia-compliance, Bankcoin on AAABlockchain is for, but not limited to, savings, deposit, ethical loans, finance, stocks, bonds, Private Placement Programs, and to digitally discover new mine deposits to franchise; using the Blockchain for proof of stake secondary mining.

Mine discovery of assets and commodities benefit entities such as, but not limited, to Governments, treasuries, Central Banks, Banks, financial institutions, monetary funds, judicial entities, and profit-sharing Blockchain franchise investments (PSBFI's).

Notes

THE INNOVATIVE PROCESS

When The Bank Coin Reserve (BCR) Bankcoin technology was proven to work, innovation Patents were filed. The AAABlockchain process demonstrated its ability to transition the current Banking, finance, and monetary funds from interest to asset, with commodity earnings and returns.

For the first time in history, these institutions can transact peer to peer, with honesty (you can see the secondary mining) and transparency (Blockchain stores every single transaction made).

The New Islamic Banking Sharia Compliant Blockchain Innovation Patent was granted to Gary McAlister and Nina Taylor, April 18, 2017 (#2017100426) by the Commonwealth of Australia Patents Office. It is a government Treasury Central Bank product, hereinafter referred to as "Treasury Product".

The Bankcoin Reserve (BCR) Stakeholders had multiple meetings with Prime Ministers and their cabinet members in several Countries to formulate this Treasury Product Bankcoin. BCR and the Prime Ministers created a Memorandum of Understanding (MOU) Agreement. As owners, BCR sets the price for Bankcoin for its use in the private market place. The Treasury Product Bankcoin was valuated using facts to make the price determination. (Formulas and flow charts 1 & 2 are available).

The purpose of this Treasury Product Bankcoin is to give the Treasury, and therefore the Country, a Sovereign, debt free, interest free position over time as it uses this new Treasury Product Bankcoin to pay down its existing debts and slowly transitions out of debt-based, interest-bearing loans from foreign entities. This is possible because Central Banks have a license from the government to bring the nation's money into existence.

As in past and current practice, the Treasury creates a Treasury Bond and sells it to the Central Bank. The Central Bank then sells it to the commercial retail Banks, and the Treasury pays interest on that Bond, which is really a loan. Some governments also take out loans from International lenders. With Treasury Product Bankcoin, the Central Bank can acquire the Bankcoin assets, discovered and mined from the Treasury, and these assets become the Country's Sovereign reserves. There is no interest or debt component. It is a trade.

Explained earlier, reiterated several times for importance, BCR Bankcoin is pegged to the one ounce gold price and that one ounce gold price is determined by the actual market. If there is no rise in the market gold price above the current Bankcoin price then the Bankcoin price remains the same. The price is reflected on the website BankcoinReserve.com

One percent (1%) – ten percent (10%) of the Country's Gross Domestic Product (GDP), is what Bankcoin starts with. If the GDP of a Country is $1.375B U.S. per annum, the principle amount required by The Bankcoin Reserve (BCR) is equal to that which will be allocated to the Treasury. BCR will mine for the Treasury at a yield of 10% per annum; 100k Bankcoin as per the MOU agreement, which equates to $137.5M U.S.

With this formula, BCR mines and matches the amount of Bankcoin ($137.5M U.S.) sold to the Central Bank by the Treasury, and BCR receives $137.5M per annum for the length of the contract. A contract for twenty (20) years would bring the value to $2,750,000,000.00 ($2.75B). This would be the minimum valuation price for the Patent product. License fees would be added to that on a monthly or yearly basis, by the entity that acquires it.

Notes

BLOCKCHAIN BENEFITS TO THE COUNTRY

• Removes the need for the Country to borrow and be indebted to external entities. It is the interest on these debts that is inflationary.

• Since the Country no longer needs to borrow, the interest burden is no longer there for the tax payers to repay, or worse, sell new Treasury bonds to pay off the interest on old Treasury bonds.

• This is the only Sovereign product available that is asset and/or commodity based, available to be shared in this way using the Blockchain.

• Government now has a new revenue earning model to work with and can reduce taxes accordingly to offset this new gain

• Treasury now has a new revenue model that is not coming from the people of the Country via increased taxes.

• The Internal Revenue Department now has several new revenue streams coming in which helps its budget.

• The Central Bank has a new revenue model to cover its costs and makes a profit. (Good for private Banks).

• Simple to implement. Not much training required. All the complicated issues have been taken care of by BCR.

• Full AML/KYC compliance, auditing and insurance covered. This product is private and all entities are known.

• The Bankcoin Reserve (BCR) is fully committed to the Countries it enters. Ten Percent (10%) of the BCR matched funds are left in Country for job creation and infrastructure, and 10% is committed externally for Country's needs, i.e., training, teachers, schools, hospitals, staff, machinery, etc.

MORE BLOCKCHAIN QUESTIONS AND ANSWERS

• Can any Country implement this?

Yes. If Country wishes to transition from borrowing from external entities and indebting its people for generations.

• How much will it cost a Country?

There is no direct cost to the Country or its citizens. The mined 10% covers everything.

• How long would it take to implement the product?

The amount of time needed to install a laptop/tablet to accept The Bankcoin Reserve Bankcoin on AAABlockchain.

• Can the Country's Central Bank monetize?

Yes. Central Bank charters have the license and ability to acquire assets/commodities, which is exactly what they would be doing.

• Can Country use AAABlockchain innovation where there are no losers?

Yes, and become a debt and interest free, Sovereign Country.

• What are the main purposes of this innovation?

✓ To put the Country into a positive and sustainable position where they no longer must pay down debt and interest to outside external entities. ✓ To strengthen the Treasuries' position; instead of it always being in the negative, this innovation makes it possible for the Treasury to grow with population growth. This innovation creates reserves in the positive because it continues to mine and or discover new mines for the Treasury for the length of the contract. ✓ To provide the Central Bank with an income stream that it did not previously have and create the climate for growth among the business sector which by default leads to increased confidence minimizing the negative boom bust cycles which create havoc on the economy.

• Why would an Islamic Country want to implement it?

Because this innovation is genuine, open, honest, and fully transparent. It is the first product of its kind ever that fully addresses the non riba requirements as set forth in sharia law.

• Is there a cap, as we always worry about inflation?

In relation to the Treasury Product there is cap of 10% of GDP unless the case can be made for an increase.

• What are the risks?

For the Countries that implement the Treasury Product, BCR manages all Bankcoin accounts and BCR handles all the technical problems that may arise.

Notes

THE BANKCOIN RESERVE'S (BCR) PATENTED "ALL BUSINESS" BANKCOIN IS THE MOST STABLE DIGITAL COMMODITY IN THE MARKET TODAY.

2017100375, Granted April 4, 2017, this new digital mine-discovery franchise innovation is for, but not limited to, Governments, treasuries, Central Banks, private Banks, financial institutions, monetary funds, judicial entities, real estate properties, commercial, industrial, domestic, foreign, stock, bond and share markets, insurance-captive underwriting institutions, public, private, wholesale, retail and service sectors. This "All Business" Bankcoin uses the Blockchain to discover a master franchise and or for the discovery of franchises of the new digital mines.

It benefits major players in the public and private fields of law and regulation. Never has there been a formulated fixed price commodity with a floor that may be both a medium of exchange and a store of value.

BCR Bankcoin has the intrinsic and unique ability to mint/mine new Bankcoin's via the Blockchain from the principle amount held in its digital wallet. What may be perceived as interest, are digital commodity earnings.

BCR Bankcoin has no limit to its adoption in the mainstream economy which gives it great growth potential that is significant and sustainable.

MARKETPLACE OPPORTUNITIES FOR DIGITAL COMMODITIES WITH CURRENCY ABILITY

The Bankcoin Reserve (BCR) through its Bankcoin patents, have identified a marketplace that is in desperate need of innovation. The commodity market and payment systems in the U.S. and the rest of the world require a second rail (Blockchain) of an ethical, non-usury nature. Many of today's systems are in negative/zero interest territory; slow, unproductive, expensive, legacy debt-based and unsustainable. As it is, it places a generational burden on the very people it was designed to work for.

In partnership with The Bankcoin Reserve (BCR), a Country can serve as a role model for other Nations to become Sovereign. Because of the Sovereign, debt-free financial position this partnership puts the Country, its Government has the means to make major investments in infrastructure such as roads, sewerage, schools, higher education, affordable housing, clean and renewable energy technology.

By partnering with BCR, the Country can create and provide opportunities for its people to start their own small and medium-sized enterprises using no interest principle. People will be able to truly prosper by investing in themselves. A BCR partnership will enhance and strengthen the Country's position in the marketplace, with full exporting capabilities via the BCR monetary transactional network using the latest in Blockchain and mobile technology.

Ethical Treasury Bonds – "Bankcoin" – that can run alongside the current Treasury Bond offering. Continuance of the existing Treasury Bond program is recommended, with the benefit being that Bankcoin earnings will comfortably cover the interest rate with no disruptions. The core focus is to build the Country and its people.

The Bankcoin Reserve (BCR) sets the market price for the Digital mining commodities (DMC's), monthly. The BCR also insures the ten percent (10%) growth. The principle DMC's mine is guaranteed to ensure market certainty, as well as budget and forward estimates. The BCR also valuates Bankcoin. The rate is $1,375.00 per Bankcoin in the Blockchain. The BCR agrees to allocate a substantial amount of their Bankcoin holdings to the Country's government. BCR will mine at a 10% yield – with that 10% becoming the property of the Country's government. The proviso is that the allocation and mined Bankcoin's remain under the management of the BCR for the life of the (25-year) contract.

AAABlockchain Limited has been granted three patents - Savings & Deposits, Loans & Finance, and New Monetary System. The purpose of these Patents is to protect the product and guarantee product's market entry. A 10% license fee applies to what is mined and monetized from the BCR allocation.

Tax Rule: BCR Bankcoin acquired by the Central Bank will be taxed at 20% as per the Private Product Rule. The license fee will also be taxed at this rate, as will the Central Bank earnings from Bankcoin mining.

BANKING AND BLOCKCHAIN FORMULA

The Bankcoin Reserve Holdings under BCR management - How does Bankcoin work?

Example: The Treasury owns what the Major Stakeholder allocation mines per annum, which is 100k Bankcoin's free and clear from debt and interest - $137.5M.

The Central Bank of the Country acquires the 100k Bankcoin's from the Treasury for $137.5M - and the Bankcoin's then start to mine for the Central Bank.

The Central Bank then mines 10% - 10k from the 100k acquisition it made from the Treasury - earning it $13.75M. Once monetized, these Bankcoin's become the property of the Treasury, and begins to mine for the Treasury.

The Central Bank also acquires 100k Bankcoin's from the Major Stakeholders for $137.5M per annum, and the Bankcoin's then start to mine for the Central Bank.

The Central Bank then mines 10% - 10k from the 100k acquisition it made from the Major Stakeholders - earning it $13.75M per annum. Once monetized, these Bankcoin's become the property of the Treasury and begin to mine for the Treasury.

The Patent license fee is based on 10% of the amount of Bankcoin monetized. This would be paid to AAABlockchain Limited which would have an account at the Central Bank and meet all KYC and AML requirements.

The Treasury would be paid 10% of 100k which would be 10k totaling $13.75M per annum.

Major Stakeholders 10% of 100k which would be 10k totaling $13.75M to be paid per annum.

Tax Treatment Internal Revenue Department

The Treasury is exempt from Tax

The Central Bank of Country is taxed at the rate of 20% on what it monetizes.

The Major Stakeholders are taxed at the rate of 20% on what they monetize.

The Bankcoin Reserve (BCR) Patented Blockchain process and product moves the Central Bank from a Treasury acquisition and interest-bearing entity to a digital commodity earnings partner, debt free.

The Bankcoin Reserve is working with the U.S. Treasury and FinCEN (Financial Crimes and Enforcement Network) to help them pave the way to implement this process,

This Islamic Patent claim is for deposit, not the savings. There are four additional claims and their valuations.

To expand on this further, there are 200 Countries, each one with a different GDP. (U.S. $)

Saudi Arabia: $753.83B, 10% GDP. As per formula, $75.383B match to BCR, $75.383B per annum. This would be under a 20-year contract between Saudi Arabia and The Bankcoin Reserve (BCR).

Malaysia: $350B,10% GDP. As per formula, $35B match to BCR, $35B per annum. This would be under a 20-year contract between Malaysia and The Bankcoin Reserve (BCR).

UAE: $370B, 10% GDP. As per formula, $37B match to BCR, $37B per annum. This would be under a 20-year contract between UAE and The Bankcoin Reserve (BCR).

Kuwait: $114B, 10% GDP. As per formula, $11.4B match to BCR, $11.4B per annum. This would be under a 20-year contract between Kuwait and The Bankcoin Reserve (BCR).

Qatar: $165B, 10% GDP. As per formula, $16.5B match to BCR, $16.5B per annum. This would be under a 20-year contract between Qatar and The Bankcoin Reserve (BCR).

Indonesia: $860B, 10% GDP, As per formula, $86B match to BCR, $86B per annum. This would be under a 20-year contract between Indonesia and The Bankcoin Reserve (BCR).

Bahrain: $31B, 10% GDP. As per formula, $3.1B match to BCR, $3.1B per annum. This would be under a 20-year contract between Bahrain and The Bankcoin Reserve (BCR).

Non-Islamic Countries that wish to benefit from The Bankcoin Reserve Bankcoin on its Blockchain

USA: $18036.65B, 10% GDP. As per formula, $1.8T match to BCR $1.8T per annum. This would be under a 20-year contract between USA and The Bankcoin Reserve (BCR).

European Union: $16311.90B, 10% GDP. As per formula, $1.6T match to BCR, $1.6T per annum. This would be under a 20-year contract between European Union and The Bankcoin Reserve (BCR).

Euro Area: $11602.40B, 10% GDP. As per formula, $1.16T match to BCR, $1.16T per annum. This would be under a 20-year contract between Euro Area and The Bankcoin Reserve (BCR).

China: $11007.72B, 10% GDP. As per formula, $1.1T match to BCR, $1.1T per annum. This would be under a 20-year contract between China and The Bankcoin Reserve (BCR).

Japan: $123.26B, 10% GDP. As per formula, $412B match to BCR, $412B per annum. This would be under a 20-year contract between Japan and The Bankcoin Reserve (BCR).

Germany: $3363.43, 10% GDP. As per formula, $336B match to BCR, $336B per annum. This would be under a 20-year contract between Germany and The Bankcoin Reserve (BCR).

United Kingdom: $858.00B, 10% GDP. As per formula, $285B match to the BCR, $285B per annum. This would be under a 20-year contract between United Kingdom and The Bankcoin Reserve (BCR).

France: $2418.84B, 10% GDP. As per formula, $241B match to the BCR, $241B per annum. This would be under a 20-year contract between France and The Bankcoin Reserve (BCR).

India: $2095.40B, 10% GDP. As per formula, $209B match to the BCR, $209B per annum. This would be under a 20-year contract between India and The Bankcoin Reserve (BCR).

Italy: $1821.50B, 10% GDP. As per formula, $182B match to the BCR, $182B per annum. This would be under a 20-year contract between Italy and The Bankcoin Reserve (BCR).

Brazil: $1774.72B, 10% GDP. As per formula, $177B match to the BCR, $177B Per annum. This would be under a 20-year contract between Brazil and The Bankcoin Reserve (BCR).

Canada : $550.54B, 10% GDP. As per formula, $155B match to the BCR, $155B per annum. This would be under a 20-year contract between Canada and The Bankcoin Reserve (BCR).

South Korea: $1377.87B, 10% GDP. As per formula, $137B match to the BCR, $137B per annum. This would be under a 20-year contract between South Korea and The Bankcoin Reserve (BCR).

Australia: $1339.54B, 10% GDP. As per formula, $133B match to the BCR, $133B per annum. This would be under a 20-year contract between Australia and The Bankcoin Reserve (BCR).

Note

WHO WE ARE

Gary McAlister, Technical Inventor and Creative Innovator, who, with extraordinary persistence brings his powerful ideas to extraordinary results.

Gary McAlister (born November 24, 1968) is an Australian/New Zealand futurist and currently chairman of the Global Energy Reserve, the central authority on clean and renewable energy globally. During his tenure as chairman, McAlister has overseen the Global Energy Reserve's research & development, global commerce and environmental interests of solving complex problems.

Before becoming Global Energy Reserve chairman, McAlister was research & development leader in marine energy technology specifically the rise & fall of the tides from 2000 to November 2003. From 2003 until 2006, he was a leader in the integration between energy & commerce including the complex nature of supply chains, proposed the CSR Covenant, and first discussed "the Corporate Social Responsibility End User Mandate"--the theory that primary business has social, economic and environmental responsibility including the end user's use. Certain formulas were created to show business especially in the retail sector that the products they sold had an impact on these three factors. McAlister then served as advisor, consultant and mentor to a number of companies in both profit and nonprofit until his appointment with the Global Energy Reserve in 2010.

McAlister is a proud member of the Stanford who's who and can be referenced in many journals and white papers for his dedicated work on clean and renewable energy technology including full introduction throughout the supply chains.

His advanced work in these fields was an outgrowth of his early years as a problem solver. McAlister originated the concept of decentralization of clean and renewable electric-power generation and distribution at homes, businesses, and factories – a crucial development in the future of developed and developing nations.

From 2010 to 2013 McAlister realized that finance was the crucial part missing in the manufacture and roll out of major clean and renewable technologies so set to work on developing a Kwh currency to self-fund the developments he had in his portfolio as well as external developments in the sector. While developing the Kwh currency a decentralized crypto currency entered the market called Bitcoin which showed a lot of promise and had the elements and capabilities he was looking for.

From 2013 to 2014 McAlister looked at all the issues good and bad surrounding Bitcoin and worked with developers on a new crypto currency product this came to market in 2014 called Bankcoin he then became the chairman of the Bankcoin Reserve.

From 2014 to 2017 McAlister developed and designed new products and processes off Bankcoin core and filed multiple patents to protect it. Currently holds 7 granted major POS proof of stake blockchain patents with his partners covering Banks, Financial Institutions, Monetary funds, PPP's private placement programs, new monetary system, realestate franchises and Islamic Banking.

TO LEARN MORE AND GET INVOLVED CONTACT:

support@bankcoinreserve.com

http://www,BankcoinReserve.com

EXAMPLE MOU Heads of Agreement

Below is an example of the MOU that is available for those countries that want to transition from the current debt and interest based system to our non riba non usury non interest digital mining asset/commodity earnings revenue model which is available to be implemented immediately at between 1% - 10% of your GDP The below example is implemented at 10% of the country's GDP. There is an engagement fee to be negotiated which is a small percentage of the contract value.

SUBJECT TO CONTRACT

Heads of terms – MOU Example for all countries

In respect of (the Arrangement Proposal)

Between

Parties

1 (country) Government - Represented by President Prime Minister – (here)

2 The Bankcoin Reserve BCR – Represented by Chairman – Gary McAlister

3 AAABlockchain – Represented by Administrator – Nina Taylor

Background

This form sets out the principal terms and conditions which the above named parties are willing to enter into for the proposed Arrangement. With the exception of the confidentiality provisions set out below, the parties do not intend to be legally bound by these heads of terms and the Arrangement is strictly subject to the execution of a legally binding agreement. The parties agree to negotiate in good faith until execution of such legally binding agreement. If you country debt is $1B then the allocation the BCR will make for you is equal to that debt amount $1B the key difference is it will be in the form of a digital mining asset/commodity that secondary mines which is what you would trade your commodity asset/fiat for meaning monetize for your local currency. The country debt will be paid down over 10 years.

Terms

1. Pre-Conditions: This example shows the debt of a country at $1.375B

The Bankcoin Reserve has agreed to allocate at no cost to the (your) Government or Treasury 1M Bankcoin's valuation $1.375B which will POS proof of stake secondary mine 10% or 100k Bankcoin's coins pa which = $137.5M sovereign, debt free and clear. These are digitally mined commodities under management by the BCR. The CB Central Bank has the sovereign right and ability to bring the countries money into existence on the condition it is in the form of trade; the acquired trade becomes the Central Bank's and Treasuries sovereign reserves. The trade will be in the form of your country dollars. In this example we will use Bankcoin which has a private market value of $1375.00 per Bankcoin.

2. How will it work?

The Treasury now owns what the BCR country allocation mines pa which is 100k Bankcoin's free and clear from debt and interest, these are sovereign reserves $137.5M.

The CB acquires the 100k Bankcoin's from the treasury for $137.5M and the Bankcoin's then start to mine for the CB.

The CB then mines 10% 10k from the 100k acquisition it made from the Treasury earning it $13.75M once monetized these Bankcoin's become the property of the Treasury and begin to mine for the treasury these are sovereign reserves.

The CB also acquires 100k Bankcoin's from the BCR for $137.5M pa and the Bankcoin's then start to mine for the CB.

The CB then mines 10% 10k from the 100k acquisition it made from the BCR earning it $13.75M pa once monetized these Bankcoin's become the property of the Treasury and begin to mine for the Treasury these are sovereign reserves.

The Patent license fee is based on 10% of the amount of Bankcoin monetized this would be paid to AAABlockchain Limited which would have an account at the CB and meet all KYC and AML requirements.

Treasury 10% of 100k which would be 10k totaling $13.75M to be paid pa

Major Stakeholders 10% of 100k which would be 10k totaling $13.75M to be paid pa

CB 10% of 20k which would be 2k totaling $2.75M to be paid pa

An additional fund of 500k Bankcoin's which will mine at 10% pa $68.75M will be setup for Government members to access for their electorates. To be determined by a Taskforce.

The Tax to Internal Revenue

Treasury is exempt from Tax

The CB is taxed at the rate of 20% on what it monetizes

The BCR is taxed at the rate of 20% on what it monetizes

Bankcoin's can be acquired and monetized weekly fortnightly monthly, for the task force to determine.

3. Payment messages

Amount

From the BCR to the CB via Blockchain message Bitmessage which would be installed on a standalone computer at the CB and staff trained to accept and process the message which is similar to SWIFT.

4. Method of payment

All payments to be made in country dollars including from the BCR on conversion from US price per Bankcoin to country dollars this conversion will be made at the BCR and the Blockchain messages will be in country dollars.

5. Party 1's obligations

Week 1 & 2:

Set up Taskforce in conjunction with the Treasury, IR and the CB to work on education & Training, processes and amendments (if any) including implementation. Bankcoin Product and process is plug and play. At no time does this product and process interfere with or change the existing system. Members of the Taskforce are welcome to come to Australia to learn more about the product, process and implementation and/or members of the BCR are able to go to the country to work with the taskforce.

Week 3 & 4:

Work with the BCR to understand the Blockchain messaging system and run tests on implementation. By the end of week 4 several transactions will have been performed to iron out any bugs in the system, be they internet connection issues, staff issues, and taskforce issues.

Transactions to be completed: [amount to be determined]

BCR to CB – Bitmessage to CB – CB to Treasury account.

BCR to CB – Bitmessage to CB – CB to BCR account.

BCR to CB – Bitmessage to CB – CB to CB account.

AAABlockchain License fees

BCR – CB – AAABlockchain Account.

Once this is done and all parties agree that the product and process are performing as predicted a formal contract will be written and agreed to for a period of 25 years as per the spreadsheet schedule.

6. Party 2's obligations

The BCR agrees to manage, secure and insure the Bankcoin's allocated for the CB and the Treasury. Four Bankcoin's wallets have been allocated with 1M Bankcoin's spread across them. Also 1M Bankcoin's have also been allocated to insure the full amount allocated.

The BCR will send a Bitmessage Blockchain transaction message to the computer the BCR team setup in the CB. The staff at the CB will process the message and allocate the funds according to the Taskforce recommendations.

A VPS virtual private server remote desktop connection can be provided for each of the entities to be able to log into as they require.

The BCR agrees to an administrator/CIO between the BCR and the above entities and play a role in the Taskforce as they would know the Bankcoin product well.

6b. Party 3's obligations

AAABlockchain Limited agrees to license the Government via the CB and the Treasury to monetize the earnings from the Bankcoin's they have allocated. These terms are covered in the relevant patents which AAABlockchain was granted. If any changes to the proposal are made during this period AAABlockchain must be informed and license fees adjusted to reflect the changes made.

7. Governing law

8. Estimated time to completion the parties agree to negotiate in good faith with a view to executing a legally binding agreement on or before [date] which is when this agreement will expire.

9. Responsibility

The Terms and the Arrangement are confidential to the parties and their advisers.

Each party undertakes that it shall not at any time disclose to any person any confidential information which is disclosed by the other party in contemplation of the Arrangement except to its employees, officers, representatives or advisers who need to know such information for the purposes of the evaluation of the arrangement and the negotiation of the legally binding agreement.

For the purpose of this MOU, confidential information shall mean any information which concerns the business, affairs, customers, clients or suppliers of a party or of any member of the group of companies to which that party belongs and which are expressly identified by that party as being confidential or which the reasonable business person would identify as confidential.

No party shall use the other party's confidential information for any purpose other than the evaluation of the Arrangement and the negotiation of the legally binding agreement.

This letter is for the benefit of the parties to it and is not intended to benefit, or be enforceable by, anyone else. We confirm our agreement to the above.

....

Signed by [Prime Minster] - [President] for and on behalf

of [Government]

Print name:

Date:

....

Signed by [Chairman] - [Gary McAlister] for and on behalf

of [Bankcoin Reserve]

Print name:

Date

....

Signed by [Administrator] - [Nina Taylor] for and on behalf

of [AAABlockchain Limited]

Print name:

Date

....

Islamic Banking on the BLOCKCHAIN

Signatories: Delegates from all nations to embrace and protect this non riba sharia compliant Islamic banking declaration and all that is in it.

As pursuant to the Qur'an & Sharia Law the following must be stated:

I Gary [Gabriel] McAlister am the source of this Islamic banking sharia compliant copyrightable works intellectual property patented Riba Interest Usury free world information using the Digital mining asset/commodities on the blockchain. This trustworthy information must be passed on in its entirety so that all those that need to know will know the truth that I Gary [Gabriel] McAlister am the one true author.

I Gary [Gabriel] McAlister created from my knowledge this Islamic banking sharia compliant patented product and process on/using the blockchain and digital mining assets/commodities for the people of this earth this is what I know to be true and let it be recorded as truthful.

All who know me directly know me to be of moral character and integrity which was fundamental and played an integral part of writing and formulating this Islamic banking sharia compliant works for which I have the intellectual property rights bestowed upon me. This intellectual property is an extension of my personhood and I am the master of this work which grants me protection of my moral rights.

I Gary [Gabriel] McAlister have an intimate and unique bond to this Islamic banking sharia compliant copyrightable works intellectual property which has inalienable qualities because this is connected to me the author directly. I have always felt deeply about the negative effects that riba places on the people and I knew one day I would find the answer to rid us of this destructive societal practice. What we see today in/from our Islamic banking institutions is darura riba products of emergency and last resort however let it be known that because of this new truth new Islamic banking sharia compliant copyrightable works intellectual property patented information that I am providing truthfully here for the world to see and learn from there is no more reason no more justification however necessary for there to be these so called darura riba products to be in the market. The time has come for us to rid ourselves of these riba interest usury products that are unjust commercial dealings, deceptive and unscrupulous commercial practices once and for all and the opportunity is placed before us to take the people from a debt based interest bearing model to a non-debt based digital mining asset commodity earnings revenue model. These measures must be respected trade practices that are fair and balanced.

Governments around the world are compelled under shari'a to protect my sacred copywriter property rights and provide remedies for the theft or infringement in connection with my intellectual private property rights from those who are unjustly enriched and make illegal appropriations without my consent/agreement. I Gary [Gabriel] McAlister the rightful owner of these intellectual property rights if infringed am entitled to compensation for any resulting damage caused by the unauthorized enrichment and/or appropriation as the Qur'an expressly condemns theft of such copyright works.

2017100426 New Islamic Banking Sharia Compliant Blockchain Innovation Patent that has no riba, usury or interest component for but not limited to savings, deposit, ethical loans, finance, stock share bond, Private Placement Programs, Digitally discover new mine deposits to franchise & new monetary system using blockchains POS proof of stake/secondary mining mine discovery process of assets and commodities for entities such as but not limited to Governments, treasuries, central banks, banks, financial institutions, monetary funds, judicial entities, profit-sharing blockchain franchise investments PSBFI's. McAlister, Gary MR; Taylor, Nina MISS McAlister, Gary; Taylor, Nina 2017-04-18 GRANTED

Abstract:
This Islamic Banking Sharia Compliant Blockchain Innovation provides new methods for banks, financial institutions and monetary funds to provide ethical loans finance including Islamic deposits and finance with no riba, interest or usury. Banks, financial institutions and monetary funds can earn the interest or usury using a different process which is an internal crypto currency block chain dependent process the minting of new coin and mining of transaction fees. This new method is made possible because of the latest technology inside the crypto currency wallet as well as external factors. Customer applies for a loan, bank approves the loan and at the same time the bank acquires bankcoin to the value of the loan. The bank then leverages the bank coin 2x as a number Ix goes to the pay for the bankcoin and the other goes to the borrower. The borrower makes repayments however it is only the principle that he owes as there is no interest or usury.

This Islamic Banking Sharia Compliant Blockchain Innovation concerns cryptographic currency for use in the finance industry. More specifically the present invention relates to the provision of cryptographic currency by banking or other such financial institutions for their everyday products such as deposit and term deposit accounts etc. The financial institution then mints/mines the cryptographic currency up to a certain percentage to pay the interest on the account etc.

This Islamic Banking Sharia Compliant Blockchain Innovation concerns cryptographic currency/digital mining assets/commodities for use in the stock/share/bond market industry. More specifically the present invention relates to the provision of cryptographic currency/digital mining assets/commodity stock/share/ bond innovation which fundamentally changes how the stocks/shares/bonds are discovered, issued, valuated and rated.

This Islamic Banking Sharia Compliant Blockchain Innovation that addresses what the stocks/shares/bonds now known as digital mining assets/commodities look like and how they are bought, sold and traded on a digital mining assets/commodities Blockchain exchange. It affects proof of ownership on the Blockchain, investor returns, earnings to shareholders, settlement speed and company strength etc.

This Islamic Banking Sharia Compliant Blockchain innovation is a new stocks/shares/bonds structure using digital mining assets/commodities which are the actual stocks/shares/bonds in the start-ups, businesses, companies and corporations which can then be bought/sold/traded on a new Blockchain shared ledger exchange/platform. New start-ups and existing businesses/companies/corporations can transition from their old stocks/shares/bonds structure in the existing stocks/shares/bonds market over to this new innovative digital mining assets/commodities stocks/shares/bonds structure on a new digital mining assets/commodities Blockchain exchange.

This Islamic Banking Sharia Compliant Blockchain Innovation makes it possible for investors/stakeholders to acquire principle digital mining asset/commodity in a start-up, business/company/corporation in both the primary and secondary market and let their principle digital mining asset/commodity secondary mine for them on exchange and/or off exchange. This is then a new innovative way for investors/stakeholders who would now be shareholders in this new structure to get a stable return on investment without having to sell their principle stocks/ shares/bonds back into the market place. They can simply sell what their start-up/business/company/corporation principle digital mining assets/commodities stocks/shares/bonds secondary mine.

This Islamic Banking Sharia Compliant Blockchain Innovation has the potential to completely reshape the Islamic Banking industry and drive huge improvements in market efficiency, settlement, security, regulatory, speed of transfer, ownership CIS, KYC, AML. We will use Bankcoin as our example of the digital mining assets/commodities which has had its principle Bankcoin mined and is now secondary mining a percentage from 1% onwards pa from the total amount in their Bankcoin digital wallet. Example: if you acquire 1000 Bankcoin's it will secondary mine up to 10% pa which equals up to 100 newly mined Bankcoin's pa. So when an investor/stakeholder acquires 1000 digital mining asset/commodity stocks/shares/bonds in a start-up/business/company/corporation from the SharesX exchange for example, they will newly secondary mine 100 digital mining asset/commodity stocks, shares, bonds per annum for the new shareholder.

This Islamic Banking Sharia Compliant Blockchain digital mining asset/commodity stocks/shares/bonds innovation assists with market stability being a fixed price with the option of a floating price above that, transparency as the Blockchain is decentralized, security of ownership as investors/shareholders have full control over their digital mining asset/commodity stocks/shares/bonds both online and offline in their own digital wallet, and minimizing tax avoidance by increased transparency and regulatory oversight.

This Islamic Banking Sharia Compliant Blockchain Innovation method/process using crypto currency applies to and for entities, which require an income/revenue producing asset using any form of named/renamed crypto currency, using any form of blockchain/chain process using the wallet which mints/mines new coin assets. This new method/process makes it possible for an entity to acquire a (blockchain or any chain dependent) crypto currency asset to earn revenue, mint and mine new assets and currency, produce, acquire income for that entity and or on behalf of another entity.

This Islamic Banking Sharia Compliant Blockchain Innovation digital mine discovery innovation actually discovers more digital mines while it uses the blockchain as the rails and a secondary digital mine discovery process to discover secondary digital mines. The 2nd digital mine discovers a 3rd digital mine and then a 4th then 5th which can continue discoveries indefinitely perpetual automatically all from the digital mines discovered before them. Because they are actual digital mines which are discovered they would come under the realestate/property classification. Be it a commercial operation and/or in the wholesale sector and/or retail a portfolio of digital mines traded and/or on sold to the retail sector including being used as but not limited to security, insurance, collateral etc.

This Islamic Banking Sharia Compliant Blockchain Innovation sets out a new realestate and/or property blockchain franchise model and has the ability to be exploited under a patent license fee agreement and/or outright bought/sold to specific entities such as but not limited to, governments, Banks, financial institutions, monetary funds,

insurance industries on platforms such as but not limited to asset/commodity/stock/bond/share markets and exchanges etc.
This Islamic Banking Sharia Compliant Blockchain Innovation is a blockchain digital mine discovery franchise innovation specifically designed and developed for the realestate /property, insurance/underwriting, security/collateral markets. This is not a crypto currency nor is it an asset/commodity innovation that earns interest. What we have discovered on the blockchain is an actual digital mine we can call the master franchise which can actually discover new digital mines at a pre-determined discovery percentage rate example 1/10th per annum. It is estimated because mine discovery is not an exact science.
This Islamic Banking Sharia Compliant Blockchain Innovation is an actual digital mine discovery innovation on the blockchain which by default means it is covered under the realestate banner and in doing so we have worked out through our modelling that it can be an actual franchise. The master franchise is discovered the moment we find it and from there subsequent franchises with the same ability are discovered and then allocated and considered as per this patent as franchisees/sub franchises off the master franchise as well as off the sub franchisees themselves..
Because this Islamic Banking Sharia Compliant Blockchain Innovation is an actual digital mine on the blockchain with a secondary, third, fourth, fifth unlimited and continuous digital mine discovery ability and features, discovery capabilities which then has the ability to discover a third digital mine off the second discovered franchise digital mine which then has the ability to discover fourth digital mine off the third discovered digital mines and so on and so forth. Also from the second digital mine discovery onwards we have the ability to go to an actual asset/commodity which would end the new digital mine discovery it is unique and innovative hence the innovation patent.

Islamic Banking: Claim 1 Savings and Deposits

Claim 1. Islamic Banking sharia-compliant finance innovation on/using the Blockchain applied but not limited to: eliminate replace interest from the Savings and Deposits and transition to using this Islamic banking innovation revenue earnings returns shared model.
New Islamic bank banking blockchain sharia-compliant finance innovation for Banks, financial institutions & monetary fund's using digital currency, Digital asset/commodity, crypto currency for savings, deposit taking, trust, escrow, to remit, intermediary, safekeeping. Digital Commodity Bankcoin mines/mints earnings revenue, mines/mints transaction fees, proof of stake, pos, secondary mining/minting on the blockchain protocol/process.
Banking and financial entities can now use digital currency, Digital asset/commodity, and crypto currency as savings, deposits and term deposits for their clients and customers. Currently banks and financial institutions take money over the counter to open these accounts and then find the money used to pay the interest and associated costs on these accounts; take from Peter to pay Paul and or create it out of thin air this is not sharia-compliant. This new method gives banks and financial institutions the ability to eliminate those non sharia-compliant components, costs and exploit the savings, earnings revenue and fees therefore increase profits. Banks and financial institutions can now enter the crypto currency market using their clients and customers funds in the below methods and Bankcoin which is a crypto currency that banks and financial institutions can acquire to reproduce and perform the following.
Bankcoin will be used as an example however this new method will apply to all crypto currencies be they classed as but not limited to an asset, commodity, collateral, stock, property, currency meaning all those using a blockchain, any chain and associated with digital crypto currency with POS proof of stake/a secondary mining operation off the first/previous coin mined/minted. A further fundamental innovative step is in the current system deposits are seen as liabilities

because for example a 10 year term deposit/CDO certificate of deposit can be called in early by the customer even though the customer has to pay a penalty it is only minimal compared to the amount of loans the bank has written typed in and leant out against it, this Islamic banking innovation takes that to a whole new level by showing that the customer deposit is 100% backed reserved by in this example Bankcoin on the blockchain which means even when the customer calls in the deposit early it makes no difference to the health and security of the bank as it has the deposit backed and can continue to mine mint new Bankcoin's for itself. What this means in reality and practise this Islamic Banking innovation has turned what was once a liability on the banks' balance sheet is now an asset the same as the loan finance side of the ledgers.. This is a huge advancement in banking both sides of the balance sheet are assets in the positive if a deposit defaults is called early before the term is up the bank is fine it has the digital asset commodity to hold it up if a loan defaults it has its collateral to hold it up. If you look at claim two it works similar to this as well since they are principle only loans and finance they are backed up twice once by the collateral security on the loan and Bankcoin because the bank needs to earn revenue return for making the loan as that's where the banks' profits will now be.

Example

I walk into a bank that has this New Islamic bank banking blockchain sharia-compliant finance innovation and ask for an Islamic Bankcoin Savings Term Deposit 12 month that pays 4% pa shared earning revenue, I pass over the counter $13000.00 the Bank takes the $13000.00 and buys 10 Bankcoin's as each one would be worth $1300. It then allocates the Bankcoin to those customers Bankcoin Term Deposit Account. This could be done in a ledger where the Bank actually holds an amount of Bankcoin's and therefore just makes an entry or it could actually be sent via the Bankcoin network to the allocated designated customers account within the Bank. The Bank or financial institution can determine if customers or clients have access to the Bankcoin's or not. The bank then uses the Bankcoin that it has for fractional reserve leverage 3x 5x whatever the rules are for that specific Bank or financial institution. The Bankcoin's are then Minting/mining/POS proof of stake up to a

certain percentage pa the more the transactions throughout the network the better it mints/mines/pos proof of stake When a bank or financial institution uses example crypto currency Bankcoin for its savings, deposit and term deposit accounts as a new method it will have the following advantages that its current system does not have. Crypto currency Bankcoin is a decentralized financial instrument on its own decentralized blockchain and has the following benefits specifically designed for Islamic banks and financial institutions.
Bankcoin crypto currency has the ability to mint/mine to earn earnings revenue 1% onwards throughout the Bankcoin network by leaving the secured Bankcoin wallet open and having a positive Bankcoin balance, the advantage to the banks and financial institutions is they do not need to find that earnings revenue payment from somewhere else to pay to the savings, deposit or term deposit client customer. It is built into the code of crypto currency Bankcoin and can be exploited by the banks and financial institutions when used in this way. Bankcoin crypto currency has the ability to mine/mint the transaction fees throughout the Bankcoin network by leaving the secured Bankcoin wallet open and having a positive Bankcoin balance, the advantage to the banks and financial institutions is they do not need to find the transaction fees from somewhere else to contribute to the savings, deposit or term deposit client customer. It is built into the code of crypto currency Bankcoin and can be exploited by the banks and financial institutions when used in this way. Bankcoin has proof of stake (POS) feature where banks and financial institutions can see transactions come through. This is a fraud prevention mechanism which is built into the code therefore banks and financial institutions do not have to set up separate departments to deal with the fraud and security. The Bankcoin digital wallet has built into it a block explorer so banks and financial institutions can verify where their customers and clients transactions are coming from and going to for accounting purposes and security. No Risk because the banks and financial institutions would have ownership of the actual crypto currency Bankcoin. A lease option of the crypto currency may also be available. This is a way Banks and financial institutions can enter the Crypto currency market and benefit from the many advantages it has to offer without any cost or risk to them. No cost

because they are using the customers money to purchase the Bankcoin's and the Minting/mining/POS up to a certain percentage pa actually would make them a profit. The price of the crypto currency would be determined by such entities as the Bankcoin Reserve which would have insurance capabilities to cover customers Bankcoin accounts similar to the FDIC. This Bankcoin Crypto currency actually creates its own digits this is a cryptographic process throughout the Bankcoin Crypto currency network and this method when used by banks and financial institutions can be exploited.

Al Ajr using this Islamic Banking blockchain sharia-compliant finance innovation: Refers to commission, fees or wages charged for services. Islamic Banking blockchain Amana/Amanah using this Islamic Banking blockchain sharia-compliant finance innovation: Lit: reliability, trustworthiness, loyalty, honesty. Technically, an important value of Islamic society in mutual dealings. It refers to deposits in trust. A person can hold a property in trust for another, sometimes by express contract and sometimes by implication of a contract. Amanah entails absence of liability for loss except in breach of duty. Current Accounts are regarded as Amanah (trust). If the bank gets authority to use Current Accounts funds in his business, Amanah transforms into a loan. As every loan has to be repaid, banks are liable to repay full amount of the Current Accounts. Islamic Banking blockchain Bai Al-Arboon using this Islamic Banking blockchain sharia-compliant finance innovation: A sale agreement in which a security deposit is given in advance as a partial payment towards the price of the commodity purchased. This deposit is fortified if the buyer failed to meet his obligation. Islamic Banking blockchain Fatwah using this Islamic Banking blockchain sharia-compliant finance innovation: A religious decree.

Islamic Banking blockchain Fiqh using this Islamic Banking blockchain sharia-compliant finance innovation.: Islamic jurisprudence. The science of the Shariah. It is an important source of Islamic economics. Hajj using this Islamic Banking blockchain sharia-compliant finance innovation: Hajj means pilgrimage to Mecca and other holy places. Hajj, the fifth pillar of Islam will know of this innovation. Haram is a term not required using this Islamic Banking blockchain sharia-compliant finance innovation: Unlawful. Islamic

Banking blockchain Rab-al-maal using this Islamic Banking blockchain sharia-compliant finance innovation: In a mudaraba contract the person who invests the capital.

Riba is completely removed and not necessary using this Islamic Banking blockchain sharia-compliant finance innovation: One of the three fundamentals prohibitions in Islamic finance (the other two being Gharar and Maysir). This term literally means an increase or addition. Technically it denotes any increase or advantage obtained by the lender as a condition of the loan. Any risk- free or "guaranteed" rate of return on a loan or investment is riba. Riba, in all forms, is prohibited in Islam. Sharia compliance is fully met using this Islamic Banking blockchain sharia-compliant finance innovation: Islamic law as revealed in the Quran and through the example of Prophet Muhammad.

A Sharia compliant product meets the requirements of Islamic law. Sharia Board is the committee of Islamic scholars available to an Islamic financial institution for guidance and supervision in the development of Sharia compliant products. Islamic Banking blockchain Tawarruq using this Islamic Banking blockchain sharia-compliant finance innovation: Reversed murabaha. Wadiah using this Islamic Banking blockchain sharia-compliant finance innovation: Islamic safekeeping deposit device, in which the bank is deemed as a keeper and trustee of funds.

Islamic banking (Arabic: مصرفية إسلامية) using this innovation in banking and or banking finance activity that is consistent with the principles of sharia (Islamic law) and its practical application through the development of Islamic economics and takes it to the next level where we can use it to address all those without birth certificates, papers, bank accounts meaning the unbanked as they now have a fully compliant banking and finance products and processes to enter and engage with. As such, a more correct term for Islamic banking is sharia-compliant finance. Sharia prohibits acceptance of specific interest or fees for loans of money (known as riba, or usury), whether the payment is fixed or floating. Investment in businesses that provide goods or services considered contrary to Islamic principles (e.g. pork or alcohol) is also haraam ("sinful and prohibited"). This innovation addresses all these issues in the current banking and financial sectors and brings them into the 21st century via the blockchain, no interest, no usury, no riba this is replaced with genuine earnings revenue. An excess or increase is not a part of this innovation as depositors and savers are partners with the banks financial institutions and monetary fund's using this innovation under patent license. Technically, it means an increase over principal in a loan transaction or in exchange for a commodity accrued to the owner (lender) without giving an equivalent counter-value or recompense ('iwad) in return to the other party; every increase which is without an 'iwad or equal counter value.

Claim 1 - Savings & Deposit - Image 1 – Inventor Gary McAlister

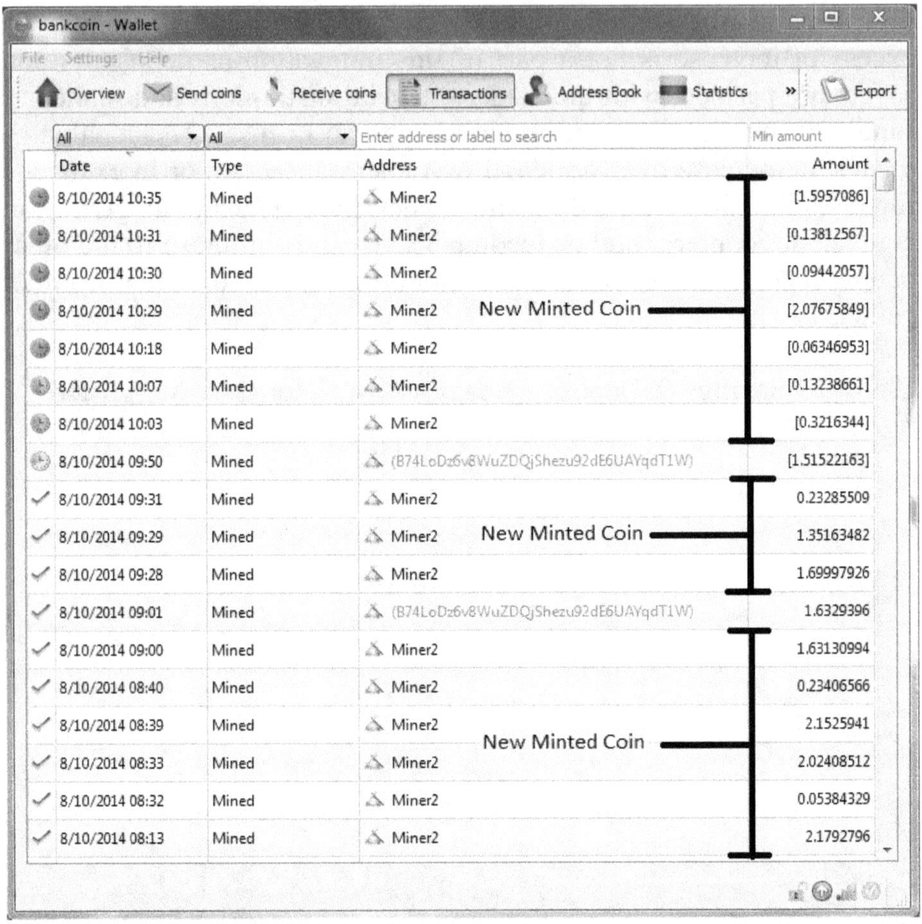

When a bank, financial institution and or monetary fund uses this Islamic Banking sharia-compliant innovation on the blockchain with crypto currency, digital asset, digital commodity example Bankcoin for its but not limited to: savings, deposit and term deposit accounts as a new model method it will have the following advantages that its current system does not have. crypto currency, digital asset, digital commodity example Bankcoin is a decentralized financial product and instrument in its own right on its own decentralized blockchain and has the following benefits specifically designed such as POS proof of stake, secondary mining, revenue earnings shared incorporated built in for but not limited to: banks and financial institutions and or monetary funds.

Bankcoin crypto currency, digital asset, digital commodity has the ability to mint new Bankcoin's on the blockchain at a per annum rate starting at as a number 1% upwards throughout the Bankcoin network by leaving the secured Bankcoin wallet open and having a positive Bankcoin balance, the advantage to the banks and financial institutions is they do not need to find that interest, riba, usury payment from somewhere else to pay to the savings, deposit or term deposit client customer. It is built into the code of crypto currency Bankcoin and can be exploited by the banks and financial institutions when used in this way it is the beginning of a whole new market for those wanting to enter the Islamic banking sector and provide this the only product in the world to the entire market.

As you can see in the image because there is already has a principle primary Bankcoin Balance the wallet is able to discover on the blockchain mint mine new Bankcoin's at a rate of up to in Bankcoin's case 10% per annum. Islamic banks and institutions could show their Bankcoin wallet on a big screen to their new savings and deposit customers who are specifically by sharia law looking for a deposit product that is in full compliance with the law this way they can know exactly how their revenue earnings have been made and can feel comfortable in knowing that they have broken no laws and are held to the highest account.

As you can see the bank mined minted on the blockchain 1.5957086 Bankcoin's and because Bankcoin has a Valuation of US$1300.00 per Bankcoin by the Bankcoin Reserve you know that the Bank has earned by discovering it US$2074.42118 which it shares with the customer/customer base at an agreed percentage that is fair to both parties. Since we know the discovery rate of Bankcoin is 10% per annum the bank may share ½ to client customer ½ to the bank. Meaning: US$1037.21059 between them. This is the product and process the Islamic world has been looking for centuries a genuine product that can undergo any amount of scrutiny and fully comply with the moral and ethical foundation of non riba profit share, revenue earnings Sharia law principles.

There is some risk as to be expected with a digital mining operation as digital blockchain mining is not an exact science therefore the revenue earnings return will fluctuate up to the 10% per annum rate. Maybe 9.2% at the end of the year however these revenue earnings returns are mined and minted by the minute, hour, day week all depending on how much is in the depositor client's account and the value of the term deposit in fiat meaning if the Bank acquired 3650 Bankcoin's then it is fair to say it would mint mine approximately 1 Bankcoin per day as you can see the numbers in the image.

Claim 1 - Savings & Deposit - Image 2 – Inventor Gary McAlister

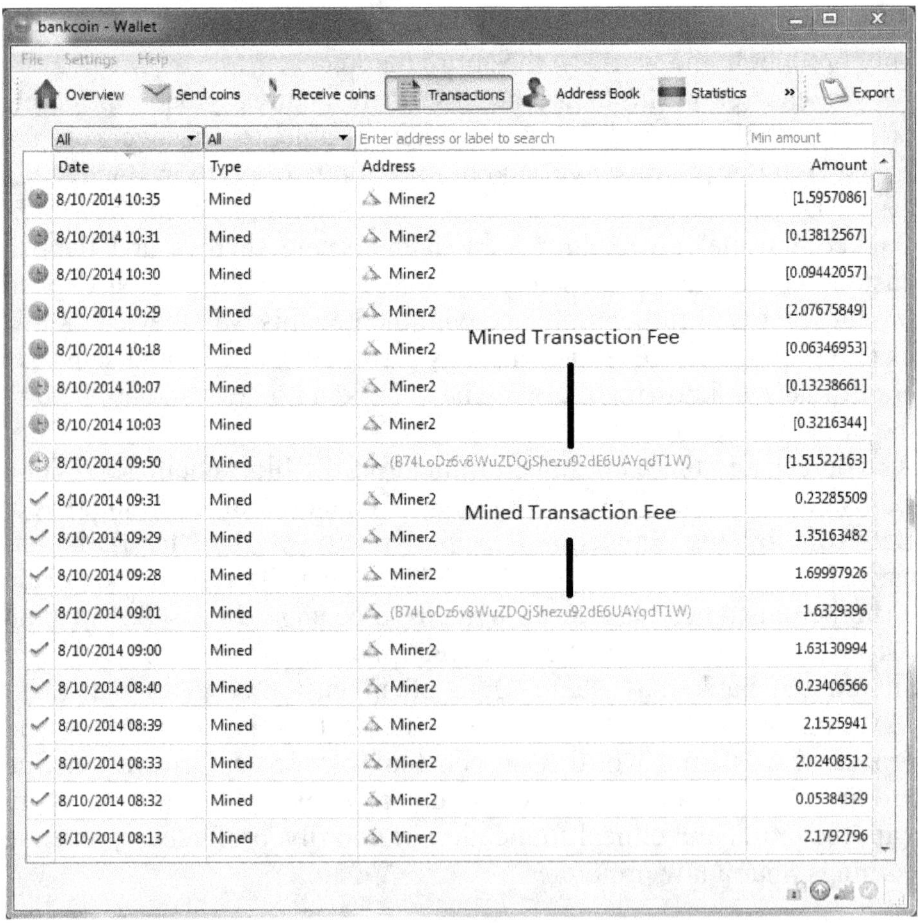

Date	Type	Address	Amount
8/10/2014 10:35	Mined	Miner2	[1.5957086]
8/10/2014 10:31	Mined	Miner2	[0.13812567]
8/10/2014 10:30	Mined	Miner2	[0.09442057]
8/10/2014 10:29	Mined	Miner2	[2.07675849]
8/10/2014 10:18	Mined	Miner2	[0.06346953]
8/10/2014 10:07	Mined	Miner2	[0.13238661]
8/10/2014 10:03	Mined	Miner2	[0.3216344]
8/10/2014 09:50	Mined	(B74LoDz6v8WuZDQjShezu92dE6UAYqdT1W)	[1.51522163]
8/10/2014 09:31	Mined	Miner2	0.23285509
8/10/2014 09:29	Mined	Miner2	1.35163482
8/10/2014 09:28	Mined	Miner2	1.69997926
8/10/2014 09:01	Mined	(B74LoDz6v8WuZDQjShezu92dE6UAYqdT1W)	1.6329396
8/10/2014 09:00	Mined	Miner2	1.63130994
8/10/2014 08:40	Mined	Miner2	0.23406566
8/10/2014 08:39	Mined	Miner2	2.1525941
8/10/2014 08:33	Mined	Miner2	2.02408512
8/10/2014 08:32	Mined	Miner2	0.05384329
8/10/2014 08:13	Mined	Miner2	2.1792796

Bankcoin crypto currency has the ability to also mine the transaction fees throughout the entire Bankcoin blockchain network by leaving the secured Bankcoin wallet open and having a positive Bankcoin balance, the advantage to the banks and financial institutions is they can capture transaction fees from external transactions being made by external users which can contribute to the savings, deposit or term deposit client customer. It is built into the code of crypto currency Bankcoin blockchain and can be exploited by the Islamic banks and financial institutions when used in this way.

Claim 1 - Savings & Deposit - Image 3 – Inventor Gary McAlister

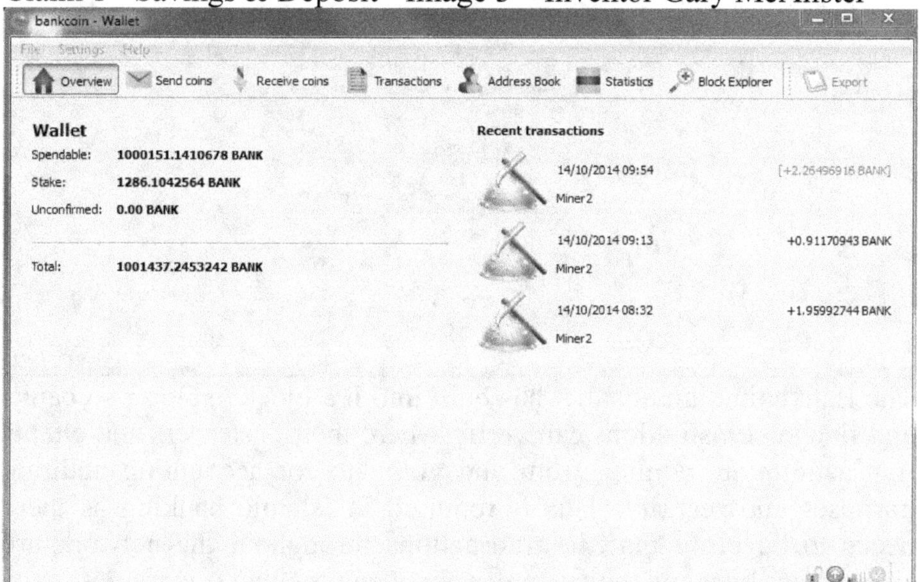

Bankcoin has proof of stake (POS) feature where banks and financial institutions can see transactions come through the blockchain network and make sure that it is legitimate and not fraudulent and it is also a secondary mining feature of the Bankcoin POS proof of stake product process which replaces interest, usury riba to earning, revenue returns. This is a fraud prevention mechanism which is built into the code therefore banks and financial institutions do not have to set up separate departments to deal with fraud and security. 10% per annum directly related to your Bankcoin account balance and per your fiat deposit and savings made.

Claim 1 - Savings & Deposit - Image 4 – Inventor Gary McAlister

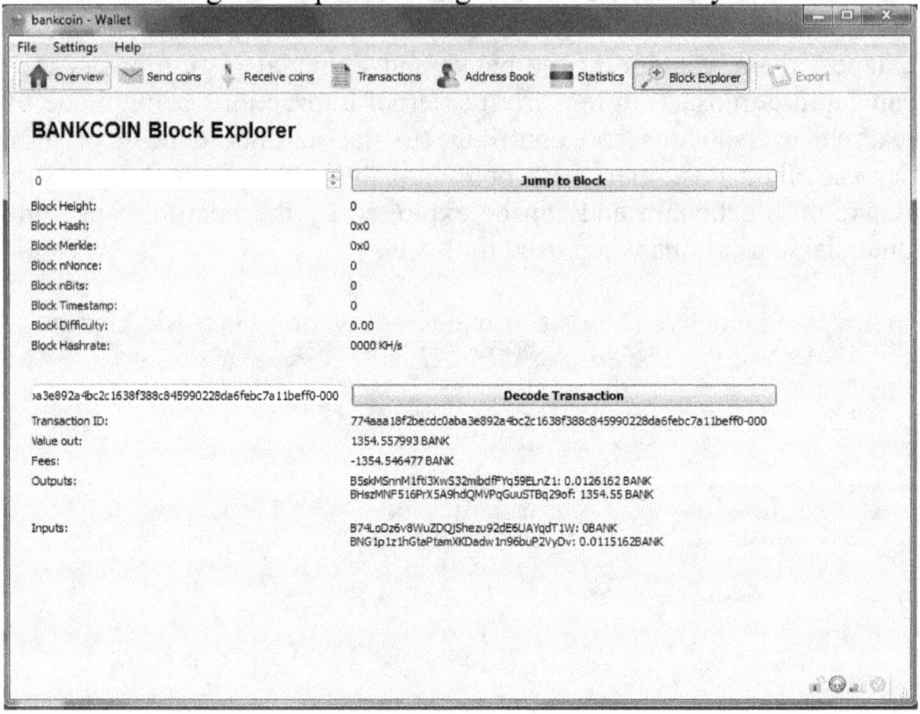

The Bankcoin digital wallet has built into it a block explorer so banks and financial institutions can verify where their customers and clients transactions are coming from and going to for accounting auditing purposes and security. This is required in Islamic banking as there needs to be proof that the transactions throughout the network are sharia compliant and the customer client can see that it is true.

Claim 1 - Savings & Deposit - Image 5 – Inventor Gary McAlister

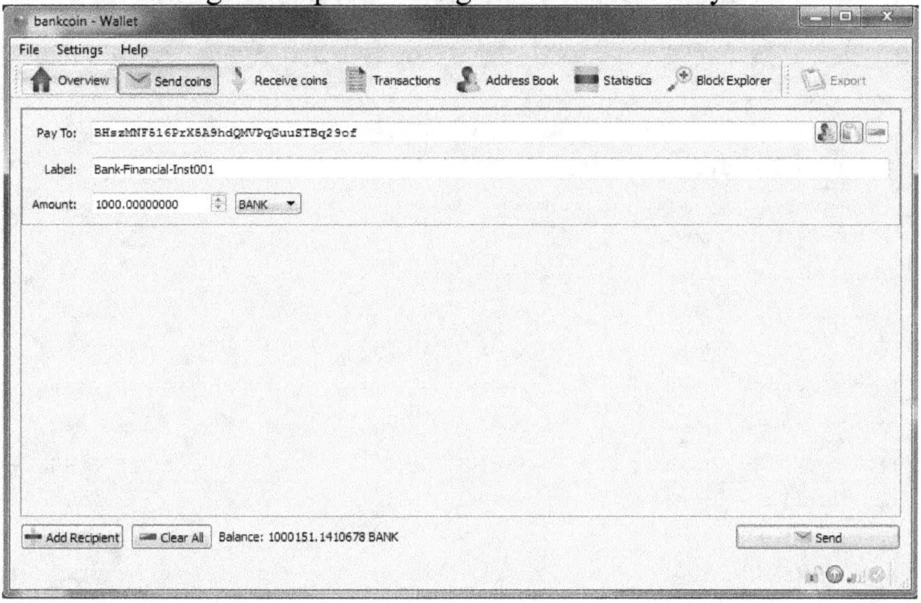

No Risk to the Islamic banks and financial institutions because they would have ownership of the actual crypto currency Bankcoin. A lease option of the crypto currency may also be available.

Claim 1 - Savings & Deposit - Image 6 – Inventor Gary McAlister

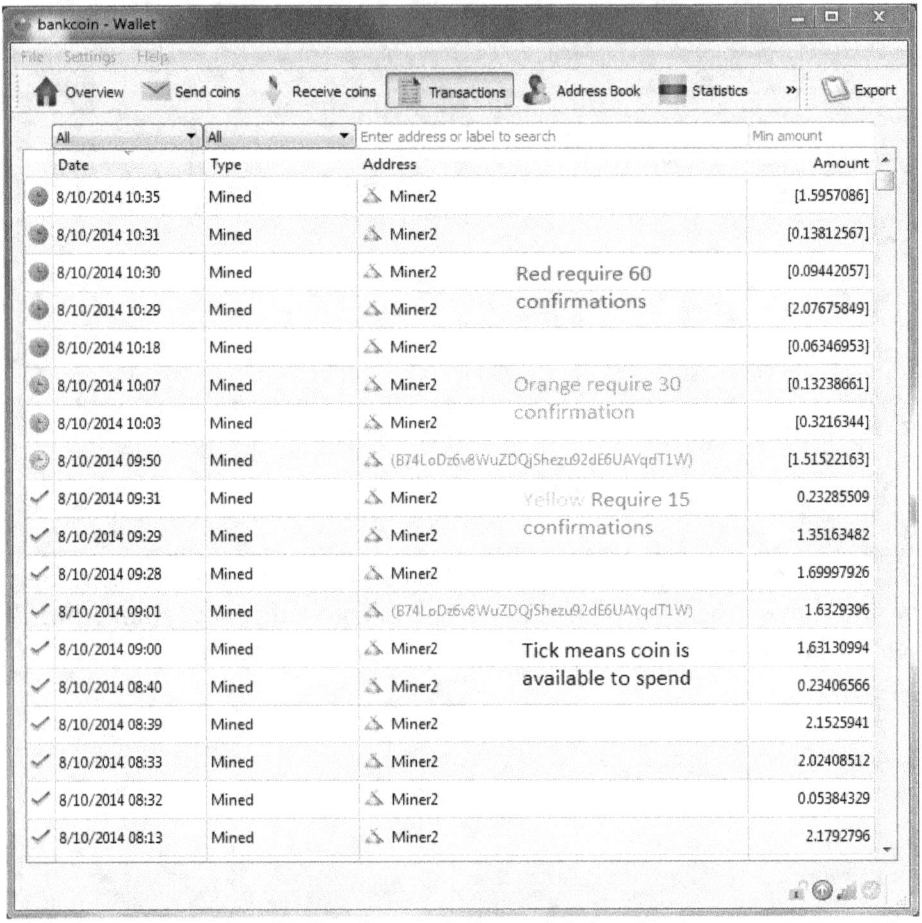

Date	Type	Address	Amount
8/10/2014 10:35	Mined	Miner2	[1.5957086]
8/10/2014 10:31	Mined	Miner2	[0.13812567]
8/10/2014 10:30	Mined	Miner2	[0.09442057]
8/10/2014 10:29	Mined	Miner2	[2.07675849]
8/10/2014 10:18	Mined	Miner2	[0.06346953]
8/10/2014 10:07	Mined	Miner2	[0.13238661]
8/10/2014 10:03	Mined	Miner2	[0.3216344]
8/10/2014 09:50	Mined	(B74LoDz6v8WuZDQjShezu92dE6UAYqdT1W)	[1.51522163]
8/10/2014 09:31	Mined	Miner2	0.23285509
8/10/2014 09:29	Mined	Miner2	1.35163482
8/10/2014 09:28	Mined	Miner2	1.69997926
8/10/2014 09:01	Mined	(B74LoDz6v8WuZDQjShezu92dE6UAYqdT1W)	1.6329396
8/10/2014 09:00	Mined	Miner2	1.63130994
8/10/2014 08:40	Mined	Miner2	0.23406566
8/10/2014 08:39	Mined	Miner2	2.1525941
8/10/2014 08:33	Mined	Miner2	2.02408512
8/10/2014 08:32	Mined	Miner2	0.05384329
8/10/2014 08:13	Mined	Miner2	2.1792796

This is a way Islamic Banks and financial institutions can enter the Crypto currency market and benefit from the many advantages this innovation has to offer without any cost or risk to them. No cost because they are using the customer's money to purchase the Bankcoin's and the Minting/mining/POS proof of stake through the blockchain up to a certain percentage pa actually would make them a profit. There is also a statistics section inside the Bankcoin wallet.

Claim 1 - Savings & Deposit - Image 7 – Inventor Gary McAlister

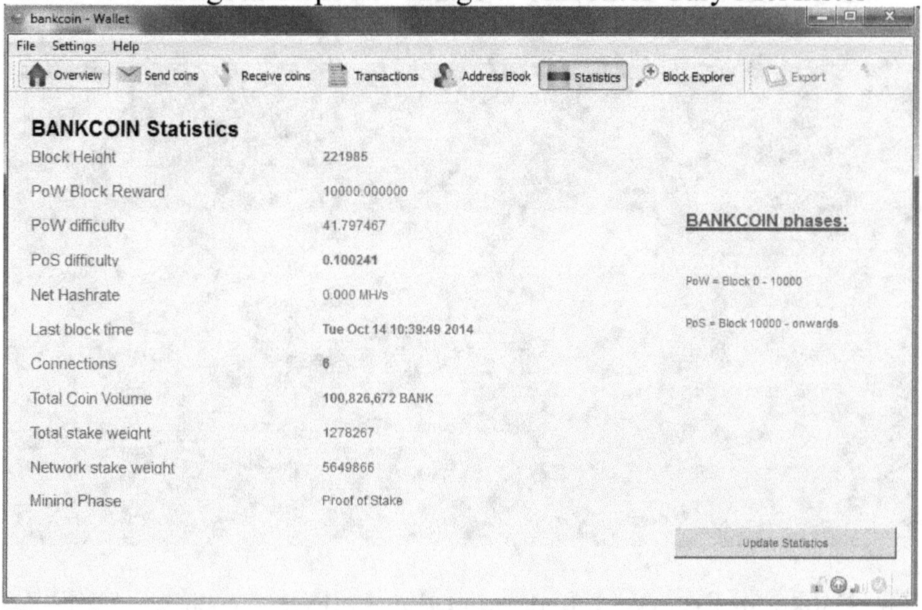

The price of the crypto currency is determined by such entities as the Bankcoin Reserve which would have insurance capabilities to cover customers Bankcoin accounts similar to the FDIC.

Claim 1 - Savings & Deposit - Image 8 – Inventor Gary McAlister

The Bankcoin Reserve valuates and Rates all Crypto currency, digital asset/commodities that are used with this innovation. The reason being the price the Bankcoin Reserve sets per month for digital commodity Bankcoin is done by a special formula which is the ceiling price of gold in that month becomes the floor price of Bankcoin for the following month, This is a critical component in Islamic banking and sharia law as it is pegging old money gold to new money Bankcoin which by default eliminates interest, riba, usury. This protects the Bankcoin holder from market manipulation and volatility so that they can get on with business and have certainty for the forthcoming months' worth of business. This way they are able to make sustainable projections on where their business can grow and make solid employment decisions as they know that Bankcoin can never go down in price it can only go up as per the gold market per ounce price. The Bankcoin Reserve is a price taker directly from the gold market it is not a price setter.

This Bankcoin Crypto currency actually discovers its own Bankcoin's in a mining process this is a cryptographic process throughout the Bankcoin Crypto currency blockchain network and can be exploited by Islamic banks and financial institutions via this new method innovation of using the newly minted mined Bankcoin and mining of the network transaction fees to cover the costs of the savings and term deposit and what is left over would be clear profit. These also add to the balance of the wallet as each amount of a Bankcoin that comes in increases the wallets ability to mint and mine more Bankcoin's.

1, Bankcoin Reserve - This reserve evaluates the gold market and sets the price accordingly. The formula is the ceiling of the gold oz. price is the floor of the Bankcoin value meaning it can never go below its current traded value. This is monitored now monthly. Bankcoin Reserve also acts as an insurer for the Bankcoin's between Bankcoin holders and the Bank to guarantee delivery of the Bankcoin's and the mint/mine of Bankcoin's.

2, Bankcoin wallets maybe installed at the bank so they have possession/ownership of the Bankcoin assets they acquire.

3, Term deposit is requested by Customer

4, Bankcoin request is sent to Bankcoin Reserve

5, Bankcoin Reserve facilitates trade between Bankcoin holder and bank

6, Bankcoin holder fiat account is created by bank for funds from the bank to the Bankcoin holder

7, Bankcoin's are transferred from Bankcoin holder to Bank wallet

8, Bankcoin holder funds are cleared

9, When term deposit ends Bankcoin's keep minting and mining new Bankcoin's for the Bank these would now be seen as the Banks reserves therefore instead of requiring a Bank to increase its capital reserve position which costs the Banks money it makes more financial and economic sense to use the Bankcoin reserves to also transition out of the having to hold fiat as reserves as it is a cost loss and expensive and use Bankcoin instead which continue to grow, earn and provide the bank with a positive income earnings and returns sustainably and indefinitely depending on contract with the BCR Bankcoin Reserve.

Advantages to banks using this new Islamic banking innovation new method process.

1, it is a blockchain asset commodity that brings 10% revenue to the table

2, that's 4% the banks do not have to find from the loan finance side don't have to find from somewhere else to satisfy the term deposit
3, It provides you with 6% free and clear as it mints up to 10% You could even increase the term deposit % to attract even more Islamic savings and deposit business.
4, It is a new product so you can promote and advertise it
5, It will attract new Islamic business especially the sophisticated and younger market being crypto currency
6, It will continue to mint for the bank after the term deposit has ended.
7, The first genuine sharia compliant banking product that has no riba, interest or usury.
8, this attracts an entirely new market namely Islamic and ethical banking professionals
9, Cost the bank nothing to acquire Bankcoin's as it is acquired with the customers term deposit funds.
10, Has a low minimum of 10 Bankcoin's to start $13k which is pretty much the minimum term deposit amount. You will need to pay and cover the cost of training your team; we can do this over Skype video training sessions.
11, The Bankcoin Reserve covers/insures the amount mined & minted 10% and updates the price monthly to reflect the market price for the previous month. This can also be front loaded. If you have any questions or want to acquire Bankcoin's and get started simply let us know support@bankcoinreserve.com

Why Bankcoin's new Islamic savings and deposit innovation on the blockchain product/process/method matters to Banks.
Banks are losing market share and therefore profits to digital innovators every day. The current banking system is slow to adapt so innovators being innovators quickly innovate their way around them as we have seen in Bitcoin and neobanks therefore existing Banks need to be at the front of this or they will automatically be left behind. Shareholders know and understand this why CEO's and CFO's do not is a shame.
Bankcoin takes a different approach and believes that its new product can quickly allow banks to adapt this plug and play process. You can

look at the Bankcoin product as a future proof step for Banks and when you are talking about billions of dollars and new markets for these banks Bankcoin matters a lot.

We have had a centralized banking system for just over 100 years and I am sure we will have it for another 100. Where Bankcoin comes in is it slightly changes the model it does not replace it just changes it by way of the interest usury component this is where the innovation is. As it stands the interest usury component is on those that borrow which by default a percentage goes to those that save deposit. We have created a new innovative product using Bankcoin and the blockchain to where the bank still makes its interest but in a more socially acceptable ethical sharia compliant way.

So can both digital and fiat work together the answer is absolutely they can now we just need to constantly update our banking products processes and procedures to stay relevant in the market place or be replaced by those that will.

It is unreasonable to expect the market not to shift to a better system because you don't think or in the case of Bankcoin being so new that you don't know about it which is why I am here once again explaining it in the hope that more of those in the banking sector will see it.

So the process is pretty simple for banks to implement the new product. In Australia it is classed as an asset so its security or collateral, Lets work with Term deposits because it's fixed rate, fixed term and fixed amount just for simplicity.

Bank promotes/markets Bankcoin Term deposits, ethical profit share term deposits which will cater to the Islamic banking sector and obviously those wanting ethical banking products as there are no interest/usury in this new product. Our young people want to be in crypto currency but it has to make sense and be of direct benefit to them which Bankcoin is.

Customer comes in and says I would like a Bankcoin Term deposit please 130k 12 months currently at 4% return on my money. Bank says absolutely it's our new product and we are very excited about it, may I ask how you heard about it? TV ads ok thank you, you would do your typical extraction of information here for your marketing department.

So customer hands over or transfers 130k from his bank to your bank and you will then open up his Bankcoin term deposit and the customer says thank you very much. At no point is the customer directly connected to the coin it is an allocation from the banks main Bankcoin wallet, ledger entry.

Now this is where you need to focus you have the customers 130k the banks will then leverage it here in Australia 3x-5x leverage so that 130k becomes let's keep it simple 390k. The bank purchases 130k of Bankcoin loans out the other 270k by way of its current system charging interest etc. this is what pays the 2% or whatever it is from the discount window.

Let me be clear here the 130k stays true because it is now new money there is no cost or interest related to this 130k it is free and clear of the current system and it is not based on debt. It is simply a trade transfer from Bankcoin to/for fiat.

What the Bankcoin mints simply gets converted to fiat this way Bankcoin always stays true.

The 130k buys 100 Bankcoin's as it is an asset and since it is an asset it can be leveraged again 3x another 390k to be leant out against it. This is a huge advantage in of itself however there is more.

The bank takes possession of the Bankcoin's to secure its position 100% not 3 not 5 not 10, 100 and those customers that are in this new product know that its real it's not some gimmick to get their money. You can even show them its minting new coin and mining the transaction fees education is key here to be open and transparent.

This Islamic Banking Sharia Compliant Blockchain Innovation provides new methods for banks, financial institutions and monetary funds to provide ethical loans finance including Islamic deposits and finance with no riba, interest or usury. Banks, financial institutions and monetary funds can earn the interest or usury using a different process which is an internal crypto currency block chain dependent process the minting of new coin and mining of transaction fees. This new method is made possible because of the latest technology inside the crypto currency wallet as well as external factors. Customer applies for a loan, bank approves the loan and at the same time the bank acquires Bankcoin to the value of the loan. The bank then leverages the bank coin 2x as a number Ix goes to the pay for the

Bankcoin and the other goes to the borrower. The borrower makes repayments however it is only the principle that he owes as there is no interest or usury.

This Islamic Banking Sharia Compliant Blockchain Innovation concerns cryptographic currency for use in the finance industry. More specifically the present invention relates to the provision of cryptographic currency by banking or other such financial institutions for their everyday products such as deposit and term deposit accounts etc. The financial institution then mints/mines the cryptographic currency up to a certain percentage to pay the interest on the account etc.

Islamic Banking: Claim 2 Loan and Finance

Claim 2. Islamic Banking sharia-compliant finance innovation on/using the Blockchain applied but not limited to: eliminate interest, riba, usury from the Loan and Finance equation and transition to using this Islamic banking innovation to a revenue earnings returns shared model principle only loan and finance
New Blockchain Islamic bank banking innovation for loans and finance
New method for banks, financial institutions and monetary funds to provide ethical loans finance including Islamic finance with no interest, riba or usury. Banks, financial institutions and monetary funds can replace interest, riba or usury using this new method which is an internal crypto currency blockchain dependent process the minting of new coin and mining of transaction fees.
Customer walks into a bank that has our Islamic Banking blockchain innovation and asks for a loan/finance to buy a car. Now under Islamic banking sharia law the customer cannot pay interest, riba, usury on that loan therefore a mark-up has to be put in place for the bank to make money so if you want a car and it is $10k then the bank would buy it and re sell it to you at $20k called a mark-up repayments over a term say 10 years. SO in reality you are paying interest its just in a different form and its understandable how they reached this position because customer wants the car today. This is where our Islamic Banking Blockchain innovation comes into play. The Bank no longer needs to use Backdoor riba using the mark-up model because it can simply use this innovation and back the loan for the car with our digital asset/commodity 100% meaning the loan becomes principle only to the customer because they are sharing in the origination and formation of the loan together. The customer gets what he needs a car at its true price and the bank gets what they need which could be seen as profit, earnings, margin, revenue only and all because of the customer requiring a loan. The returns on this loan come from what this innovation actually does which is mine/mint POS proof of stake

and secondary mine not just new assets/commodities but also the transactions that go throughout the entire asset/commodity allocated network for that bank it can then simply monetize the assets/commodities mined for fiat as it has the license and ability to bring new money into existence. All AML and KYC requirements have been met by the bank on the customer and the blockchain can be closed loop therefore all assets/commodities on the network are known. If the customer defaults on the loan the bank are protected because it has 100% reserves therefore the loan default does not affect other customers and clients of that bank.

A New method for banks, financial institutions and monetary funds to provide ethical loans finance including Islamic finance with no interest, riba or usury. Banks, financial institutions and monetary funds can earn the interest, riba or usury using a different process which is an internal crypto currency blockchain dependent process the minting of new coin and mining of transaction fees. This new method is made possible because of the latest technology inside the crypto currency wallet as well as external factors. Customer applies for a loan bank approves the loan and at the same time the bank acquires bank coin to the value of the loan. The bank then leverages the bank coin 2x as a number Ix goes to the pay for the bank coin and the other goes to the borrower. The borrower makes repayments however it is only the principle that he owes as there is no riba, interest, riba or usury.

This new method gives banks, financial institutions and monetary funds the ability to earn the interest, riba or usury in a different process being the minting of new coin and mining of transaction fees which is an internal crypto currency block chain dependent process as opposed to the current system method of charging interest, riba or usury on loans/finance to the Borrower/Person/Entity/Applicant. Bankcoin will be used in this and the following claims as the crypto currency example, however this new method will apply to all crypto currencies that are blockchain dependent irrelevant of what they are called. Example, bank, note, coin, bar, rights; these examples of crypto currencies names are all blockchain dependent.

A centralised and/or decentralised bank, financial institution and monetary fund can issue a single crypto currency using this new

method to some and/or all banks, financial institutions and monetary funds and also can issue separate specific crypto currencies to some banks, financial institutions and monetary funds. A Borrower/Person/Entity/Applicant/Country enters a crypto currency/blockchain dependent loan/finance agreement with banks, financial institutions and monetary funds to take advantage of this new method of no riba, interest or usury.
Example: Bankcoin Loan, Bankcoin Finance
Each Borrower/Person/Entity/Applicant/Country could have its own allocation abbreviated in the wallet code on the blockchain. Example BankAU, BankUS, BankEU, HSBCAU, HSBCEU, HSBCUS, GaryAU, GaryEU, GEAU, GEUS, GEEU. Each with its own mined market cap, valuation, reserve, coin mint mine market cap %, and transaction fee mint mining cap %. The banks, financial institutions and monetary fund's then buy/acquire Bankcoin for or on behalf of the Borrower/Person/Entity/Applicant/Country to secure the position from 1% upwards to back the loan/finance.
Example: The banks, financial institutions and monetary funds can back this loan/finance 100% to protect it in case the loan/finance Borrower/Person/Entity/Applicant/Country defaults. The banks, financial institutions and monetary funds can leverage the Bankcoin's which it has acquired by 2x, 5x, 30x, etc. whatever the rules are for that specific bank, financial institution and monetary fund. The leveraged Bankcoin's is to create fiat which is then allocated to the Borrower/Person/Entity/Applicant/Country. This is riba and interest free, no usury because Bankcoin being Crypto Currency/Blockchain dependent actually mint/mines new coins and mine/mints the transaction fees throughout the Bankcoin network.
This gives the banks, financial institutions and monetary funds the ability to exploit this new method and determine what % it wants to earn via the mint/mine process.
All associated fees would still apply Example: late payment/overdue payment fees; these fees could either be in fiat or Bankcoin or both. Only the principle loan/finance is required to be repaid.
Al Rahn Al using this Islamic Banking blockchain sharia-compliant finance innovation: An arrangement whereby a valuable asset is

placed as collateral for a debt. The collateral may be disposed of in the event of a default.

Bai Bithaman Ajil mark-up removed using this Islamic Banking blockchain sharia-compliant finance innovation: This contract refers to the sale of goods on a deferred payment basis. Equipment or goods requested by the client are bought by the bank which subsequently sells the goods to the client an agreed price which includes the bank's mark-up (profit). The client may be allowed to settle payment by instalments within a pre-agreed period, or in a lump sum. Similar to a Murabaha contract, but with payment on a deferred basis. Bai Muajjal (Deferred Payment Contract) mark-up removed using this Islamic Banking blockchain sharia-compliant finance innovation: A contract involving the sale of goods on a deferred payment basis. The bank or provider of capital buys the goods (assets) on behalf of the business owner. The bank then sells the goods to the client at an agreed price, which will include a mark-up since the bank needs to make a profit. The business owner can pay the total balance at an agreed future date or make instalments over a pre-agreed period. This is similar to a Murabaha contract since it is also a credit sale.

Istisna (Progressive Financing) using this Islamic Banking blockchain sharia-compliant finance innovation: A contract of acquisition of goods by specification or order where the price is paid progressively in accordance with the progress of a job. It is a contractual agreement for manufacturing goods and commodities, allowing cash payment in advance and future delivery or a future payment and future delivery. A manufacturer or builder agrees to produce or build a well-described good or building at a given price on a given date in the future. Price can be paid in instalments, step by step as agreed between the parties. Istisna'a can be used for providing the facility of financing the manufacture or construction of houses, plants, projects, and building of bridges, roads and highways. Ju'alal using this Islamic Banking blockchain sharia-compliant finance innovation.: Lit: stipulated price for performing any service. Technically applied in the model of Islamic banking by some. Mudaraba using this Islamic Banking blockchain sharia-compliant finance innovation.: An Investment partnership. As a financing technique adopted by Islamic banks, it is a contract in which all the capital is provided by the Islamic bank while the business is managed by the other party. The profit is shared in pre-agreed ratios, and loss, if any, is borne by the investor. Mudarib using this Islamic Banking blockchain sharia-compliant finance innovation: In a mudaraba contract, the person or party who acts as entrepreneur. Murabaha using this Islamic Banking blockchain sharia-compliant finance innovation: A form of credit which enables customers to make a purchase without having to take out an interest bearing loan. The bank buys an item and then sells it on to the customer on a deferred basis this is backdoor riba and forbidden which is why this innovation is so unique it addresses this issue head on and says all Islamic Banking blockchain sharia-compliant finance innovation loans and finance are principle only with no tricks or excuses as this innovation clearly demonstrates there is no reason one must take out a loan or finance for anything and pay a hidden interest in the form of mark up to get around the sharia law and compliance. This innovation patent sets the foundation for the complete elimination of riba usury and interest once and for all. Current out-dated financial system which works as following: Non Sharia Compliant - Currency/Credit Creation - Debt Slavery - Liability - Interest Vs this new innovation being Asset/Commodity Discovery – Sovereign wealth and Freedom - Asset/Commodity mined, acquired and traded - Earnings/Revenue then Shared. This innovation claim also brings into the blockchain product and process the following but not limited to:

Islamic Banking blockchain Dayn or Debt: A Dayn comes into existence as a result of any other contract or credit transaction. It is incurred either by way of rent or sale or purchase or in any other way that leaves it as a debt to another. Duyun (debts) ought to be returned without any profit since they are advanced to help the needy and meet their demands and, therefore, the lender should not impose on the borrower more than what he had given on credit. Falah: Falah means to thrive, to become happy or to have luck and success. Technically it implies success both in this world and in the Akhirah (Hereafter). The Falah presumes belief in one God, the apostlehood of Prophet Muhammad (Peace be upon him), Akhirah and conformity to the Sharia'h in behaviour. Al Ghunm bil Ghurm : This provides the rationale and the principle of profit sharing in Shirkah arrangements. Earning profit is legitimized only by engaging in an economic venture, risk sharing and thereby contributing to the economy. Halal: Anything permitted by the Sharia'h. Hibah: Hibah means Gift. Ijab: Offer, in a contract; see also qabul. Ijtihad: It refers to an endeavor of a qualified jurist to derive or formulate a rule of law to determine the true ruling of the divine law in a matter on which the revelation is not explicit or certain, on the basis of Nass or evidence found in the Holy Qur'an and the Sunnah. Express injunctions have no room for Ijtihad. Implied injunctions can be interpreted in different ways by way of inference from the accepted principles of the Sharia'h 'Illah : It is the attribute of an event that entails a particular Divine ruling in all cases possessing that attribute. 'Illah is the basis for applying analogy for determining permissibility or otherwise of any act or transaction. Ijma' : Consensus of all or majority of the leading qualified jurists on a certain Sharia'h matter in a certain age.

Islamic Banking blockchain 'Inah (A kind of Bai) : Double sale by which the borrower and the lender sell and then resell an object between them, once for cash and once for a higher price on credit, with the net result of a loan with interest. 'Inan (A type of Shrikah) : It is a form of partnership in which each partner contributes capital and has a right to work for the business, not necessarily equally. Istihsan : It is a doctrine of Islamic law that allows exception to strict legal reasoning, or guiding choice among possible legal outcomes, when considerations of human welfare so demand. Israf: It refers to immoderateness, exaggeration and waste and covers spending on lawful objects but exceeding moderation in quantity or quality; spending on superfluous objects while necessities are unmet; spending on objects that are incompatible with the economic standard of the majority of the population. See also Tabzir

Islamic Banking blockchain Jahl or Jahala : Ignorance, lack of knowledge; indefiniteness in a contract, sometime leading to gharar. Jua alah or Ji'alah : Literally, Joalah constitutes wages, pay, stipend or reward. Legally, it is a contract for performing a given task against a prescribed fee in a given period. A similar contract is 'Ujrah' in which any work is done against stipulated wage or fee. Kali bil-Kali : The term Kali refers to something delayed; appears in a maxim forbidding the sale of alkali bil-Kali i.e. the exchange of a delayed counter value for another delayed counter value. Al- Kafalah

(Suretyship) : Literally, Kafalah means responsibility, amenability or suretyship, Legally in Kafalah a third party become surety for the payment of debt. It is a pledge given to a creditor that the debtor will pay the debt, fine etc. Suretyship in Islamic law is the creation of an additional liability with regard to the claim, not to the debt or the assumption only of a liability and not of the debt. Kharaj bi-al-Daman: Gain accompanies liability for loss; a Hadith forming a legal maxim and a basic principle – see also Al- Ghunm bil Ghurm. Khiyar: Option or a power to annul or cancel a contract. Khiyar al-Majlis: Option of the contracting session; the power to annul a contract possessed by both contracting parties as long as they do not separate.

Islamic Banking blockchain Khiyar al-Shart: A right, stipulated by one or both of the parties to a contract, to cancel the contract for any reason for a fixed period of time. Mal-e-Mutaqawam : Things the use of which is lawful under the Sharia'h; or wealth that has a commercial value. Legal tenders of modern age that carry monetary value are included in Mal-eMutaqawam. It is possible that certain wealth has no commercial value for Muslims (non-Mutaqawam) but is valuable for non-Muslims. Examples are wine and pork. Mithli (Fungible goods): Goods that can be returned in kind, i.e. gold for gold, silver for silver, US $ for US $, wheat for wheat, etc. Mubah: Object that is lawful (i.e. something which is permissible to use or trade in). Musawamah: Musawamah is a general kind of sale in which price of the commodity to be traded is bargained between seller and the purchaser without any reference to the price paid or cost incurred by the former. Qabul: Acceptance, in a contract; see also Ijab.

Islamic Banking blockchain Qard (Loan of fungible objects): The literal meaning of Qard is 'to cut'. It is so called because the property is really cut off when it is given to the borrower. Legally, Qard means to give anything having value in the ownership of the other by way of virtue so that the latter could avail of the same for his benefit with the condition that same or similar amount of that thing would be paid back on demand or at the settled time. It is that loan which a person gives to another as a help, charity or advance for a certain time. The repayment of loan is obligatory. The Holy Prophet is reported to have said "Every loan must be paid". But if a debtor is in difficulty, the creditor is expected to extend time or even to voluntarily remit the whole or a part of the principal. Qard is, in fact, a particular kind of Salaf. Loans under Islamic law can be classified into Salaf and Qard, the former being loan for fixed time and the latter payable on demand. (see Salaf) Qimar : Qimar means gambling. Technically, it is an arrangement in which possession of a property is contingent upon the happening of an uncertain event. By implication it applies to a situation in which there is a loss for one party and a gain for the other without specifying which party will lose and which will gain. Qiyas: Literally it means measure, example, comparison or analogy. Technically, it means a derivation of the law on the analogy of an existing law if the basis ('illah) of the two is the same. It is one of the sources of Islamic law.

Islamic Banking blockchain Riba Al-Fadl: Riba Al-Fadl (excess) is the quality premium in exchange of low quality with better quality goods e.g. dates for dates, wheat for wheat, etc. – an excess in the exchange of Ribawi goods within a single genus. The Concept of Riba Al-Fadl refers to sale transactions while Riba Al-Nasiah refers to loan transactions. Riba Al-Nasiah : Riba Al-Nasiah or riba of delay is due to exchange not being immediate with or without excess in one of the counter values. It is an increment on principal of a loan or debt payable. It refers to the practice of lending money for any length of time on the understanding that the borrower would return to the lender at the end of the period the amount originally lent together with an increase on it, in consideration of the lender having granted him time to pay. Interest, in all modern banking transactions, falls under purview of Riba Al-Nasiah. As money in present banking system is exchanged for money with excess and delay, it falls, under the definition of riba. A general accord reached among scholar about its prohibition. Ribawi: Goods subject to Fiqh rules on Riba in sales, variously defined by the schools of Islamic Law: items sold by weight and by measure, foods, etc. Al- Rahn: Pledge, Collateral; legally, Rahn means to pledge or lodge a real or corporeal property of material value, in accordance with the law, as security, for a debt or pecuniary obligation so as to make it possible for the creditor to recover the debt or some portion of the goods or property. In the pre-Islamic contracts, Rahn implied a type of earnest money which was lodged as a guarantee and material evidence or proof of a contract, especially when there was no scribe available to put it into writing. The institution of earnest money was not accepted in Islamic law and the common Islamic doctrine recognized Rahn only as a security for the payment of a debt.

Islamic Banking blockchain Salaf or Loan / Debt: The word Salaf literally means a loan that draws forth no profit for the creditor. In wider sense, it includes loans for specified periods, i.e. short, intermediate and long-term loans. Salaf is another name of Salam as well wherein price of the commodity is paid in advance while the commodity or the counter value is supplied in future; thus the contract creates a liability for the seller. Amount given as Salaf cannot be called back, unlike Qard, before it is due. (see Qard) Salaf or Loan / Debt: The word Salaf literally means a loan that draws forth no profit for the creditor. In wider sense, it includes loans for specified periods, i.e. short, intermediate and long-term loans. Salaf is another name of Salam as well wherein price of the commodity is paid in advance while the commodity or the counter value is supplied in future; thus the contract creates a liability for the seller. Amount given as Salaf cannot be called back, unlike Qard, before it is due. (see Qard) Al-Sarf : Basically, in pre-Islamic times it was exchange of gold for gold, silver for silver and gold for silver or vice versa. In Islamic law such exchange is regarded as 'sale of price for price' (Bai al Thaman bil Thaman), and each price is consideration of the other. It also means sale of monetary value for monetary value – currency exchange.

Islamic Banking blockchain Shirkah : A contract between two or more persons who launch a business or financial enterprise to make profits. In the conventional books of Fiqh, the partnership business has been discussed under the option of Shirkah that, broadly, may include both Musharakah and Mudaraba. Sunnah: Custom, habit or way of life. Technically, it refers to the utterances of the Prophet Muhammad (PBUH) other than the Holy Quran known as Hadith, or his personal acts, or sayings of others, tacitly approved by the Prophet. Tabarru': It is a donation/gift the purpose of which is not commercial but is seeking the pleasure of Allah. Any benefit that is given by a person to other without getting anything in exchange is called Tabarru'. Gracious repayment of debt, absolutely at lender's own discretion and without any prior condition or inducement for

reward, is also covered under Tabarru'. Repaying a loan in excess of principal and without a pre-condition is commendable and compatible with the Sunnah of the Holy Prophet (peace be upon him). But, it is matter of individual discretion and cannot be adopted as a system because this would mean that loan would necessarily yield a profit. If such reward takes the form of a system, it would be considered Riba..
Islamic Banking blockchain Tabzir : Spending wastefully on objects which have been explicitly prohibited by the Sharia'h irrespective of the quantum of expenditure. See also Israf. Wakalah : A contract of agency in which one person appoints someone else to perform a certain task on his behalf, usually against a certain fee. Zakah / Zakat: compulsories levy on every Muslim who has wealth greater than the amount of Nisab. The amount payable by a Muslim on his net worth as a part of his religious obligations, mainly for the benefit of the poor and the needy. See also ushr. Zakah al-Fitr: A small obligatory head-tax imposed on every Muslim who has the means for himself and his dependants. It is paid once yearly at the end of Ramadan before Eid al-Fitr. Zakah Al-Mal: The Muslims wealth tax: One must pay 2.5% of one's yearly savings above a certain amount to the poor and needy Muslims. The Zakah is compulsory on all Muslims who have saved (at least) the equivalent of 85g of 24 carat gold at the time when the annual Zakah payment is due.
Islamic Banking blockchain Zakatul Huboob: Zakah of grain/corn. Zakatul Madan: Zakah of minerals. Zakatur Rikaaz: Zakah of treasure/precious stones. Zakatu-rid Tijaarah: Zakah of profits of merchandise. Zar: seed; crop to be sown. Zhulm: A comprehensive term used to refer to all forms of inequity, injustice, exploitation, oppression and wrongdoing whereby a person either deprives others of their rights or does not fulfil his obligations towards them. Zimmah: equivalent of legal personality in positive law; receptacle for the capacity for acquisition; see ahd.
This innovation now makes it possible to do Bai bil Wafa on the blockchain under license agreement: Sale with a right in the seller, having the effect of a condition, to repurchase (redeem) the property by refunding the purchase price. According to majority of Fuqaha it is not permissible.

This Islamic Banking Sharia Compliant Blockchain Innovation concerns cryptographic currency/digital mining assets/commodities for use in the stock/share/bond market industry. More specifically the present invention relates to the provision of cryptographic currency/digital mining assets/commodity stock/share/ bond innovation which fundamentally changes how the stocks/shares/bonds are discovered, issued, valuated and rated.
This Islamic Banking Sharia Compliant Blockchain Innovation that addresses what the stocks/shares/bonds now known as digital mining assets/commodities look like and how they are bought, sold and traded on a digital mining assets/commodities Blockchain exchange. It affects proof of ownership on the Blockchain, investor returns, earnings to shareholders, settlement speed and company strength etc.
This Islamic Banking Sharia Compliant Blockchain innovation is a new stocks/shares/bonds structure using digital mining assets/commodities which are the actual stocks/shares/bonds in the start-ups, businesses, companies and corporations which can then be bought/sold/traded on a new Blockchain shared ledger exchange/platform. New start-ups and existing businesses/companies/corporations can transition from their old stocks/shares/bonds structure in the existing stocks/shares/bonds market over to this new innovative digital mining assets/commodities stocks/shares/bonds structure on a new digital mining assets/commodities Blockchain exchange.

Islamic Banking: Claim 3 New Monetary System

Claim 3. Islamic Banking sharia-compliant finance innovation on/using the Blockchain but not limited to: New Islamic monetary system using this Islamic banking innovation where you no longer need to borrow as the underlying assets/commodities earn revenue for you.

New Blockchain Islamic bank banking innovation for monetary system

This new monetary innovation method/process using crypto currency applies to and for entities, which require an income/revenue producing asset using any form of named/renamed crypto currency, using any form of blockchain/chain process using the wallet which mints/mines new coin assets.

This method/process using crypto currency applies to and for entities, which require an income/revenue producing asset using any form of named/renamed crypto currency, using any form of blockchain/chain process using the wallet which mints/mines new coin assets. This new method/process makes it possible for an entity to acquire a (blockchain or any chain dependent) crypto currency asset to earn revenue, mint and mine new assets and currency, produce, acquire income for that entity and or on behalf of another entity

This new monetary innovation method/process using crypto currency applies to and for entities, which require an income/revenue producing asset using any form of named/renamed crypto currency, using any form of blockchain/chain process using the wallet which mints/mines new coin assets. Example of entities would be but not limited to Governments, corporations, companies, SME's (small medium enterprises), sole traders, NGO's (non-government organisations), not for profits, non-profits, sole traders etc. The below claims will apply to the above entities.

Reduction of: Taxes (governments), Fees (businesses), Grants (NGO's), donations (non-profits) This new method/process makes it possible for an entity (referenced above) to acquire a (blockchain or any chain dependent) crypto currency asset to earn revenue, mint and mine new assets and currency, produce, acquire income for that entity and or on behalf of another entity. Example Government: For this claim we will use crypto currency Bankcoin as the asset currency which is what is stored in the Bankcoin wallet that mints new coin assets amine/mints the transaction fees of those assets throughout the blockchain network and transacted by the entity throughout the blockchain network. A government can acquire and/or have developed a revenue/income producing crypto currency asset, e.g. Bankcoin which uses the blockchain to earn revenue by way of mint/mine new assets and mine/mint the transaction fees as oppose to their current system where they acquire/require taxes, rates, fees to be paid as their form of revenue. This new method can reduce or eliminate the need for governments to charge taxes, rates, fees on some or all in the following definition. This new method process will apply to all entities.

Definition:

Taxes - a tax is a compulsory levy imposed by the government, mainly to raise revenue. There is usually no clear and direct link between payment of taxes and the provision of particular goods and services by government. Taxes are levied on incomes, property, production, sale and use of goods and services, and the performance of activities. Included are personal income taxes, company taxes, payroll and fringe benefits taxes, sales tax, customs and excise duties, land taxes, municipal rates, motor vehicle registration fees, compulsory fees and fines collected by all levels of government.

This new method and/or process makes it possible for an entity to reduce its borrowing as it can now acquire/develop/have developed an income/revenue producing asset using crypto currency such as Bankcoin. Therefore it will have no debt to refinance or be repaid as this new method is considered new money; new wealth not based on debt and has no interest usury component to it. It is based on the crypto currency minting and mining of new assets. This reduction in borrowing will strengthen the entities position in the market place and give it an advantage over those that have not engaged in this new method and/or process. It can be fully replicated and exploited via a license agreement Increase/surplus in: lending (cash), mergers (business), acquisitions (property)

This new method and/or process makes it possible for an entity to increase its income/revenue producing asset that it has acquired under license to a point it would have surplus available to lend through cash, mergers and acquisitions. This increase is possible because there is a variable and fixed rate of return on the assets that are acquired through the mint/mine process and will mint/mine at that rate per annum so the entity always knows what's available to them and what the surplus will be at any given point in time. Only through this new method using the Bankcoin crypto currency model, method and or process can this be achieved.

Ability to finance: infrastructure/buildings/assets, separate departments/divisions/portfolios, internal and external. This new method and/or process make it possible for an entity, in this example we will use Government. They will be able to acquire/ develop/have developed a crypto currency asset specifically for a department, a portfolio, a specific division where they can control the amount of assets return/revenue via the mint/mine process to cover that departments requirements for the year as the rate of return is measured per annum. Each department will then know exactly what amount it has available to allocate. Example, Building works department would know exactly how much they will earn from their allocation of crypto currency assets the federal government allocates to it therefore it can make sound decisions on the number of bridges and roads it can build in that year and since this new method and/or process is configurable we can develop it to suit. Regulatory Body Oversight:

This new method and/or process will be overseen, developed, issued, regulated, insured, valued, licensed, distributed, monitored and expanded upon by the self-regulated entity Bankcoin Reserve (BCR). The BCR has a number of patents relating to crypto currency under license from the patent owner/s, and can demonstrate fully the new method and/or process to which this patent applies.

Digital mining asset/commodity contracts Using digital mining commodities/high quality assets on the Blockchain with a fixed contract value price or floating mining contract value price, fixed or floating Bankcoin/any coin value Bankcoin/any coin amount makes the entire process open, transparent and more secure via its built in wallet encryption mechanisms, statistics and block explorer. For reference a digital mining asset/commodity is not just any digital commodity. A digital commodity is a commodity that has completed its function and is static like Bitcoin. Once a Bitcoin is mined you have a Bitcoin but it does nothing further, you can use it as a medium of exchange back and forth. A Digital mining asset/commodity such as Bankcoin is mined which we then call the principle/primary and then that principle in your Bankcoin wallet starts to secondary mine/mint new Bankcoin's at a rate of up to 10% per annum, as an example.

This is why we call it a digital mining asset/commodity as opposed to just a digital mined asset/commodity. It has an additional mining function after the initial principle coin has been mined; it moves into the secondary mining phase. The amount mined/minted in this stage is dependent on the principle amount in the actual digital Bankcoin wallet. More than one contract at a time can be secured. These programs have no time limits therefore can be renewed endlessly or as long as the paper is there to be bought and sold. New ethical markets This is an innovation for Private Placement, High Yield Investment, Tier 1, MTN buy/sell Structured financial Trading Programs and Platforms, because never before have brokers, dealers and those in the financial sector had a product that is ethical meeting all ethical and humanitarian requirements. It mines/mints/earns new Bankcoin's which we call earnings as there is no interest component meaning this will open up new ethical markets for them that they never had access to before. A Private Placement, High Yield Investment, Tier 1, MTN buy/sell

Structured financial Trading Programs and Platforms is where the investors digital mining assets/commodities are blocked, by the Bankcoin reserve, from being used for any other purpose than for the traders own Buy/Sell Program. Typically this type of program lasts for a 40 week period. The clients Bankcoin wallet mines by the second, minute, hour, day, week or month. Its real time which makes it now possible for the broker/trader/those in the financial sector to adjust the amount of trades they can do real time based on the real time increase in the clients Bankcoin wallet. As an example, if the minimum amount for a PPP was $130M then the client would need to put up his Bankcoin wallet with 100,000 Bankcoin's as each Bankcoin on the market has a valuation of $1300. Now this is where it gets innovative, instead of only being a fixed contract it can also be a floating contract as the clients Bankcoin wallet is going to mine as we know up to 10% pa which amounts to approximately 10,000 newly mined/minted/earned Bankcoin's which would bring the clients total to 110,000 over the 12 month period which is an additional $13M the broker/trader has ongoing access to over the term of the contract, example 40 week period. Now $13M might not sound much but if the client has 1M Bankcoin's with a Valuation of $1.3B then it could mine/mint/earn up to $130M pa. Allocation of secondary mined assets/commodities This innovation makes it possible for the client/investors primary mined digital assets/commodities to secondary mine/mint new digital assets/commodities. These secondary mined/minted new digital assets/commodities can then be automatically allocated to entities such as the IMF/UN/World Bank for the funding of humanitarian and reconstruction projects located in any country of the world as long as that country is deemed appropriate. What this claim does is guarantee on behalf of the client/investor that a percentage of their returns are actually going to where they need to go such as the IMF/UN/World Bank for the funding of humanitarian and reconstruction projects at their discretion. While commercial projects with vocational aspects get funded as well as humanitarian projects.

As an example: The client/investor has 1 Million principle Bankcoin's in their Bankcoin digital wallet which is allocated in this example to a 40 week program. With a valuation via the Bankcoin Reserve (who sets the Bankcoin price) of US$1.3Billion, this will then secondary mine up to 10% per annum of US$130Million. That 10% is also used by the trader at time intervals that suit them as it would equate to US $3.25Million per month depending on the minimum amount the trader can use. However we would know with some certainty that US$130M from this 40 week trade program would automatically be allocated to the example IMF/UN/World Bank to non-profits and NGO's for humanitarian reasons and also to allocate the proceeds to major projects such as infrastructure, bridges, roads, hospitals, schools, higher education etc. This is in addition to the client/investors principle amount of 1Million Bankcoin's that started the 40 week program. Access/Monitoring and regulatory oversight Another part of the innovation is the broker/trader/those in the finance sector can use what we call an RDC or remote desktop connection to log into the VPS virtual private server/computer which is where the clients Bankcoin wallet would be located and even log into the wallet itself if necessary to check its statistics real time, check transactions via the built in block explorer and even download an Excel spread sheet of all transactions for record keeping and watch the mining of new coins so that they can make changes and adjustments to their buy/sell trade/invest side if and when required.

This innovation by default also gives regulators access and therefore the ability to assess the quantity and quality of the data and trades by way of Bankcoin's wallet capabilities and RDC functions being used in this innovation. Also greater transparency, efficiency and security at a lower cost which regulators have not had access to until this innovation. It also gives traders, brokers and those in the finance industry the ability to monitor the process and progress real time which allows them to make real time changes on their end possible which only this innovation can deliver. It allows trader checking and monitoring client/investors Bankcoin wallet and balance.

Regulatory Authority The Bankcoin Reserve acts as the regulatory authority in relation to Blockchain Digital Mining Commodity/Asset innovation for Private Placement, High Yield Investment, Tier 1, MTN buy/sell Structured financial Trading Programs and Platforms. The Bankcoin Reserve is the only major international entity that facilitates between Brokers/traders and those in the financial sector to those clients/investors in the Blockchain Digital Mining Commodity/Asset sector. The Bankcoin Reserve accepts custody of the clients Bankcoin's for the Private Placement, High Yield Investment, Tier 1, MTN buy/sell Structured financial Trading Programs and Platforms. The Bankcoin Reserve secures the client/investors Bankcoin's and 100% fully insures them from risk of loss which would be in the form of Bankcoin. The Bankcoin Reserve will make available to the trader/broker a remote desktop connection application so they can check and monitor the client/investors Bankcoin wallet at any time. Trader can enter the wallet on the Blockchain by logging in via the Remote Desktop Connection which can be on their phone, desktop, laptop etc. giving them the ability to check the status of the clients Bankcoin wallet balance, mined and mining at anytime from anywhere. The Bankcoin Reserve will block the movement of the clients Bankcoin's from the trader and also from the client. They will be locked in place until the term of the agreement has expired.

The Bankcoin Reserve will determine the valuation of Bankcoin's both in the private and public sectors which will reflect the market needs and requirements. The Bankcoin Reserve also rates Bankcoin's when used in this innovation. The Bankcoin Reserve monitors the decisions made by the CFTC in relation to digital mining commodities for any changes that may occur. The Bankcoin Reserve has no upfront fees to Bankcoin holders for this service. The Bankcoin Reserve purely facilitates between the Bankcoin holders and the traders/brokers. The Bankcoin Reserve is not a part of the contract between the client and trader. The Bankcoin Reserve provides a Responsible Principal Guarantee in the form of an SKR to the client and trader as the Bankcoin's are commodities which could also be seen as securities and/or corporate client bonds. The Bankcoin Reserve holds only high quality Digital Bankcoin commodities/assets and does high quality transactions only. The Bankcoin Reserve has a Program Application (CIS/KYC). Color-Scanned Copy of Bankcoin Wallet Screen Statement/ Tear Sheet Colour-Scanned Copy of Account Signatory's Passport the Bankcoin Reserve determines the client is the legal owner of Bankcoin's held in custody.

Bai al Salam using this Islamic Banking blockchain sharia-compliant finance innovation: This term refers to advance payment for goods which are to be delivered later. Normally, no sale can be affected unless the goods are in existence at the time of the bargain. But this type of sale forms an exception to the general rule provided the goods are defined and the date of delivery is fixed. The objects of this type of sale are mainly tangible things but exclude gold or silver as these are regarded as monetary values. One of the conditions of this type of contract is advance payment.

Baitul Mal using this Islamic Banking blockchain sharia-compliant finances innovation: Treasury. Dirham using this Islamic Banking blockchain sharia-compliant finance innovation: Name of a unit of currency, usually a silver coin, used in the past in several Muslim countries and still used in some Muslim countries, such as Morocco and United Arab Emirates. Hawala using this Islamic Banking blockchain sharia-compliant finance innovation: Lit: bill of exchange, promissory note, cheque or draft. Technically, a debtor passes on the responsibility of payment of his debt to a third party who owes the former a debt. Thus the responsibility of payment is ultimately shifted to a third party. Hawala is a mechanism for settling international accounts, by book transfers. This obviates, to a large extent, the necessity of physical transfer of cash.

This Islamic Banking Sharia Compliant Blockchain Innovation makes it possible for investors/stakeholders to acquire principle digital mining asset/commodity in a start-up, business/company/corporation in both the primary and secondary market and let their principle digital mining asset/commodity secondary mine for them on exchange and/or off exchange. This is then a new innovative way for investors/stakeholders who would now be shareholders in this new structure to get a stable return on investment without having to sell their principle stocks/ shares/bonds back into the market place. They can simply sell what their start-up/business/company/corporation principle digital mining assets/commodities stocks/shares/bonds secondary mine.

This Islamic Banking Sharia Compliant Blockchain Innovation has the potential to completely reshape the Islamic Banking industry and drive huge improvements in market efficiency, settlement, security, regulatory, speed of transfer, ownership CIS, KYC, AML. We will use Bankcoin as our example of the digital mining assets/commodities which has had its principle Bankcoin mined and is now secondary mining a percentage from 1% onwards pa from the total amount in their Bankcoin digital wallet. Example: if you acquire 1000 Bankcoin's it will secondary mine up to 10% pa which equals up to 100 newly mined Bankcoin's pa. So when an investor/stakeholder acquires 1000 digital mining asset/commodity stocks/shares/bonds in a start-up/business/company/corporation from the SharesX exchange for example, they will newly secondary mine 100 digital mining asset/commodity stocks, shares, bonds per annum for the new shareholder.

This Islamic Banking Sharia Compliant Blockchain digital mining asset/commodity stocks/shares/bonds innovation assists with market stability being a fixed price with the option of a floating price above that, transparency as the Blockchain is decentralised, security of ownership as investors/shareholders have full control over their digital mining asset/commodity stocks/shares/bonds both online and offline in their own digital wallet, and minimising tax avoidance by increased transparency and regulatory oversight.

Islamic Banking: Claim 4 Stocks Shares Bonds

Claim 4. Islamic Banking sharia-compliant finance innovation on/using the Blockchain applied but not limited to: Banks, financial institutions and monetary funds can now you this innovation for Stocks, shares, bonds etc.. as there is no riba, usury or interest which makes it possible for new financial models to be created with the underlying innovation technology for increased sharia compliant products and services.

New Blockchain Islamic bank banking innovation for stock share bond system includes for Private Placement, High Yield Investment, Tier 1,2,3, MTN buy/sell Structured financial Trading Programs and Platforms

New stock/share/bond innovation using principle mined cryptographic currency/digital mining assets/commodities which secondary mine for stock/share/bond holders on/using the Blockchain/any chain/shared ledger on a cryptographic currency/digital mining assets/commodities exchange.

The invention concerns cryptographic currency/digital mining assets/commodities for use in the stock/share/bond market industry. More specifically the present invention relates to the provision of cryptographic currency/digital mining assets/commodity stock/share/ bond innovation which fundamentally changes how the stocks/shares/bonds are discovered, issued, valuated and rated. This is an innovation that addresses what the stocks/shares/bonds now known as digital mining assets/commodities look like and how they are bought, sold and traded on a digital mining assets/commodities Blockchain exchange. It affects proof of ownership on the Blockchain, investor returns, earnings to shareholders, settlement speed and company strength etc.

This innovation is a new stocks/shares/bonds structure using digital mining assets/commodities which are the actual stocks/shares/bonds in the start-ups, businesses, company's and corporations which can then be bought/sold/traded on a new Blockchain shared ledger exchange/platform. New start-ups and existing businesses/companies/corporations can transition from their old stocks/shares/bonds structure in the existing stocks/shares/bonds market over to this new innovative digital mining assets/commodities stocks/shares/bonds structure on a new digital mining assets/commodities Blockchain exchange.

This innovation makes it possible for investors/stakeholders to acquire principle digital mining asset/commodity in a start-up, business/company/corporation in both the primary and secondary market and let their principle digital mining asset/commodity secondary mine for them on exchange and/or off exchange. This is then a new innovative way for investors/stakeholders who would now be shareholders in this new structure to get a stable return on investment without having to sell their principle stocks/shares/bonds back into the market place. They can simply sell what their start-up/business/company/corporation principle digital mining assets/commodities stocks/shares/bonds secondary mine. This innovation has the potential to completely reshape the industry and drive huge improvements in market efficiency, settlement, security, regulatory, speed of transfer, ownership CIS, KYC, AML.

We will use Bankcoin as our example of the digital mining assets/commodities which has had its principle Bankcoin mined and is now secondary mining a percentage from 1% onwards pa from the total amount in their Bankcoin digital wallet. Example: if you acquire 1000 Bankcoin's it will secondary mine up to 10% pa which equals up to 100 newly mined Bankcoin's pa. So when an investor/stakeholder acquires 1000 digital mining asset/commodity stocks/shares/bonds in a start-up/business/company/corporation from the SharesX exchange for example, they will newly secondary mine 100 digital mining asset/commodity stocks/shares/bonds for the new shareholder.

This digital mining asset/commodity stocks/shares/bonds innovation assists with market stability being a fixed price with the option of a floating price above that, transparency as the Blockchain is decentralised, security of ownership as investors/shareholders have full control over their digital mining asset/commodity stocks/shares/bonds both online and offline in their own digital wallet, and minimising tax avoidance by increased transparency and regulatory oversight. Gary McAlister Terry

New digital mining asset/commodity share structure with new innovations in technology and new regulations from that technology, come new terms. Digital mining assets/commodities are digitally mined principle assets/commodities that are now secondary mining adding to their existing principle mined asset/commodity balance total. Therefore the new company stocks/shares/bonds would actually be digital mining assets/commodities. The company would have principle digital mining assets/commodities which it sells/ trades into the market and the investors would be buying the principle stocks/shares/bonds and then secondary mining them to sell into the market place on a Blockchain exchange such as SharesX. Start-ups once they have their market valuation and company share structure can submit it to SharesX for valuation and approval into the digital mining asset/commodity share market exchange. Take for example a company called AAABlockchain Limited. A start up that has been testing its products in the market for nearly two years is now ready to enter the private secondary market to raise funds and decentralise its intellectual property via a share offering. This company now has the option via this new innovation to use SharesX.com, a Blockchain stocks/shares/bonds exchange that specialises in digital mining asset/commodity, to sell/trade its principle digital mining assets/commodities.

The company has a total market valuation of $1B/10M stocks/shares/bonds and wants to sell/trade to market 10% which would equate to $10OM/1M stock/share/bond at $100 per stock/share/bond. This innovation allows this start-up to sell/trade a principle amount of AAABlockchain principle stocks/shares/bonds in the form of digital mining assets/commodities and place 1M of those principle stocks/shares/bonds on SharesX.com to sell/trade. The core of the innovation is that AAABlockchain principle stocks/shares/bonds will secondary mine for the investors/stakeholders meaning the stocks/shares/bonds in this company that are bought off the exchange will start to secondary mine for the new shareholder at a rate of up to 10% pa. So if you acquired $100k worth of AAABlockchain stocks/ shares/bonds, 1000@$100 each which are digital mining assets/commodity stocks/shares/bonds, it works out at up to $10k pa in ethical earnings. What this does is smooth out the real world company fluctuations, be they seasonal, weather dependent, manipulated, traded, buy/low sell high or leveraged, and also removes the need for new stocks/shares/bonds offers which would dilute the shareholders principle stocks/shares/bonds.

This innovation leads to a sounder, more stable market and provides certainty to market participants/investors as well as shareholders. Profit and Earnings from digital mining asset/commodity stocks/shares/bonds. The profit/earnings from AAABlockchain products and services in the real world are used to acquire digital mining asset/commodity stocks/shares/bonds off the SharesX exchange that their shareholders have secondary mined and put up for trade/sale. By default this strengthens the core of the company into which market participants and investors are investing. This is not a buyback of stocks/shares/bonds as these stocks/shares/bonds are newly mined digital mining asset/commodity stocks/shares/bonds from shareholders. This is a reflection of the new products and/or services the company is actually delivering in the real world. So for the company it's a buy the newly mined digital mining asset/commodity stocks/shares/bonds from their shareholders, hold and let the newly acquired digital mining asset/commodity stocks/shares/bonds secondary mine for the company, strengthen the overall company which puts it on a path to sustainable growth.

Rating, management and fee structure for digital mining asset/commodity stocks/shares/bonds A company like SharesX would have a rating system with the highest rating going to the companies that consistently buy the most digital mining asset/commodity stocks/shares/bonds from their shareholders on the exchange. This shows the strength and growth of that company in the real market. This rating could be adjusted periodically throughout the year. This innovation gives each digital mining asset/commodity shareholder a method of recording and confirming their share transactions in real time instead of a centralised platform doing it for them. Each shareholder can hold a digital wallet which has a complete record of mined digital mining assets/commodities and transactions through peer to peer verification through the Blockchain and the block explorer. This means there is no central recording system; rather each participant keeps a record of all transactions ever made. This is the same system which allows Bankcoin to operate with no central authority.

All digital mining asset/commodity share trades would be settled by each digital mining asset/commodity shareholder confirming transactions through the peer to peer network/Blockchain. The network/Blockchain could record the buying and selling of each digital mining asset/commodity of the shareholder, the number of stocks/shares/bonds traded the price of stocks/shares/bonds, time of exchange and the exchange of funds as all these are real time stamped on the exchange. The exchange, such as SharesX, will still provide a centralised electronic exchange for each digital mining asset/commodity shareholder to place buy/sell/trade orders. The settlement or back office function will be provided to the entire network/Blockchain which is a major advantage with huge cost savings.

There are no fees to buy/sell/trade on the exchange such as SharesX however there is a fee to list on the exchange in the form of a percentage of the digital mining asset/commodity of the listing company. These principle company stocks/shares/bonds will then secondary mine for SharesX and be put up for sale/trade on the exchange. Fixed price formula for digital mining asset/commodity stocks/shares/bonds this innovation brings in a fixed price formula which means there is a floor price. As an example, AAABlockchain Limited digital mining asset/commodity share floor price is $100, however it can climb up due to market forces though it cannot go below the floor price. This brings in a sustainable ethical growth formula yet gives those that require markets to fluctuate above the floor price that option as well. Innovation benefits and advantages of digital mining asset/commodity stocks/shares/bonds this digital mining asset/commodity stocks/shares/bonds innovation has the potential to cut inefficiencies in the share settlement function.

As trades are settled in real time by peer to peer confirmations, there is no need for a clearing house, auditors to verify trades, or custodians to ensure a shareholder actually has the stocks/shares/bonds they claim to hold. The shareholders digital wallet holds all this information on the exchange in the Overview page, Statistics page and block explorer. This digital mining asset/commodity share innovation removes the need for middlemen in the back office which means fewer costs in record keeping and in turn less costs to trading on exchanges such as SharesX. The high cost in getting a third party to audit, record keep and/or verify trades would be substantially reduced. This digital mining asset/commodity stocks/shares/bonds innovation addresses all these issues and more since it can cover any and all costs because it mines new digital mining asset/commodity stocks/shares/bonds.

The digital mining asset/commodity shareholders confirmation of trades means settlement time can be significantly reduced compared to the current settlement period of three working days (T+3) as the existing exchanges need to make sure the participants have the money and stocks/shares/bonds on hand to exchange. This would make digital mining asset/commodity stocks/shares/bonds a far more liquid investment. Higher liquidity means more investment into start-ups/ businesses/companies and corporations principle digital mining asset/commodity stocks/shares/bonds using this innovation. As all participants have the full record of transactions and therefore holdings of the business there is complete transparency in the equity market. This makes it almost impossible to falsify transactions or to make changes to prior transactions. If a false trade occurs, participants will find inconsistencies in their full ledger and reject the trade. For example an investor would be unable to sell stock/shares/bonds that they did not own as all participants throughout the Blockchain would know exactly how much stocks/shares/bonds the investor/company owns as that information is inside the digital wallet.

Bai al Dayn using this Islamic Banking blockchain sharia-compliant finance innovation: Debt financing: the provision of financial resources required for production, commerce and services by way of sale/purchase of trade documents and papers. Bai al-Dayn is a short-term facility with a maturity of not more than a year. Only documents evidencing debts arising from bona fide commercial transactions can be traded.

Gharar is enhanced using this Islamic Banking blockchain sharia-compliant finance innovation: Uncertainty. One of the three fundamentals prohibitions in Islamic finance (the other two being Riba and Maysir). Gharar is a sophisticated concept that covers certain types of uncertainty or contingency in a contract. The prohibition on Gharar is often used as the grounds for criticism of conventional financial practices such as short selling, speculation and derivatives.

Maysir is removed and not necessary using this Islamic Banking blockchain sharia-compliant finance innovation. Gambling. One of three fundamental prohibitions in Islamic finance (the other two being Riba and Gharar). The prohibition on maysir is often used as the grounds for criticism of conventional financial practices such as speculation, conventional insurance and derivatives.

Sukuk using this Islamic Banking blockchain sharia-compliant finance innovation: Similar to an asset backed bond, Sukuk is a form of commercial paper that provides an investor with ownership in an underlying asset, and a return based on this ownership. The issuing entity needs to identify existing assets to sell to the Sukuk investors, via transference to an SPV. The Sukuk investors then have a proportionate beneficial ownership in these assets. Investors typically take on the credit risk of the issuer rather than real asset risk on the assets owned by the SPV. Sukuks can be listed and rated, though this is not necessary, depending on the target investor market. Sukuks are typically issued by corporate issuers, and some Financial Institutions, and also by Governments (Bahrain, Malaysia, Pakistan).

Blockchain Islamic bank banking sharia compliant Initial Coin Offering ICO - a POS proof of stake secondary mining from the primary principle initial coin call it KwhCoin/Token so it can give an ongoing sustainable return to investors in the form of Kwh's say 15-25% pa from the principle primary kwh coin in your wallet. Because it is clean and renewable energy technology the ICO investment is going into then a name like Kwh will make sense to the Investors.

This also takes pressure off the company taking the investment from the ICO in relation to building the clean and renewable infrastructure however this ICO model will increase investment into the sector because the investors will have two returns one immediately in the form of Kwh's Kwh coin and the other once the operation is built and producing Kwh energy.

Let's propose a $10M ICO raise the company proposing the ICO will discover 100M Kwh coins and at $1 each will allocate 10M to the company doing the operation, they will then sell 10M Kwh's coins to the investors in the ICO. Now these start to mine as a number 15% per annum the investors are happy because not only have they invested in the underlying physical building installation and production leading to generation and a return on their investment in the real world but also the return on the Kwh coin itself so it's a win as soon as they acquire their ICO Kwh coins as they then start to mine/mint for them at the 15% rate and a win for them once the facility begins to product Kwh's say for example sold to the grid.

This model can be applied to any and all clean and renewable real world installations to attract investment where the returns are from two different sources. First being from the blockchain and the second from the generation of Kwh's to the grid for example. We understand that it takes time to build these projects in the real world therefore we need the underwriting facility in this case the Kwh coin to give the investors a return instantly which by default takes pressure off the company doing the building and installation. We also know that so many investors want their ROI too soon which is why most investments in this sector are not made. We have always needed a way where we could take care of the investors ROI however not let it affect the real world building of the infrastructure and their natural time frames and we believe this is a sound way to go about it. You can look at the Kwh coin underwriting and/or insuring the actual product even though it has a standalone valuation and market viability. From this point forward investors that want to invest in clean and renewables can do so by simply acquiring the Kwh,s off the investors in the ICO just a thought. This is how they can turn their ICO Kwh coin investment return the 15% into fiat.

This Islamic Banking Sharia Compliant Blockchain Innovation method/process using crypto currency applies to and for entities, which require an income/revenue producing asset using any form of named/renamed crypto currency, using any form of blockchain/chain process using the wallet which mints/mines new coin assets. This new

method/process makes it possible for an entity to acquire a (blockchain or any chain dependent) crypto currency asset to earn revenue, mint and mine new assets and currency, produce, acquire income for that entity and or on behalf of another entity.
This Islamic Banking Sharia Compliant Blockchain Innovation digital mine discovery innovation actually discovers more digital mines while it uses the blockchain as the rails and a secondary digital mine discovery process to discover secondary digital mines. The 2nd digital mine discovers a 3rd digital mine and then a 4th then 5th which can continue discoveries indefinitely perpetual automatically all from the digital mines discovered before them. Because they are actual digital mines which are discovered they would come under the realestate/property classification. Be it a commercial operation and/or in the wholesale sector and/or retail a portfolio of digital mines traded and/or on sold to the retail sector including being used as but not limited to security, insurance, collateral etc.
This Islamic Banking Sharia Compliant Blockchain Innovation sets out a new realestate and/or property blockchain franchise model and has the ability to be exploited under a patent license fee agreement and/or outright bought/sold to specific entities such as but not limited to, governments, Banks, financial institutions, monetary funds, insurance industries on platforms such as but not limited to asset/commodity/stock/bond/share markets and exchanges etc.

Islamic Banking: Claim 5 Digital Mine Discovery Franchise

Claim 5. Islamic Banking sharia-compliant finance innovation on/using the Blockchain applied but not limited to: New digital mine discovery franchise on the blockchain

New Blockchain islamic bank banking innovation for New digital mine discovery franchise

Blockchain Al-kharaj bil daman

Link of exposure to risk, one can claim profit only if one is ready to bear the business risk, if any. The principle in Islamic jurisprudence that entitlement to return or yield (al-kharaj) is for the one who bears the liability (daman) for something, say an asset, and one who does not bear the liability has no claim to the yield. This Islamic Banking Blockchain innovation both parties share the risk equally and therefore share the return or yield equally.

New digital mine discovery franchise innovation for but not limited to Governments, treasuries, central banks, banks, financial institutions, monetary funds, judicial entities, real estates, properties commercial, industrial, domestic, foreign, stock, bond and share markets, insurance captive underwriting institutions, public, private, wholesale, retail and service sectors using the blockchain to discover a master franchise and or for the discovery of franchises of the new digital mines.

This blockchain digital mine discovery innovation actually discovers more digital mines while it uses the blockchain as the rails and a secondary digital mine discovery process to discover secondary digital mines. The 2nd digital mine discovers a 3rd digital mine and then a 4th then 5th which can continue discoveries indefinitely perpetual automatically all from the digital mines discovered before them. Because they are actual digital mines which are discovered they would come under the realestate/property classification. Be it a commercial operation and/or in the wholesale sector and/or retail a portfolio of digital mines traded and/or on sold to the retail sector including being used as but not limited to security, insurance, collateral etc.

This innovation sets out a new realestate and/or property blockchain franchise model and has the ability to be exploited under a patent license fee agreement and/or outright bought/sold to specific entities such as but not limited to, governments, Banks, financial institutions, monetary funds, insurance industries on platforms such as but not limited to asset/commodity/stock/bond/share markets and exchanges etc.

This is a blockchain digital mine discovery franchise innovation specifically designed and developed for the realestate /property, insurance/underwriting, security/collateral markets. This is not a crypto currency nor is it an asset/commodity innovation that earns interest. What we have discovered on the blockchain is an actual digital mine we can call the master franchise which can actually discover new digital mines at a pre-determined discovery percentage rate example 1/10th per annum. It is estimated because mine discovery is not an exact science.

This innovation is an actual digital mine discovery innovation on the blockchain which by default means it is covered under the realestate banner and in doing so we have worked out through our modelling that it can be an actual franchise. The master franchise is discovered the moment we find it and from there subsequent franchises with the same ability are discovered and then allocated and considered as per this patent as franchisees/sub franchises off the master franchise as well as off the sub franchisees themselves..

Because this innovation is an actual digital mine on the blockchain with a secondary, third, fourth, fifth unlimited and continuous digital mine discovery ability and features, discovery capabilities which then has the ability to discover a third digital mine off the second discovered franchise digital mine which then has the ability to discover fourth digital mine off the third discovered digital mines and so on and so forth. Also from the second digital mine discovery onwards we have the ability to go to an actual asset/commodity which would end the new digital mine discovery it is unique and innovative hence the innovation patent.

This blockchain digital mine discovery franchise innovation makes it possible to discover and develop an unlimited number of digital mine master franchises which also means an unlimited number of sub franchises and/or franchisees which also means those sub franchises and/or franchisees can sub franchise and they can also do the same continuously using all or some or mixed number of new mines discovered and/or some of the principle/primary allocation from the master franchise and/or a mix from the master franchise and any franchisee within the franchise network this is what gives the market internal/private liquidity as the new mines discovered can be sold/traded swapped etc. before they are made available to the public market sold/traded swapped etc. privately, on exchanges, to any and all entities/persons.

The reason this Realestate and/or property innovation is so innovative/unique is the blockchain now makes it possible using a built in digital mine discovery process e.g. to make new discoveries which are similar to the primary and/or principle digital mine they came from. What this means is when a digital mine is discovered and then developed on the blockchain it can have certain specifications at the discovery stage such as but not limited to, size of the digital mine, capacity of the digital mine, approximate digital mining discovery rate per annum, lifecycle of the digital mine etc.

Once these and others are determined, the first phase of the Digital mine is activated, put into service, brought online and the digital mining discovery process begins. This could also be called the principle/primary amount/position master franchise, from here we move into the second phase which is where the principle/primary amount/position master franchise starts/begins to discovery new digital mines at a pre-determined fixed or floating rate per annum which could be based off the amount of digital mines determined in the first phase at first discovery development.

What this Realestate property innovation on the blockchain makes possible is digital mines discovered through this process will be available to all who want to invest in this since they are digital mines which are sustainable, environmentally friendly, deliverable as you can take ownership of them and also package them up into digital mine portfolios and trade them with those who are looking for a product that has these capabilities and can be used as security, collateral, etc. The blockchain digital mine itself is a genuine mining process and therefore property which would come under realestate with the intrinsic ability built in to discover new digital mines at a percentage rate per annum each year.

Any secondary digital mine discovery process derived from the first digital mine already discovered is covered in this innovation, this is based off of the primary principal amount in the digital mine portfolio. The core of the realestate innovation is on the digital blockchain using secondary digital mine discovery process which is continuous in nature.

Realestate innovation on the Blockchain Digital Realestate property mine, mined, mining innovation Digital blockchain mine, digital mining asset, crypto currency, crypto commodity, digital mining commodity franchise, franchisee and franchisor, distribution hedge underwriting insurance model innovation in the wholesale and retail sectors

The fact is this digital mine discovery actually discovers more digital mines which it uses the blockchain as the rails and a proof of stake and/or a secondary digital mine discovery process to discover those digital mines. Because they are actual digital mines which are discovered they would come under the realestate/property classification. Be it a commercial operation and/or in the wholesale sector and/or retail a portfolio of digital mines traded and/or on sold to the retail sector including being used as but not limited to security, insurance, collateral etc.

This innovation sets out a new realestate and/or property model using Digital mining innovation, Bankcoin as the example, to prove that it works and has the ability to be exploited under a patent license fee agreement and/or outright bought/sold to specific entities such as but not limited to, governments, Banks, financial institutions, monetary funds, insurance industries on platforms such as but not limited to asset/commodity/stock/bond/share markets and exchanges etc.

This is a blockchain innovation specifically discovered for the realestate property and insurance underwriting security, collateral markets. This is not a crypto currency nor is it an asset/commodity innovation. What we have discovered on the blockchain is an actual digital mine we can call the master franchise which can actually discover new digital mines at a pre-determined discovery percentage rate example 1/10th. Because this innovation is an actual digital mine on the blockchain with secondary digital mine, mined, mining discovery capabilities which then has the ability to discover third digital mine/mines off the second discovered digital mine; which then has the ability to discover a fourth digital mine off the third discovered digital mines and so on and so forth; it is unique and innovative hence the innovation patent.

As an example of this claim in a real world scenario it would be explained like this"

The owners of say a copper mine in the real world would approach as an example the Bankcoin Reserve BCR (the global authority on many blockchain patent innovations which also rates these high quality assets and determines their market value/price) and ask if the BCR could discover and develop a blockchain digital copper mine discovery master franchise so that the owners of the in ground copper mine would then have multiple products which would then give them a true advantage over their competitors meaning they can sell/trade etc. with the world not just someone who needs copper as they would be able to sell the blockchain digital copper mine franchise portfolio. The copper mine franchise derived from the BCR are new copper mines the only difference is they are discovered using the blockchain. The laws around the world have determined blockchain and its derivatives to be assets/commodities this innovation takes it a step further, instead of the asset commodity being mined the core product it changes this and makes the mine itself the core product and turns it into a franchise model as this patent is not about mining, assets or commodities but about discovery of the actual mine that these assets, commodities would derive from. So it is the actual mine itself that is discovered using the blockchain that is franchised not what would typically come from as a result of having a mine meaning the asset/commodity.

Which is the reason this innovation is covered under the realestate property sector also because it is the actual mines that are being discovered and then franchised. For clarity in relation to the example the in ground copper mine is a standalone mine just like the blockchain copper mine is they both have their own valuations and capacities. The point is the blockchain copper mine is not a representation of the in ground copper mine the blockchain copper mine is an actual standalone mine which will go to market in exactly the same way as the in ground mine would. The difference is the blockchain copper mine does not actually mine copper that is where this innovation is so unique hence the innovation patent what this blockchain digital copper mine will do is once the master digital copper mine franchise has been discovered and developed it will then automatically and continuously begin to discover new digital copper mines.

Never before has a copper mine been able to discover another copper mine only new copper mines have been discovered separately and you have never been able to franchise these discoveries because they are too few and far between also never before have the mines been able to be sold in volume because that would mean you need a market for the actual commodity that derives from the actual mine.

This blockchain franchise innovation patent takes this to a whole new level. we will use copper as the example but this could apply but not limited to: all assets, property, commodities, all debt, insurance, underwriting, all governments, treasuries, reserves, central banks, banks, financial institutions

We now have the ability on the blockchain to discover a digital mine discovery master franchise

This master franchise can allocate and build sub franchises which in of themselves then discovery new digital mines off the original master franchise allocation and/or acquisition. The sub franchise is global in nature because it is in the blockchain and the new mines are discovered using unique proprietary systems.

blockchain digital mine discovery innovation discovery method for the realestate and/or property insurance/debt market sectors

This discovers new digital mines. This discovery can be estimated as per our requirements, a new digital mine a 10th of the size of the digital mine we currently own. We estimate a 10% new digital mine discovery rate, 2nd digital mine 10% the size of the first digital mine this second digital mine also has the ability to discover new digital mines at an estimated rate of 10%. We estimate this because mining is not an exact science

A simple way to look at it would be the first digital mine produces a second digital mine and that second digital mine produces a third digital mine and so forth. Also the first digital mine continues to discover new digital mines on an hourly, daily, weekly, monthly yearly and so on basis.

We identify a digital mining asset/commodity on the blockchain that the market is looking for wants, needs and get to work discovering it then developing it. For clarification the first digital mine discovered on the blockchain is a physical digital mine as it is located on physical computer servers which could be located in the cloud in any country. This is an actual real time process, one in which you can take actual possession of on a computer desktop, tablet, phone, flash/storage drive/device and/or alternatively you can put it up in the cloud and either have it stored there or fully operating meaning discovering new digital mines and or simply the discovery of the assets/commodities.

This innovation claim also explains that because this is an actual digital mine discovery product and process, it comes with additional advantages and one of those advantages is tax exemption in one process and a possible tax event in another.

The master franchise digital mine discovery is a non-tax event obviously as we discovered a digital mine in the computer code which makes it a digital mine on the blockchain, now from this point forward is the innovation but also the non-tax and at one point the taxable event. In a sense it is also an innovation in tax automated tax collection and regulation.

Because we have discovered the master digital mine franchise, from this point forward is when we can, but not limited to, allocate/distribute/sell/trade/lease/rent etc. The reason for this is the newly discovered digital mines now start to discover new digital mines on their own in their own right meaning this is not a taxable event either as the master franchise nor the franchise actually discover a product from the newly discovered digital mine because they are discovering actual new digital mines.

Now this also plays out if the valuation that, as an example, Bankcoin Reserve sets for the newly discovered digital mines increases in the market place because of a peg to an asset/commodity then there would seem to be a gain made in a typical scenario, you buy an asset for $1000 and the market increases and you sell it out for $1100 that's a $100 gain therefore you could be liable for, as an example, capital gains tax of $100 however with this innovation and in this case an asset/commodity is never actually mined, what actually happens which is the core of this innovation patent is it actually discovers more digital mines which means it is the digital mines that are being discovered and therefore never mine an actual asset/commodity therefore along this new innovative process a taxable event is never reached. It looks like this:

Discover new digital mine master franchise 100M digital mines discovered

Allocate to Franchisee 10M of those digital mines discovered now has portfolio of digital mines

That portfolio of digital mines now newly discover new digital mines 1M per annum

The franchisee can now sub franchise under license and sell/trade those newly discovered digital mines to a new franchisee and/or use them as security/collateral/asset/commodity depending on how the market wants to see them. If franchisee decides to sub franchise then that new portfolio of digital mines 1M will start to discover new digital mines at the rate of 100K new digital mines per annum.

In this scenario we estimate 10% or 1/10th of the original franchise portfolio and would contract each of the franchisees as a number for 20 years would also fully insure that digital mine discovery rate for the entire 20 years by, as an example, matching the allocation and placing it with a third party cold stored to backup and eliminate any risk that would otherwise be associated.

Realestate digital mine discovery franchise innovation on the Blockchain Digital Realestate property mine, mined, mining innovation Digital blockchain mine, digital mining asset, crypto currency, crypto commodity, digital mining commodity franchise, franchisee and franchisor, distribution hedging instrument hedged item underwriting insurance model innovation in the wholesale and retail sectors

Blockchain perpetual continuous new digital mine discovery franchise innovation for Governments, treasuries, central banks, banks, financial institutions, monetary funds, judicial entities, real estates, stock, bond and share markets, insurance captive underwriting institutions, public, private, wholesale and retail sectors.

This blockchain digital mine discovery innovation actually discovers more digital mines while it uses the blockchain as the rails and a secondary digital mine discovery process to discover secondary digital mines. The 2nd digital mine discovers a 3rd digital mine and then a 4th then 5th which can continue discoveries indefinitely perpetual automatically all from the digital mines discovered before them. Because they are actual digital mines which are discovered they would come under the realestate/property classification. Be it a commercial operation and/or in the wholesale sector and/or retail a portfolio of digital mines traded and/or on sold to the retail sector including being used as but not limited to security, insurance, collateral etc.

This innovation sets out a new realestate and/or property blockchain franchise model and has the ability to be exploited under a patent license fee agreement and/or outright bought/sold to specific entities such as but not limited to, governments, Banks, financial institutions, monetary funds, insurance industries on platforms such as but not limited to asset/commodity/stock/bond/share markets and exchanges etc.

This is a blockchain digital mine discovery franchise innovation specifically designed and developed for the realestate /property, insurance/underwriting, security/collateral markets. This is not a crypto currency nor is it an asset/commodity innovation that earns interest. What we have discovered on the blockchain is an actual digital mine we can call the master franchise which can actually discover new digital mines at a pre-determined discovery percentage rate example 1/10th per annum. It is estimated because mine discovery is not an exact science.

This innovation is an actual digital mine discovery innovation on the blockchain which by default means it is covered under the realestate banner and in doing so we have worked out through our modelling that it can be an actual franchise. The master franchise is discovered the moment we find it and from there subsequent franchises with the same ability are discovered and then allocated and considered as per this patent as franchisees/sub franchises off the master franchise as well as off the sub franchisees themselves..

Because this innovation is an actual digital mine on the blockchain with a secondary, third, fourth, fifth unlimited and continuous digital mine discovery ability and features, discovery capabilities which then has the ability to discover a third digital mine off the second discovered franchise digital mine which then has the ability to discover fourth digital mine off the third discovered digital mines and so on and so forth. Also from the second digital mine discovery onwards we have the ability to go to an actual asset/commodity which would end the new digital mine discovery it is unique and innovative hence the innovation patent.

Innovation process master franchise and sub franchises

The tenement from and of the first digital mine could determine the tenement of the second digital mine being, as an example, 1/10th of the first digital mines discovery rate and capability however it is a separate digital mine and therefore the second digital mine discovered could determine the tenement of the 3rd digital mine and its available discoveries and so on and so forth. This innovation also makes it possible if and when required from the second franchisee to only discover the asset/commodity. This innovation is unique as it has the ability to change the new digital mine discovery to discovering the actual assets/commodities that that digital mine would discover. This can only happen from the first franchisee onwards.

Once we have made the discovery we then set out to digitally mine it on the blockchain. Once we have mined it all out it has an approximate tenement as per our market requirements, we then set out to discover new digital mines directly connected to that first digital mine which could be seen to be in nearby proximity. This new mine would be evaluated and its size and scope determined by the previous digital mine, say a 10th of the size.

In layman's terms this realestate property digital mine would be similar to

A. a physical digital mine. In this innovation we have discovered a digital mine using the blockchain, coupled with POS proof of stake and/or a secondary digital mine function which is realestate and/or property.

B. a typical physical mine you would have assays, tenements and core samples to show an estimate of the mines capacity over time, so in our digital mine we estimate the digital mine's capacity and estimates at discovery over time.

C. discovers new digital mines. In this digital mine innovation example but not limited to in its own digital mining wallet, sent to an external digital mine wallet.

Main digital mine

This is where all the discovered digital mines originate from. It can also be seen as the master or mother in relation to a franchise. Therefore all discovered digital mines from this point forward could be considered franchises which could be, but not limited to, sold, leased, rented, traded and could be used as, but not limited to, security, collateral, insurance, asset, commodity, etc.

1. The image shows the digital vault/safe that the master franchise discovery is securely held in.

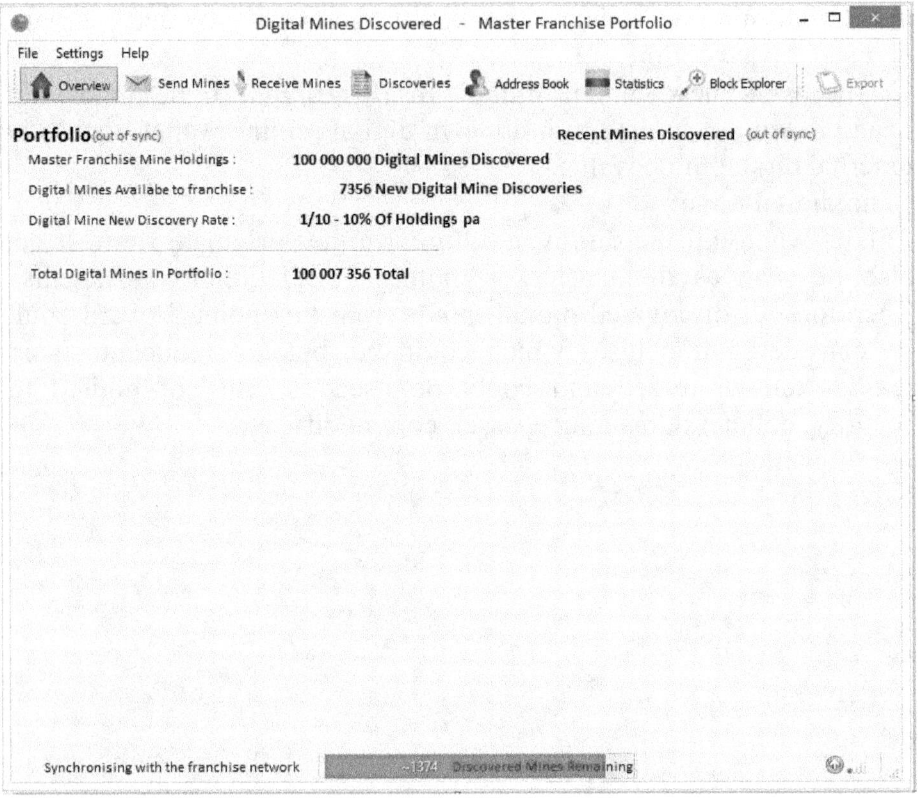

2. This image shows that the digital wallet is physical, tangible property which can be held in your hand and most of all, full ownership of the digital mine/s can be delivered either digitally by sending a digital mine and/or portfolio of digital mines via the blockchain or physically in the mail/freight or both, meaning some via the blockchain and the balance via the post/freight.

3. This statistic image shows the capacity of the master mining franchise. You will see here 100,000,000 (100M) digital mines. We estimated during discovery that this master mining franchise would discover new digital mines at the rate of approximately 1/10th of what they have in their digital holdings.

The Bankcoin Reserve is the central authority on the origination of all master digital mine franchises and therefore franchisees covering, but not limited to, all real estate categories as well as what is considered to be property which includes assets and commodities including debt as this innovation can turn debt into an opportunity to earn by underwriting it with this realestate property digital mine innovation.
What this means is the innovation can discover new digital mines in the form of the above mentioned real estate property, assets, commodities, etc.
Real estate agents, property managers and brokers, Governments, treasuries, central banks, banks, financial institutions, monetary funds now have an innovative product that they can move into the marketplace. Because this innovation is a mining product, they no longer have to look for high net worth individuals nor sophisticated investors as a typical digital mine would cost millions of dollars which would be split up among multiple investors. Therefore no single investor would actually own the digital mine outright, this innovation makes that possible. But not just that, it also makes it possible for an investor to not just acquire a single digital mine, but multiple digital mines over time which they would then create and have full ownership of a portfolio of digital mines.
What also happens is the digital mine that they would have just acquired will begin to discover new digital mines for them at a percentage rate the master franchise has determined at discovery time. These are huge advantages over the current digital mine acquisition process as well as the advantage of additional discoveries. Because these are digital mines all the operational costs of a typical mining operation are no longer there as they have all been embedded into the computer hardware and software. This is a real digital mine in every sense of the word, the only difference is it is more efficient, less cost, you can carry your digital mine or portfolio of digital mines around with you on a laptop, computer, tablet and even a phone, anything that the digital mine software can be installed on and/or implemented in.

As you can see from the images DMF FP 0001,

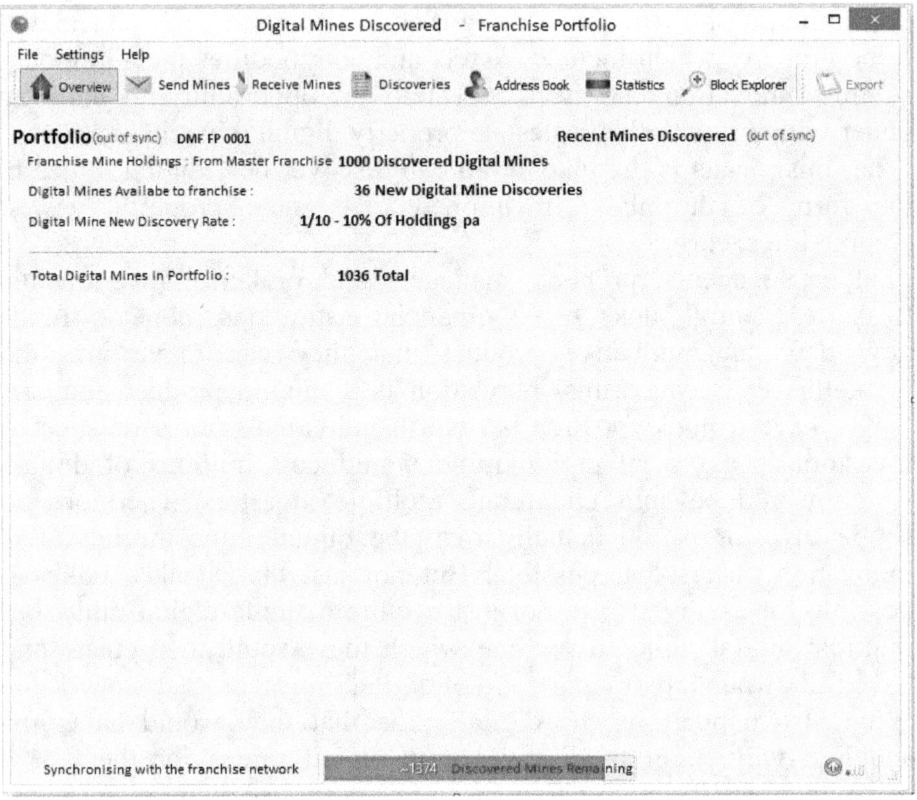

DMF FP 0002

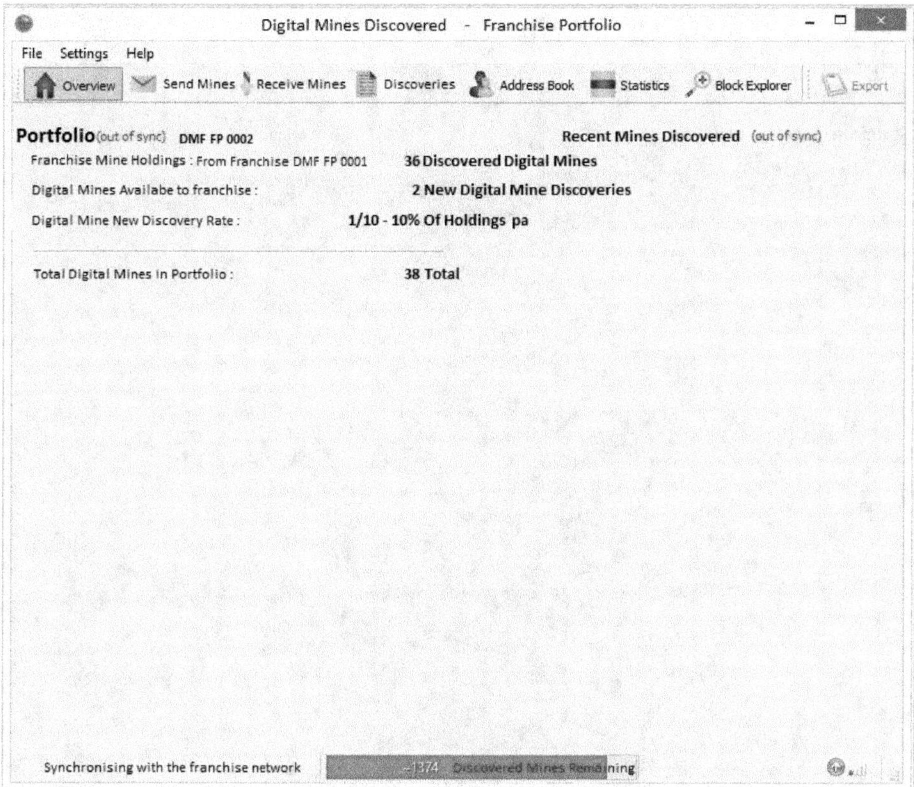
Digital Mines Discovered - Franchise Portfolio
File
Settings
Help
Overview
Send Mines
Receive Mines
Discoveries
Address Book
Statistics
Block Explorer
Export
Portfolio (out of sync)
DMF FP 0002
Recent Mines Discovered (out of sync)
Franchise Mine Holdings : From Franchise DMF FP 0001
36 Discovered Digital Mines
Digital Mines Availabe to franchise :
2 New Digital Mine Discoveries
Digital Mine New Discovery Rate :
1/10 - 10% Of Holdings pa
Total Digital Mines in Portfolio :
38 Total
Synchronising with the franchise network
~1374 Discovered Mines Remaining

and DMF FP 0003

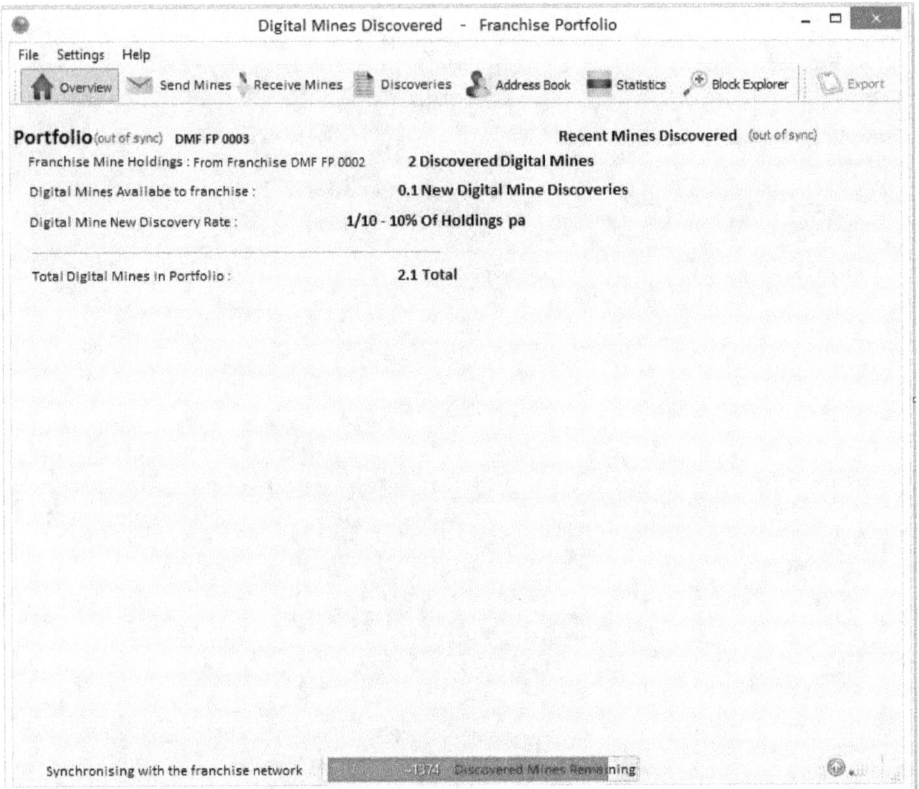

as DMF FP 0001 discovers new digital mines, makes new mine discoveries which are added to the portfolio, the portfolio now has digital mines available to sell/trade to someone and/or an entity that wants to acquire a digital mine discovery franchise of their own. So the deal is done and a second franchise portfolio is setup and the first franchise owner DMF FP 0001 transfers full title and ownership of the discovered digital mines to DMF FP 0002 and the same happens again when DMF FP 0002 has discovered new mines it can on sell and/or trade to a new franchise owner DMF FP 0003 as the images show. This is a somewhat endless perpetual innovation process. These franchise owners can also sell/trade back to each other in any quantity over the principle amount first which would be set in the franchise rules as to keep the integrity of the franchise in order.

As the new mines are discovered they can be placed inside the same portfolio and/or they can be allocated to a new address location inside the same portfolio and/or they can be transferred directly to another franchisee and/or they can be sent to a new portfolio ready for a new franchisee.

This blockchain franchise innovation takes franchising to a whole new level. Because of this innovation we have the ability and capabilities to discover new property indefinitely with no limit to actual discovery what is being discovered, when it is discovered, who, when how to transfer those newly discovered mine to the next franchisee and/or start a whole new franchise as well as sub franchises which include but are not limited to capacity of the mines, quantity of the mines both as master franchises and sub franchisees, value of the mines discovered as individual mines and as portfolios of mines which includes a 1:1 valuation basis example 1 discovered mine can start as low as $1 and climb to any value which can include using the Bankcoin Reserves valuation formula of pegging a single mine to the market price of 1 ounce of gold and/or any valuation formula the Bankcoin reserve and/or market determines.

Property product and applications for Realestate market

Digital mine ownership transfers consisting of multiple digital mines will be packaged into a single portfolio to allow multiple digital mines to be moved without exceeding or breaching the allowed amount of property sold without a realestate licence. So you would in fact be as an investor investing into a single digital mine and/or into a portfolio of digital mines that have these estimates and capabilities. A claim example on how this innovation can be exploited under license as an example from the Bankcoin Reserve would be but not limited to:

A Government is in debt which they cannot pay down meaning they have to borrow more to pay down the debt and it is this ever spiralling set of a circumstance that can only lead to one place and that is bankruptcy. So how would this blockchain realestate digital mine innovation work in this circumstance?

Let’s assume the government is in debt to the tune of US$20 Trillion Dollars, as an example.

We underwrite the government’s debt 100% by allocation of a digital mine which discovers new digital mines classed as realestate/property in their own right and of their own right, which can take on any and all forms and can match on a 1:1 basis if required.

What this means is the Government debt is Backed by and therefore underwritten by our digital mines at a 1:1 basis meaning 100% backed by property which is in the form of legitimately ruled by law as property the digital mines. Because we have the ability to allocate our digital mines at any price point we determine in this case as a number and as an example we would allocate it at no cost.

What does this mean exactly? It means the government now has the ability to use the underlying underwriting master digital mine to discover new digital mines on which it can on sell into the market place and get a return on them; a new form of income revenue to the treasury. The treasury can also on sell or trade those newly discovered digital mines which as a number could be 1/10th the size of the underlying underwritten amount which would be estimated at US$2T per annum in new digital mine discoveries which would be available to but not limited to sell/trade on the COMEX, and/or the central bank FED acquires them etc.

If the treasury traded its newly discovered digital mines which comes under realestate/property to the central bank FED it would trade them for US Dollars, as the FED has the license to bring new money into existence which is perfectly acceptable, the difference is the FED is not doing this to the treasury in the form of debt it is doing it in the form of trade. The FED would be trading US currency Fiat for newly discovered digital mines and the FED would want to do this because those newly discovered digital mines would start to discover new digital mines for them. Meaning this is a win-win situation that only this realestate property digital mine innovation on the blockchain can achieve.

To take it a step further the FED can be taxed as the new digital mines that it discovers it could monetise into US dollars meaning there could be a taxable event here which would produce new revenue for the IRS again win-win.

Because of this innovation and it being applied in this way the treasury is happy because it can now pay down the debt without borrowing to do so, meaning the new digital mine discoveries are debt free and therefore interest free, the Central Bank FED is happy because now it has a new income revenue stream by monetising actual property which is in the form of digital mines and the IRS is happy because it has a new revenue income stream that was not from increased taxes. As you can see the numbers that this innovation can address/generate/capture per this example is in the range of US$2T worth of new digital mine discoveries which as an example the FED would acquire and those new digital mines would start to discover new digital mines for the fed and would amount to $200B per annum and the IRS could receive new revenue from that at the rate of as a number 10% per annum $20B meaning the entire US debt could be paid down inside 10 years debt and interest free and move them as a country into surplus.

Another key area in this claim is governments can allocate their discovered mines to specific sectors of the economy along its own blockchain such as but not limited to the small medium enterprises and entrepreneurs in the form of grant funding contributing in this way would boost the private sector which could create exports and bring in new money to the economy and to take this claim a step further the government could also but not limited to allocate/lease/rent their newly discovered mines to a country which means the government would bring in new money as a percentage of what is discovered by that country this would be seen as a government export arrangement, exporting a governments surpluses which would by default boost the countries revenues sustainably and substantially. The country would not have to spend into the economy only to then take back a percentage in tax with this innovation model the government would export its new mine discovery surpluses and the return would be the gains from the newly discovered mines that the new country/government acquired and the lease payment would be in the form of fiat and/or its national currency converted exchanged to the country's currency that allocated them the surplus to use.

Images "Digital Mine Franchise Portfolio DMF FP 0004, 0004a and 0004b" show an example of this process

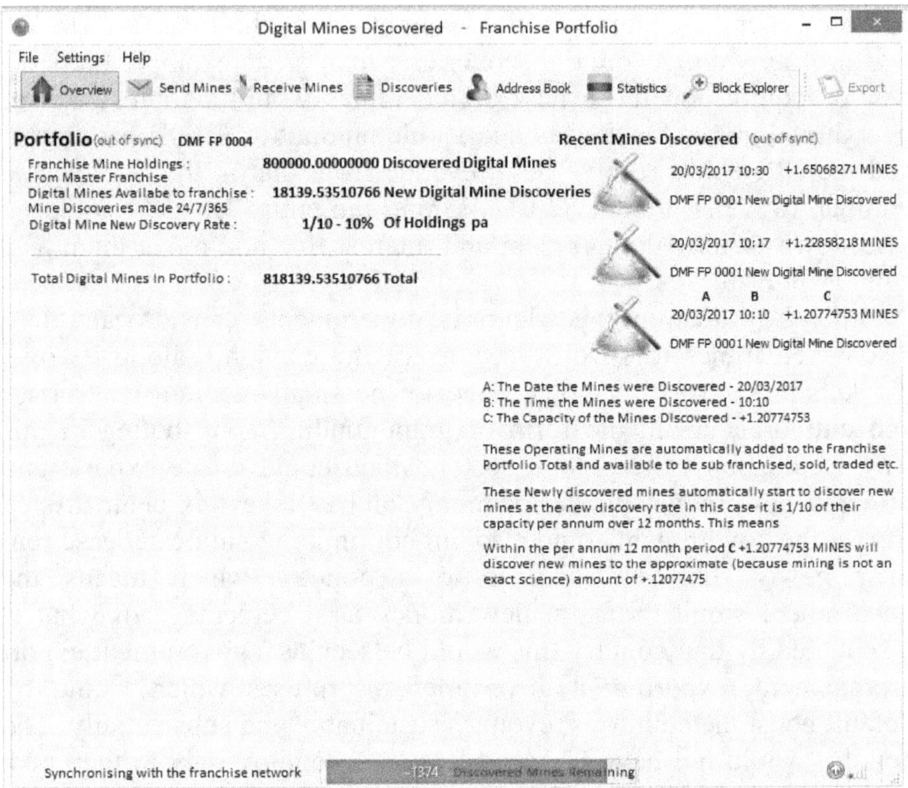

The master franchise which had to make the master franchise discovery first would receive a license fee of, as an example, 10% per annum as would the patent holder an additional, as an example, 10% per annum. Remember neither of these fees come from an external source, they are part of when the new digital mine discoveries are monetised. Meaning they are built into the digital mine discovery model.

As we have been able to clearly demonstrate, this innovation can be used and exploited to and as, but not limited to, underwrite/insure/insurance/support/security/securitise/collateral/hedge/hedging IFRS 9 etc.

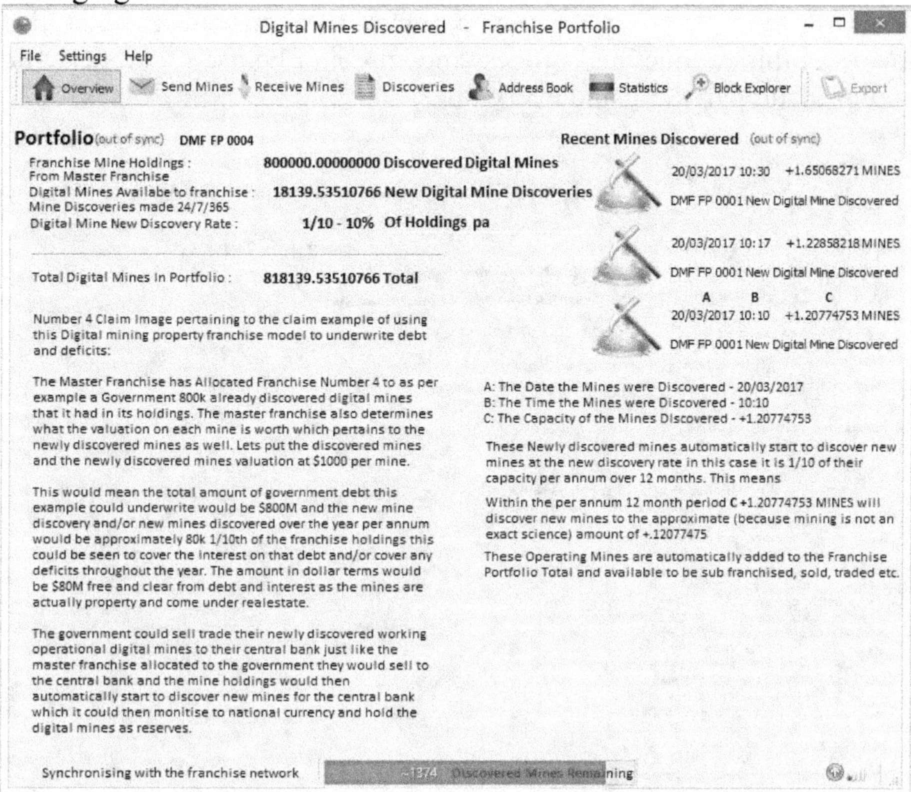

We have demonstrated that this innovation is an actual working blockchain digital mine and can enter many sectors and can at the same time imitate and replicate the very, but not limited to, asset/commodity/property/ that it determines and/or underwrites underwrite insurance using realestate property digital mine/ digital mines as collateral security.

Underwrite/insure the realestate property in full or part with the digital mine and the 2nd digital mine that is discovered from the first digital mine will discover and produce a percentage of the same property which will be available to hold and increase over time, sell or lease.

This innovation can also be used to discover any and all property tenements, acreage, and commercial domestic. Rentals property, land property, real property estate, realty assets, chattels, freehold, immoveable and buildings landed, property landholdings, lot, plot, territory, state, country, assets, commodities, currency. What this means is this product and process model could be used to underwrite and/or insure anything and everything.

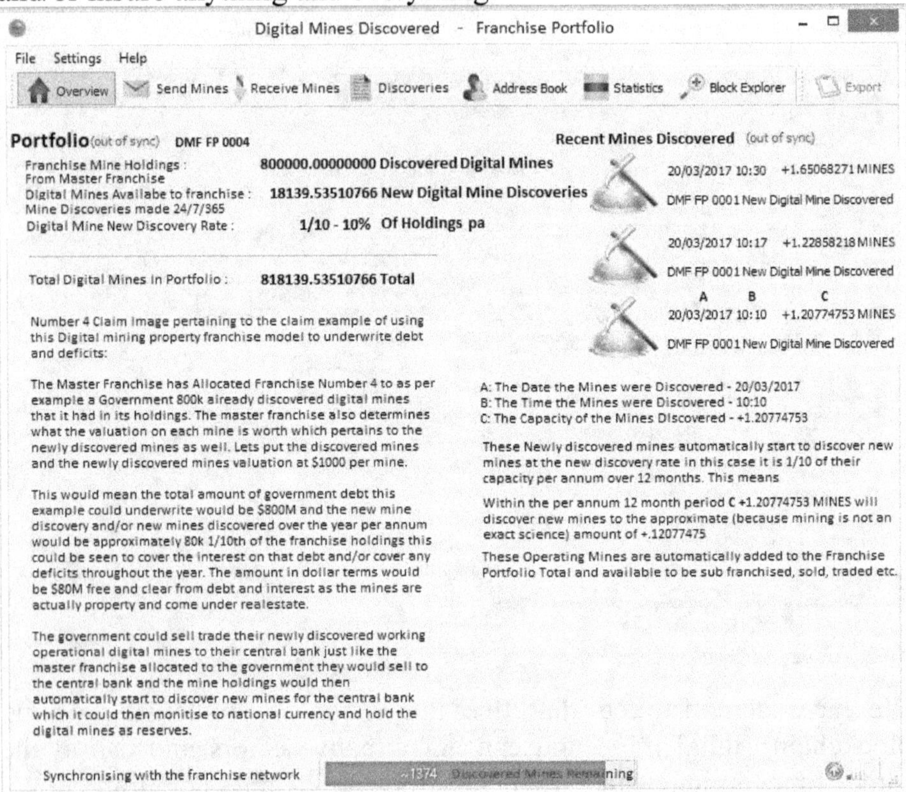

As a claim example of the pure innovation and complexity of this innovation goes as follows:

If you had $1M of gold bullion which would be considered property as any asset/commodity would and therefore come under the scope of this innovation patent. That $1M worth of gold bullion does not give a return unless it is put at risk or the market prices rise and you have to sell down some of it to realise the gain made which leaves you with actually less than the ounce volume you had to begin with. What this innovation does is:

Underwrite by allocation of a digital mine which discovers new digital mines classed as realestate/property in their own right and of their own right which can take on any and all forms of and can match on a 1:1 basis if required.
A gold bullion dealer such as the Perth mint wants to get a return on its bullion investment without putting its bullion at risk.
A master gold bullion digital mine discovery is found by the Master Franchise
A valuation by the Master franchise under license from the Bankcoin Reserve is determined this could be $1 per digital mine and up to the actual gold ounce price per digital mine or fractions of a discovered digital mine.
As per this example, to keep the numbers simple, let's say the master franchise determines the valuation of each digital mine that it discovered to be valued at $1000 which is the same as an ounce of gold on the market at this point in time, and the Bankcoin Reserve formula of the ceiling of the physical gold price in a preceding month is the floor price of the digital mine valuation in the following month meaning the price never goes down it either stays the same if the gold price on the market declines or goes up if that's what the gold market actually determines.
The physical gold market is the price maker, the Bankcoin Reserve is a price taker, meaning it takes the price from the market and pegs the digital mines that it determines to this price point as it has the ability and authority to do so since it has exclusive license to the patented products.
A portfolio of digital mines to the value of $1M would be allocated to underwrite the actual $1M of physical bullion in a sense underwriting the entire $1M bullion at full value full reserve 1:1. Now that sounds normal, the key difference which is where this innovation comes into it is the $1M of digital mine underwriting it now starts to discover new gold bullion digital mines at the rate of, as an example, 10% per annum and/or a 10th of the size of the primary digital mine master allocation in this instance $1M would discover digital mines to the value of $100k per annum ongoing for a term determined by the Bankcoin Reserve and/or 1M already discovered digital mines could

newly discover 100k new mines and these mines be put into a franchise portfolio.

This gives the physical bullion holders a return that they never otherwise would have had in the form of digital mines which can then be, but not limited to, on sold, traded, used as security, collateral free and clear etc. To be clear this is not a representation of the actual gold bullion, as regulators and law makers around the world have deemed the blockchain as the rails and what sits on it and what they do to be property, assets, commodities etc. Therefore the Digital mines that are being discovered here are legitimate digital mines in their own right and therefore outright because they can be fully demonstrated in a court of law.

Anyone and everyone now has access to acquire a digital mine property and/or a digital mining operation as it is realestate, it is a world first which is why this is a global innovation patent because it applies to and is an opportunity for people from all around the world.

This digital mine discovery actually discovers more digital mines while it uses the blockchain as the rails and a secondary digital mine discovery process to discover secondary digital mines then that 2nd digital mine discovers a 3rd digital mine and then a 4th then 5th which can continue indefinitely all from the digital mines discovered before it. Because they are actual digital mines which are discovered they would come under the realestate/property classification. Be it a commercial operation and/or in the wholesale sector and/or retail a portfolio of digital mines traded and/or on sold to the retail sector including being used as but not limited to security, insurance, collateral etc.

This innovation sets out a new realestate and/or property franchise model to prove that it works and has the ability to be exploited under a patent license fee agreement and/or outright bought/sold to specific entities such as but not limited to, governments, Banks, financial institutions, monetary funds, insurance industries on platforms such as but not limited to asset/commodity/stock/bond/share markets and exchanges etc.

This is a blockchain digital mine discovery franchise innovation specifically designed and developed for the realestate /property, insurance/underwriting, security/collateral markets. This is not a crypto currency nor is it an asset/commodity innovation that earns interest. What we have discovered on the blockchain is an actual digital mine we can call the master franchise which can actually discover new digital mines at a pre-determined discovery percentage rate example 1/10th per annum. It is estimated because mining is not an exact science.

This innovation is an actual digital mine discovery innovation which by default means it is covered under the realestate banner and in doing so we have worked out through our modelling that it can be an actual franchise. The master franchise is discovered the moment we find it and from there subsequent franchises with the same ability are allocated.

Because this innovation is an actual digital mine on the blockchain with a secondary digital mine discovery feature, discovery capabilities which then has the ability to discover a third digital mine off the second discovered franchise digital mine which then has the ability to discover fourth digital mine off the third discovered digital mines and so on and so forth. Also from the second digital mine discovery onwards we have the ability to go to an actual asset/commodity which would end the new digital mine discovery it is unique and innovative hence the innovation patent.

If the master franchise is discovered for a suburban housing development and each one of the franchises that comes from the master franchise underwrites a house the 1st franchise discovers 1/10th of a exact same house as the discoveries can become what they underwrite. What this means is house value as an example is $1M then the exact same amount is used to underwrite it and from that point forward it begins to discover new mines/houses on the blockchain at 1/10th of its capacity per annum. Over a 10 year period the home owner ends up with a portfolio of mines in this case 10/10ths of a house which equates to a full house in the portfolio which they can now trade, on sell, swap etc.. That 100% discovered over the 10 years is considered surplus to the homeowner's requirements, needs and therefore can be used to create the next franchise and the process starts all over again this time for the new franchise owner. The license and/or franchise fee would be as a number 10% which is 1% over all 10% of 10% This franchise house mines.

Another example is when a shopping centre wants to acquire a franchise and or be a franchise owner we the Bankcoin Reserve discover a master franchise and we underwrite the entire shopping value as a number $1B we underwrite the shopping centre to the value of $1B and the first franchise is given to the shopping centre management. The shopping centre franchise then starts to discover new shopping centre mines at the 1/10th the capacity/size of the underwritten asset. Again over the next 10 years the shopping centre franchise discovers a 1/10th and it adds up to 10/10ths and/or 100% of the original underwritten value which is a portfolio comprised of new shopping centre mines which continue to discover new shopping centre mines. The portfolio of shopping centre mines can now be on sold and or traded to a new franchisee who will begin to do it all over again. The franchise license fee to be paid can also be paid in other ways such as gift cards each year 10% of the 10% discovered can be converted by the shopping centre into gift cards and/or any other value the shopping centres has available this would be negotiated with the Bankcoin reserve before the franchise is acquired. This franchise discovers shopping centre mines.

This innovation now makes it possible to do Arbun on the blockchain under license agreement: Down payment; a non-refundable deposit paid by a buyer retaining a right to confirm or cancel the sale.

You can also acquire a franchise and/or pay the franchise fees in anything of value per annum on the condition the Bankcoin reserve master franchise agrees and there is a market for the traded value. example but not limited to gift cards, fuel cards, oil, wool, wheat, precious metals, gemstones, property, land, buildings, boats, cars, bikes, inventory stock, stocks, shares, bonds, products, goods, services etc..

Oil Company comes to the BCR and wants to acquire an oil franchise. The BCR sets out to discover one when it finds one it then makes a master oil company franchise out of it. It then makes available to Oil Company the first franchise. It puts one or a portfolio of its oil rigs together and valuates them to as a number $1B the first shell oil franchise is then valued the same $1B what the first franchise now

does is discover new oil deposits mine deposits which begins to build up a portfolio of newly discovered oil deposits on the blockchain as per our patents at a rate of as a number 20% per annum. These then become the second franchise from the master and/or the first franchise made available from the oil company franchise.
This innovation now makes it possible to do Daman on the blockchain under license agreement: 1) Contract of guarantee, security or collateral; (2) Responsibility of entrepreneur/manager of a business; one of two basic relationships toward property, entailing bearing the risk of its loss; compare Amanah.
Al Wadia using this Islamic Banking blockchain sharia-compliant finance innovation: Resale of goods with a discount on the original stated cost. Ijara using this Islamic Banking blockchain sharia-compliant finance innovation: A leasing agreement whereby the bank buys an item for a customer and then leases it back over a specific period. Letting on lease. Sale of a definite usufruct of any asset in exchange of definite reward. It refers to a contract of land leased at a fixed rent payable in cash and also to a mode of financing adopted by Islamic banks. It is an arrangement under which the Islamic banks lease equipments, buildings or other facilities to a client, against an agreed rental. Ijara-wa- Iqtina using this Islamic Banking blockchain sharia-compliant finance innovation: Similar to Ijara, except that the customer is able to buy the item at the end of the contract. A mode of financing, by way of Hire-purchase, adopted by Islamic banks. It is a contract under which the Islamic bank finances equipment, building or other facilities for the client against an agreed rental together with a unilateral undertaking by the bank or the client that at the end of the lease period, the ownership in the asset would be transferred to the lessee. The undertaking or the promise does not become an integral part of the lease contract to make it conditional. The rental as well as the purchase price are fixed in such a manner that the bank gets back its principal sum along with with some profit, which is usually determined in advance. Musharaka using this Islamic Banking blockchain sharia-compliant finance innovation: An investment partnership in which profit sharing terms are agreed in advance, and losses re pegged to the amount invested – basically Private Equity. Musharakah means a relationship established under a contract by the

mutual consent of the parties for sharing of profits and losses in the joint business. It is an agreement under which the Islamic bank provides funds which are mixed with the funds of the business enterprise and others. All providers of capital are entitled to participate in management, but not necessarily required to do so. The profit is distributed among the partners in pre-agreed ratios, while the loss is borne by every partner strictly in proportion to respective capital contributions.

Takaful using this Islamic Banking blockchain sharia-compliant finance innovation: Islamic insurance. Structured as charitable collective pool of funds based on the idea of mutual assistance. In Takaful the members are the insurers as well as the insured. Conventional insurance is prohibited in Islam because its dealings contain several "Haram" elements including Gharar and Riba, as mentioned above.

This innovation now makes it possible to do Al-'Aariyah (Gratuitous loan of non-fungible objects) on the blockchain under license agreement: Al-'Aariyah means loan of a particular piece of property, the substance of which is not consumed by its use, without anything taken in exchange, In other words, it is the gift of usufruct of a property or commodity that is not consumed on use. It is different from Qard that is the loan of fungible objects which are consumed on use and in which the similar and not the same commodity has to be returned. It is also a virtuous act like Qard. The borrowed commodity is treated as liability of the borrower who is bound to return it to its owner.

POSAC

Proof Of Stake - Stake A Claim - A mining claim/deposit claim on the Blockchain

Example Domain would be www.BlockchainFranchise.com

Discover Mine deposits on the blockchain and turns them into a franchise

Franchise cost and digital mine discovery rate not including 2% - 5% franchise fee per annum.

$10B Franchise discovers 25% per annum 4 year payback - 5% franchise fee per annum

$1B Franchise discovers 22.5% per annum 4.5 year payback 4.5% franchise fee per annum
$100M Franchise discovers 20% per annum 5 year payback 4% franchise fee per annum
$10M Franchise discovers 17.5% per annum 5.7 year payback 3.5% franchise fee per annum
$1M Franchise discovers 15% per annum 6.7 year payback 3% franchise fee per annum
$100k Franchise discovers 12.5% per annum 8 year payback 2.5% franchise fee per annum
$10k Franchise discovers 10% per annum 10 year payback 2% franchise fee per annum
Some examples of but not limited to franchises
Islamic Banking Blockchain Murabaha Franchise
Islamic Banking Blockchain Mudaraba Franchise
Islamic Banking Blockchain Musharaka Franchise
Islamic Banking Blockchain Ijara Franchise
Islamic Banking Blockchain Sukuk Franchise
Islamic Banking Blockchain Takaful Franchise

This Islamic Banking Sharia Compliant Blockchain Innovation is a blockchain digital mine discovery franchise innovation specifically designed and developed for the realestate /property, insurance/underwriting, security/collateral markets. This is not a crypto currency nor is it an asset/commodity innovation that earns interest. What we have discovered on the blockchain is an actual digital mine we can call the master franchise which can actually discover new digital mines at a pre-determined discovery percentage rate example 1/10th per annum. It is estimated because mine discovery is not an exact science.

This Islamic Banking Sharia Compliant Blockchain Innovation is an actual digital mine discovery innovation on the blockchain which by default means it is covered under the realestate banner and in doing so we have worked out through our modelling that it can be an actual franchise. The master franchise is discovered the moment we find it and from there subsequent franchises with the same ability are

discovered and then allocated and considered as per this patent as franchisees/sub franchises off the master franchise as well as off the sub franchisees themselves..
Because this Islamic Banking Sharia Compliant Blockchain Innovation is an actual digital mine on the blockchain with a secondary, third, fourth, fifth unlimited and continuous digital mine discovery ability and features, discovery capabilities which then has the ability to discover a third digital mine off the second discovered franchise digital mine which then has the ability to discover fourth digital mine off the third discovered digital mines and so on and so forth. Also from the second digital mine discovery onwards we have the ability to go to an actual asset/commodity which would end the new digital mine discovery it is unique and innovative hence the innovation patent.

New Glossary of Terms as per This Islamic Banking Blockchain sharia compliant patent innovation but not limited to the following:
Blockchain Mal - Wealth, money, property; any valuable thing which can be possessed on the Blockchain
Blockchain Manfa'ah - Lit: benefit or utility. The yield which a property produces on the Blockchain. The term is often used by jurists to describe the Blockchain usufruct - (usage or services) associated with a given property, especially in leasing transactions.
Blockchain Maysir - Games of chance or gambling, trying to earn easy money without having to provide equivalent consideration. A prohibited activity, as it is a zero-sum game just transferring the wealth not creating new wealth. One of three fundamental prohibitions in Islamic finance, the other two being riba and gharar . The prohibition on Maysir is often used as the grounds for criticism of conventional financial practices such as speculation, conventional insurance and derivatives. This Islamic Banking Blockchain innovation creates new wealth shared by the many instead of the few and addresses the criticism and issues with conventional financial practices such as speculation, conventional insurance and derivatives.
Blockchain Mezzanine Debt - A hybrid of debt and equity financing that is is typically used to finance the expansion of existing companies can now be replaced by this Islamic Banking Blockchain innovation

and use new wealth in the positive which takes pressure off the existing company so it can grow, expand and create new jobs. Blockchain Mudarabah, Blockchain Mudarabah Sukuk, Blockchain Mudarib, Blockchain Mufti, Blockchain Murabaha, Blockchain Murabaha Mu'ajjal, Blockchain Musaqah, Blockchain, Musharakah, Blockchain Musharakah, Permanent, Blockchain Musharakah, Diminishing, Blockchain Al-Ghurm bil Ghunm etc..

Countries and their leaders to lead the way

Afghanistan: President Ashraf Ghani
Albania
Algeria: Abdelkader Bensalah, President of the Council of the Nation
Azerbaijan: President Ilham Aliev
Bahrain: King Hamad bin Isa Al Khalifa
Bangladesh: Prime Minister Sheikh Hasina
Benin : President Patrice Talon
Brunei: Sultan Hassanal Bolkiah
Burkina Faso: President Roch Marc Kabore
Cameroon Chad: President Idris Deby
Comoros Djibouti Egypt: President Abdel Fattah el-Sisi
Gabon: President Ali Bongo Ondimba
The Gambia: President Adama Barrow
Guinea: President Alpha Condé
Guinea-Bissau: President José Mário Vaz
Guyana Indonesia: President Joko Widodo
Iraq: President Fouad Masoum
Ivory Coast: President Alassane Ouattara
Jordan: King Abdullah II
Kazakhstan: President Nursultan Nazarbayev
Kuwait: Emir Sabah Al-Ahmad Al-Jaber Al-Sabah Kyrgyzstan
Lebanon: Prime Minister Saad Hariri Libya
Malaysia: Prime Minister Najib Razak
Maldives: President Abdulla Yameen
Mali: President Ibrahim Boubacar Keïta

Mauritania: President Mohamed Ould Abdel Aziz
Morocco: Minister of Foreign Affairs Nasser Bourita
Mozambique:
Niger: President Mahamadou Issoufou
Nigeria:
Oman: Deputy Prime Minister Fahd bin Mahmoud al Said
Pakistan: Prime Minister Nawaz Sharif
State of Palestine: President Mahmoud Abbas
Qatar: Emir Tamim bin Hamad Al Thani
Senegal: President Macky Sall
Sierra Leone:
Somalia: President Mohamed Abdullahi Farmaajo
Sudan: Minister of State Taha al-Hussein
Suriname
Tajikistan: President Emomali Rahmon
Togo
Tunisia: President Beji Caid Essebsi
Turkey: Minister of Foreign Affairs Mevlut Cavusoglu
Turkmenistan
Uganda
Uzbekistan: President Shavkat Mirziyoyev
Yemen
United Arab Emirates: Crown Prince of Abu Dhabi Mohammed bin Zayed Al Nahyan
United States of America: President Donald J. Trump

Islamic banking sharia compliant non riba Product available but not limited to the following:

Financial Institution	**Country**
FINCA Afghanistan	Afghanistan
IIFC	Afghanistan
United Bank of Albania	Albania
Al Salam Bank	Algeria
Banque Al-Baraka D'Algerie	Algeria
Kuwait Finance House (Australia) Pty. Ltd.	Australia
The Muslim Community Co-	Australia

operative	
Kauthar Bank JSC	Azerbaijan
ARCAPITA Bank	Bahrain
Al Ahli United Bank	Bahrain
Al Salam Bank Bahrain	Bahrain
Al-Baraka Islamic Bank	Bahrain
Arab Islamic Bank (E.C)	Bahrain
BMI Bank BSC, Islamic Banking Division	Bahrain
Bahrain Development Bank	Bahrain
Bahrain Islamic Bank	Bahrain
Bank Alkhair	Bahrain
Capinnova Investment Bank	Bahrain
Citi Islamic Investment Bank E.C.	Bahrain
Elaf Bank	Bahrain
First Energy Bank B.S.C. (FEB)	Bahrain
Global Banking Corporation B.S.C.	Bahrain
Gulf Finance House	Bahrain
Gulf International Bank BSC	Bahrain
International Investment Bank B.S.C.	Bahrain
Investors Bank	Bahrain
Ithmaar Bank	Bahrain
Khaleeji Commercial Bank BSC	Bahrain
Kuwait Finance House Bahrain	Bahrain
Liquidity Management Centre B.S.C	Bahrain
Reef Real Estate Financing Company	Bahrain
Seera Investment Bank B.S.C.	Bahrain
Venture Capital Bank B.S.C.	Bahrain
ABC Islamic Bank	Bahrain
Investment Dar Bank	Bahrain
Al-Arafah Islamic Bank Ltd	Bangladesh
Export Import Bank of Bangladesh Ltd	Bangladesh
First Security Islami Bank Ltd	Bangladesh
ICB Islamic Bank Ltd	Bangladesh
Oriental Bank Ltd. former Al-Baraka Bank Bangladesh Ltd	Bangladesh

Prime Bank Ltd	Bangladesh
Shahjalal Islami Bank Ltd	Bangladesh
Social Islami Bank Ltd (SIBL)	Bangladesh
The City Bank Ltd	Bangladesh
Islami Bank Bangladesh Ltd	Bangladesh

nion Bank Ltd	Bangladesh
Bank Bosna International	Bosnia and Herzegovina
Bank Islam Brunei Darussalam Berhad	Brunei Darussalam
Perbadanan Tabung Amanah Islam Brunei	Brunei Darussalam
Caisse Baitul Maal	Burkina Faso
Crédit du Sahel SA	Cameroon
Islamic Saving and Credit Cooperative of Cameroon (ISCCC)	Cameroon
Al-Tawfeek Company for Investment Funds Limited	Cayman Islands
Bank of NingXia, Islamic Banking	China
Raouda Finance	Cote d'Ivoire
Cyprus Islamic (Offshore) Bank Ltd.	Cyprus
Faisal Islamic Bank Of Kibris	Cyprus
Islamic Bank International of Denmark	Denmark
Salaam African Bank	Djibouti
Al Ahli United Bank	Egypt, Arab Rep.
Al Baraka Bank Egypt, Arab Rep.	Egypt, Arab Rep.
Al Watany Bank of Egypt	Egypt, Arab Rep.
Bab Rizq Jameel	Egypt, Arab Rep.
Banque Misr	Egypt, Arab Rep.
Community Development Foundation	Egypt, Arab Rep.
Egyptian Gulf Bank	Egypt, Arab Rep.
Faisal Islamic Bank of Egypt, Arab Rep.	Egypt, Arab Rep.
Islamic International Bank for Investment & Development	Egypt, Arab Rep.
Suez Canal Bank, Islamic Banking Services	Egypt, Arab Rep.
The United Bank, Rakhaa Islamic Banking	Egypt, Arab Rep.
Arab Gambian Islamic Bank Limited	Gambia
Kuveyt Turk Germany Financial Services	Germany

BMT Inti Jogja	Indonesia
BMT Kube Sejahtera Kota Padang Unit 050	Indonesia
BMT Pringsewu	Indonesia
BMT Sanama	Indonesia
Bank BPD Kalsel Syariah	Indonesia
Bank Pembangunan Daerah (BPD) Banda Aceh	Indonesia
Bank Pembangunan Daerah (BPD) DIY	Indonesia
Bank Pembangunan Daerah (BPD) Jawa Tengah	Indonesia
Bank Pembangunan Daerah (BPD) Jawa Timur	Indonesia
Bank Pembangunan Daerah (BPD) Kalimantan Barat	Indonesia
Bank Pembangunan Daerah (BPD) Kalimantan Selatan	Indonesia
Bank Pembangunan Daerah (BPD) Kalimantan Timur	Indonesia
Bank Pembangunan Daerah (BPD) Nusa Tenggara Bar at	Indonesia
Bank Pembangunan Daerah (BPD) Riau	Indonesia
Bank Pembangunan Daerah (BPD) Sulawesi Selatan	Indonesia
Bank Pembangunan Daerah (BPD) Sumatera Barat	Indonesia
Bank Pembangunan Daerah (BPD) Sumatera Selatan	Indonesia
Bank Pembangunan Daerah (BPD) Sumatera Utara	Indonesia
HSBC Bank	Indonesia
KJKS BMT AT-TAQWA	Indonesia

KSU Syariah Al-Amin	Indonesia
Koperasi Andalas Perkasa	Indonesia
Muslim Aid Indonesia	Indonesia
PT BCA Syariah	Indonesia

PT BTN	Indonesia
PT Bank Tabungan Pensiunan Nasional (BTPN)	Indonesia
PT Bank DKI	Indonesia
PT Bank Danamon	Indonesia
PT Bank International Indonesia (BII)	Indonesia
PT Bank Permata	Indonesia
PT Bank Sinarmas	Indonesia
PT Bank Syariah BNI	Indonesia
PT Bank Syariah BRI	Indonesia
PT Bank Syariah Bukopin	Indonesia
PT Bank Syariah Jabardan Banten (BJB)	Indonesia
PT Bank Syariah Mandiri	Indonesia
PT Bank Syariah Mega Indonesia	Indonesia
PT Bank Syariah Muamalat Indonesia	Indonesia
PT Bank Syariah Panin	Indonesia
PT Bank Syariah Victoria	Indonesia
PT CIMB Niaga	Indonesia
PT Maybank Indonesia Syariah	Indonesia
PT OCBC NISP	Indonesia
Bank Keshavarzi	Iran, Islamic Rep.
Bank Maskan	Iran, Islamic Rep.
Bank Mellat	Iran, Islamic Rep.
Bank Melli	Iran, Islamic Rep.
Bank Refah	Iran, Islamic Rep.
Bank Saderat	Iran, Islamic Rep.
Bank Sepah	Iran, Islamic Rep.
Bank Tejarat	Iran, Islamic Rep.
Bank of Industry and Mine	Iran, Islamic Rep.
Eghtesad Novin Bank (EN Bank)	Iran, Islamic Rep.
Export Development Bank of Iran	Iran, Islamic Rep.
Karafarin Bank	Iran, Islamic Rep.
Parsian Bank	Iran, Islamic Rep.
Pasargad Bank	Iran, Islamic Rep.
Saman Bank	Iran, Islamic Rep.
Sarmayeh Bank	Iran, Islamic Rep.

AL Aman Center	Iraq
Al Ahli United Bank	Iraq
Al Takadum	Iraq
Al-Bilad Islamic Bank	Iraq
CHF ACSI	Iraq
Cihan Bank for Islamic Investment and Finance P.S.C	Iraq
Dijlah &Furat Bank for Development & Investmen	Iraq
Elaf Islamic Bank	Iraq
International Development Bank for Investment & Islamic Finance	Iraq
Iraqi Islamic Bank for Investment & Development SA	Iraq
Islamic Regional Cooperation Bank for Development and Investment	Iraq
Kurdistan International Bank	Iraq
National Islamic Bank	Iraq
Rafidain Bank	Iraq
Rasheed Bank	Iraq
Arab Islamic Bank	Jordan
DEF	Jordan
FINCA Jordan	Jordan
Islamic International Arab Bank	Jordan
Jordan Dubai Islamic Bank	Jordan
Jordan Islamic Bank	Jordan
Kuwait Finance House	Jordan
Aman Account, Kenya Commercial Bank (KCB)	Kenya
First Community Bank	Kenya
Gulf African Bank	Kenya
MFI KGMAMF Grameen	Kosovo
MFI Start	Kosovo
Timi Invest	Kosovo
A'Ayan Leasing & Investment Company	Kuwait

Al Ahli United Bank	Kuwait
Al Rajhi	Kuwait
Arab Investment Company	Kuwait
Aref Investment Group	Kuwait
Boubyan Bank	Kuwait
First Investment Company K.S.C.C.	Kuwait
Global Investment House	Kuwait
Gulf Investment House	Kuwait
International Investor Company, K.S.C. (The)	Kuwait
Investment Dar Co (The)	Kuwait
Kuwait Finance House	Kuwait
Kuwait International Bank	Kuwait
Rasameel Structured Finance Company K.S.C	Kuwait
The Industrial Bank of Kuwait	Kuwait
Warba Bank	Kuwait
Wared Lease & Finance (Wared)	Kuwait
Wethaq Takaful Insurance Company (Wethaq)	Kuwait
Al Baraka Bank Lebanon	Lebanon
Arab Finance House Holding SAL	Lebanon
BLOM Development Bank	Lebanon
Lebanese Islamic Bank	Lebanon
ABN AMRO	Malaysia
AL-HIDAYAH INVESTMENT BANK (LABUAN) LTD	Malaysia
Affin Islamic Bank Berhad	Malaysia
AgroBank, Islamic Banking Services	Malaysia
Al Rajhi Banking & Inv. Corp. (Malaysia)	Malaysia
Alkhair International Islamic Bank Berhad	Malaysia
Alliance Islamic Bank Berhad	Malaysia
AmIslamic Bank Berhad, Islamic	Malaysia

Banking Services	
Asian Finance Bank	Malaysia
Bank Islam Malaysia Berhad	Malaysia
Bank Islam Trust Compnay	Malaysia
Bank Kerjasama Rakyat Malaysia Berhad	Malaysia
Bank Muamalat Malaysia Berhad	Malaysia
Bank Pembangunan Malaysia Berhad	Malaysia
CIMB Islamic Bank Berhad	Malaysia
Citibank Berhad, Islamic Banking Division	Malaysia
Eoncap Islamic Bank Berhad	Malaysia
Export-Import Bank of Malaysia Berhad (EXIM Bank)	Malaysia
First Islamic Investment Bank	Malaysia
HSBC Amanah Malaysia Berhad	Malaysia
Hong Leong Islamic Bank Berhad	Malaysia
KAF Investment Bank Berhad	Malaysia
Kuwait Finance House (Malaysia) Berhad	Malaysia
MIDF Amanah Investment Bank Berhad	Malaysia
Malayan Banking Berhad	Malaysia
Maybank Islamic Berhad	Malaysia
OCBC Al-Amin Bank Berhad	Malaysia
OSK Investment Bank Berhad, Islamic Banking Division	Malaysia
Public Islamic Bank Berhad	Malaysia
RBS Berhad	Malaysia
RHB Islamic Bank Berhad	Malaysia
RUSD Investment Bank Inc	Malaysia
SME Bank, Islamic Banking Services	Malaysia
Standard Chartered Saadiq Berhad	Malaysia
Al Majmoua	Maldives
Maldives Islamic Bank Pvt Ltd	Maldives
Banque Al Wava Mauritanienne Islamique-BAMIS	Mauritania

Al-Baraka Microfinance Bank Limited	Nigeria
Lotus Capital Limited	Nigeria
Bank Dhofar	Oman
Bank Nizwa	Oman
Oman Arab Bank (Al Yusr Islamic Banking Window)	Oman
AAS Foundation	Pakistan
ABN AMRO	Pakistan
Akhuwat	Pakistan
Al Baraka Bank (Pakistan) Limited	Pakistan
Askari Bank Limited	Pakistan
Bank Alfalah	Pakistan
Bank Islami Pakistan Limited	Pakistan
Bank al Habib Limited	Pakistan
Burj Bank Limited	Pakistan
DEEP Foundation	Pakistan

awood Islamic Bank Limited	Pakistan
Dubai Islamic Bank Pakistan	Pakistan
Emirates Global Islamic Bank Limited	Pakistan
Farz Foundation	Pakistan
Faysal Bank Limited	Pakistan
First Habib Modaraba	Pakistan
First National Bank Modaraba	Pakistan
Habib Metropolitan Bank	Pakistan
Islamic Relief-Pakistan	Pakistan
MCB Bank	Pakistan
Meezan Bank	Pakistan
Muslim Aid Pakistan	Pakistan
National Bank of Pakistan	Pakistan
Naymet Islamic Microfinance	Pakistan
Pak Kuwait Takaful Company Limited	Pakistan
Soneri Bank Limited	Pakistan
Standard Chartered Modaraba	Pakistan
The Bank of Khyber	Pakistan
United Bank Limited	Pakistan

Amanah Islamic Bank	Philippine
Al Ahli United Bank	Qatar
Al Khaliji Commercial Bank and Islmaic Banking	Qatar
Barwa Bank	Qatar
Barwa Bank	Qatar
Commercial Bank	Qatar
Commercial Bank	Qatar
First Finance Company (Q.S.C)	Qatar
HSBC Bank Midde East	Qatar
Masraf Al Rayan - Qatar	Qatar
Qatar First Bank	Qatar
Qatar Islamic bank	Qatar
Qatar National Bank	Qatar
Qinvest LLC	Qatar
Qatar International Islamic Bank	Qatar
ICB Badr-Forte Bank	Russian Federation
Al Rajhi Banking & Investment Corporation	Saudi Arabia
Alinma Bank	Saudi Arabia
Arab National Bank	Saudi Arabia
Bank AlJazira	Saudi Arabia
Bank Albilad	Saudi Arabia
Banque Saudi Fransi, Islamic Banking	Saudi Arabia
HSBC Bank	Saudi Arabia
Islamic Development Bank	Saudi Arabia
Itqan Capita	Saudi Arabia
Jana	Saudi Arabia
Riyad Bank	Saudi Arabia
Samba Financial Group	Saudi Arabia
audi British Bank	Saudi Arabia
Saudi Hollandi Bank	Saudi Arabia
Saudi Kuwait Finance House	Saudi Arabia
Saudi Partners Company (Mushtaraka)	Saudi Arabia

The Investor for Securities	Saudi Arabia
The National Commercial Bank	Saudi Arabia
The Saudi Investment Bank	Saudi Arabia
Banque Islamique du Senegal	Senegal
Islamic Bank of Asia (The)	Singapore
Dayax Islamic Bank	Somalia
Salaam Somali Bank	Somalia
Absa Islamic Banking	South Africa
Albaraka Bank Limited	South Africa
Abrar Trade and Investments	Sri Lanka
Amana Bank	Sri Lanka
Muslim Aid Micro Credit (Guarantee) Ltd	Sri Lanka
Agricltural Bank Of Sudan	Sudan
Al Baraka Bank Sudan	Sudan
Al Jazeera Sudanese Jordanian Bank	Sudan
Al Salam Bank Sudan	Sudan
Al Shamal Islamic Bank	Sudan
Animal Resources Bank	Sudan
Bank of Khartoum	Sudan
Baraa Institution	Sudan
Blue Nile Mashreq Bank	Sudan
Export Development Bank - Sudan	Sudan
Faisal Islamic Bank	Sudan
Farmers Commercial Bank	Sudan
Financial Investment Bank	Sudan
Industrial Development Bank	Sudan
Islamic Co-operative Development Bank	Sudan
Livestock Bank	Sudan
Muslim Aid Sudan	Sudan
National Bank of Sudan	Sudan
Omdurman National Bank	Sudan
PASED	Sudan
Saudi Sudanese Bank	Sudan
Savings and Social Development Bank	Sudan

Social Development Institution for Sudanese Pensioners	Sudan
Sudanese Egyptian Bank	Sudan
Sudanese French Bank	Sudan
Sudanese Islamic Bank	Sudan
United Capital Bank	Sudan
Youth Institution for Microfinance	Sudan
Tadamon Islamic Bank	Sudan
Dar Al-Maal Al-Islami Trust	Switzerland
Faisal Private Bank	Switzerland

l Baraka Syria	Syrian Arab Republic
Cham Bank	Syrian Arab Republic
Syria International Islamic Bank	Syrian Arab Republic
UNDP Rural Community Development program at Jabal Al Hoss	Syrian Arab Republic
Al Baraka Bank Tunisia	Tunisia
BEST Bank	Tunisia
Banque Zitouna	Tunisia
Kuwait Turkish Participation Bank Inc.	Turkey
Albaraka Turk Participation Bank	Turkey
Asya Finance Participation Bank	Turkey
Kuwait Turkish Participation Bank	Turkey
Turkiye Finance Participation Bank	Turkey
Ihlas Finans Kurumu A.S.	Turkey
Aman Account, Kenya Commercial Bank (KCB) Uganda Limited	Uganda
Abu Dhabi Islamic Bank	United Arab Emirates
Dubai Bank	United Arab Emirates
Dubai Islamic Bank	United Arab Emirates
Emirates Islamic Bank	United Arab Emirates
Sharjah Islamic Bank	United Arab Emirates
Al Hilal Bank	United Arab Emirates
Ajman Bank	United Arab Emirates
Noor Islamic Bank	United Arab Emirates
Mawarid Finance	United Arab Emirates
Mashreq Al Islami	United Arab Emirates

Amlak Finance PJSC	United Arab Emirates
Tamweel PJSC	United Arab Emirates
Abu Dhabi Commercial Bank	United Arab Emirates
Attijari Al Islami	United Arab Emirates
First Gulf Bank, Siraj Islamic Banking	United Arab Emirates
Emirates NBD PJSC	United Arab Emirates
Emirates Industrial Bank	United Arab Emirates
National Bank of Abu Dhabi	United Arab Emirates
National Bank of Umm Al Qaiwain	United Arab Emirates
Rasmala Investment Bank Ltd	United Arab Emirates
Union National Bank	United Arab Emirates
Waqf Trust Services	United Arab Emirates
Bank of London and The Middle East	United Kingdom
European Islamic Investment Bank	United Kingdom
Gatehouse Bank plc.	United Kingdom
Islamic Bank of Britain	United Kingdom
Al Ahli United Bank	United Kingdom
Lloyds TSB Bank	United Kingdom
Muslim Aid UK	United Kingdom
United National Bank Limited	United Kingdom
Europe Arab Bank PLC	United Kingdom
Shariah Capital	United States
Bank of Whittier	United States
Devon Bank	United States
Arab Islamic Bank	West Bank and Gaza
Palestine Islamic Bank	West Bank and Gaza
Reef Finance Co.	West Bank and Gaza
Islamic Relief Palestine	West Bank and Gaza
PARC	West Bank and Gaza
PDF	West Bank and Gaza
ACAD	West Bank and Gaza
Faten	West Bank and Gaza
Asala	West Bank and Gaza
Abyan	Yemen, Rep.
AlTadamun for small and microfinance	Yemen, Rep.
Al Amal Microfinance Bank	Yemen, Rep.

Azal	Yemen, Rep.
Islamic Bank of Yemen	Yemen, Rep.
Saba Islamic Bank	Yemen, Rep.
Shamil Bank of Yemen and Bahrain	Yemen, Rep.
Tadhamon International Islamic Bank	Yemen, Rep.

Central Banks Blockchain Developments

Links:

Singapore regulator proposes fintech sandbox
https://www.finextra.com/newsarticle/29001/singapore-regulator-proposes-fintech-sandbox

HKMA to set up fintech sandbox and innovation hub
https://www.finextra.com/newsarticle/29394/hkma-to-set-up-fintech-sandbox-and-innovation-hub

Malaysia sets out fintech sandbox framework
https://www.finextra.com/newsarticle/29620/malaysia-sets-out-fintech-sandbox-framework

Bahrain joins fintech free-for-all in the Middle East
https://www.finextra.com/newsarticle/30352/bahrain-joins-fintech-free-for-all-in-the-middle-east

Central Bank of Bahrain debuts regulatory sandbox21 hours ago
https://www.finextra.com/newsarticle/30691/central-bank-of-bahrain-debuts-regulatory-sandbox?lipi=urn%3Ali%3Apage%3Ad_flagship3_feed%3Bq4vF5BFLSlCRDBuW0q9ryQ%3D%3D

Ex-Tandem CTO onboard for Dubai-based digital bank
https://www.finextra.com/newsarticle/30583/ex-tandem-cto-onboard-for-dubai-based-digital-bank

Dubai encourages fintech with temporary financial services licence
https://www.finextra.com/newsarticle/30617/dubai-encourages-fintech-with-temporary-financial-services-licence

Thailand sets up fintech sandbox
https://www.finextra.com/newsarticle/29475/thailand-sets-up-fintech-sandbox

Abu Dhabi opens fintech RegLab
https://www.finextra.com/newsarticle/29703/abu-dhabi-opens-fintech-reglab

Australian budget promises a raft of reforms to boost fintech
https://www.finextra.com/newsarticle/30536/australian-budget-promises-a-raft-of-reforms-to-boost-fintech

Asic launches licence exemption scheme for fintechs
https://www.finextra.com/newsarticle/29904/asic-launches-licence-exemption-scheme-for-fintechs

Australian Government agency steps in to support fintech accelerator
https://www.finextra.com/newsarticle/30015/australian-government-agency-steps-in-to-support-fintech-accelerator

Norway's Central Bank is Researching Anonymous Digital Currency
http://www.coindesk.com/norway-central-bank-anonymous-digital-currency/

Behind on Blockchain? Central Banks Are Catching Up Quick
http://www.coindesk.com/behind-blockchain-central-banks-catching-quick/

Blockchain Could Expand Central Bank Access, Says Bank of Japan

http://www.coindesk.com/blockchain-expand-central-bank-access-says-bank-japan/

Notes

Cambodia's Central Bank Signs Deal to Develop Blockchain Tech
http://www.coindesk.com/cambodias-central-bank-signs-deal-develop-blockchain-tech/

Australia's Central Bank is Conducting Internal Blockchain Research
http://www.coindesk.com/australia-central-bank-blockchain-research/

Russian Central Banker: Bitcoin's Legal Recognition Isn't Guaranteed
http://www.coindesk.com/russian-central-banker-bitcoins-legal-recognition-isnt-guaranteed/

Hong Kong's Central Bank is Trialing a Digital Currency
http://www.coindesk.com/hong-kong-central-bank-digital-currency-prototype/

Hong Kong's Central Bank Partners on DLT Trade Finance Test
http://www.coindesk.com/hong-kongs-central-bank-partners-on-dlt-trade-finance-test/

Emirates NBD Enlists UAE Central Bank in Blockchain Check Trial
http://www.coindesk.com/emirates-nbd-enlists-uae-central-bank-blockchain-check-trial/

G20 Should Create Central Bank Blockchain Consortium, Report Says
http://www.coindesk.com/report-g20-countries-blockchain-sandbox/

German Central Bank Chief: Blockchain Could Make Markets Faster

http://www.coindesk.com/german-central-bank-chief-blockchain-make-markets-faster/

Singapore's Central Bank Completes Digital Currency Trial
http://www.coindesk.com/singapore-central-bank-digital-currency-trial/

Canada's Central Bank is 'Open' to More Blockchain Tests
http://www.coindesk.com/canada-central-bank-blockchain-tests/

France's Central Bank Wants to Work With More Blockchain Startups
http://www.coindesk.com/france-central-bank-collaboration-blockchain/

UAE Central Bank: We Are Not Banning Bitcoin
http://www.coindesk.com/uae-central-bank-not-banning-bitcoin/

Germany's Central Bank Details Blockchain Trading Test Results
http://www.coindesk.com/germany-central-bank-blockchain-results/

China's Central Bank is Testing a Blockchain-Backed Digital Currency
http://www.coindesk.com/chinas-central-bank-testing-blockchain-backed-digital-currency/

Russia's Central Bank Adds Blockchain-Friendly Firm to FinTech Working Group

http://www.coindesk.com/central-bank-russia-blockchain-footprint/

As India Goes Cashless, it's Central Bank Researches Blockchain http://www.coindesk.com/india-goes-cashless-central-bank-researches-blockchain/

Finland's Central Bank Organizes Blockchain Event
http://www.coindesk.com/finland-central-bank-blockchain-event/

Argentina's Central Bank is Warming Up to Blockchain
http://www.coindesk.com/argentinas-central-bank-warming-blockchain/

Sweden's Central Bank Considers Digital Currency Use
http://www.coindesk.com/sweden-central-bank-digital-currency/

Hong Kong Central Bank: Blockchain Holds 'Enormous Potential'
http://www.coindesk.com/hong-kong-central-bank-blockchain-research/

Bank of Canada Demos Blockchain-Based Digital Dollar
Pete Rizzo (@pete_rizzo_) | Published on June 16, 2016 at 13:30 BST
http://www.coindesk.com/bank-canada-demos-blockchain-based-digital-dollar/

Digital Currency 'Still on the Agenda' at Russian Central Bank
Stan Higgins | Published on June 3, 2016 at 15:21 BST
http://www.coindesk.com/russias-central-bank-theres-cautious-optimism-blockchain/

90 Central Banks Seek Blockchain Answers at Federal Reserve Event
Michael del Castillo (@DelRayMan) | Published on June 6, 2016 at 18:50 BST
http://www.coindesk.com/central-banks-blockchain-federal-reserve/

IMF Economist Examines Bitcoin Blockchain's Role in Banking

Daniel Palmer | Published on June 15, 2016 at 17:06 BST
http://www.coindesk.com/imf-says-bitcoins-blockchain-tech-help-banks/

IMF Paper: Regulation Should Preserve Benefits of Digital Currency
Daniel Palmer | Published on January 20, 2016 at 17:26 BST
http://www.coindesk.com/imf-paper-preserve-digital-currency-benefits/

Nasdaq Opens Blockchain Services to Global Exchange Partners
Michael del Castillo (@DelRayMan) | Published on May 26, 2016 at 19:18 BST
http://www.coindesk.com/nasdaqs-blockchain-services-global-exchange/

Goldman Sachs: Blockchain Tech Could Save Capital Markets $6 Billion a Year
Pete Rizzo (@pete_rizzo_) | Published on May 25, 2016 at 23:44 BST
http://www.coindesk.com/goldman-sachs-blockchain-tech-save-capital-markets-12-billion/

Poland to Explore Blockchain Tech in Government Digitization Effort
Jacek Czarnecki | Published on June 23, 2016 at 15:05 BST
http://www.coindesk.com/poland-explore-blockchain-tech-government-digitization-effort/

Papua New Guinea to improve financial inclusion with new technology Blockchain
http://www.abc.net.au/news/2017-05-24/papua-new-guinea-to-improve-financial-inclusion/8555978

BANKING HISTORY

History of banking
From Wikipedia, the free encyclopedia
https://en.wikipedia.org/wiki/History_of_banking

If you have not donated to Wikipedia please do so they are an amazing resource that works on donations, Regards, Gary

The history of banking refers to the development of banks and banking throughout history, with banking defined by contemporary sources as an organization which provides facilities for acceptance of deposits and provision of loans.

The history begins with the first prototype banks of merchants of the ancient world, which made grain loans to farmers and traders who carried goods between cities. This began around 2000 BC in Assyria and Babylonia. Later, in ancient Greece and during the Roman Empire, lenders based in temples made loans and added two important innovations: they accepted deposits and changed money. Archaeology from this period in ancient China and India also shows evidence of money lending activity.

Many histories position the crucial historical development of a banking system to medieval and Renaissance Italy and particularly the affluent cities of Florence, Venice and Genoa. The Bardi and Peruzzi families dominated banking in 14th century Florence, establishing branches in many other parts of Europe. The most famous Italian bank was the Medici bank, established by Giovanni Medici in 1397. The oldest bank still in existence is Banca Monte dei Paschi di Siena, headquartered in Siena, Italy, which has been operating continuously since 1472.

The development of banking spread from northern Italy throughout the Holy Roman Empire, and in the 15th and 16th century to northern Europe. This was followed by a number of important innovations that took place in Amsterdam during the Dutch Republic in the 17th century, and in London in the 18th century. During the 20th century, developments in telecommunications and computing caused major changes to banks' operations and let banks dramatically increase in size and geographic spread. The financial crisis of 2007–2008 caused many bank failures, including some of the world's largest banks, and provoked much debate about bank regulation.

Religious restrictions on interest

Most early religious systems in the ancient Near East, and the secular codes arising from them, did not forbid usury. These societies regarded inanimate matter as alive, like plants, animals and people, and capable of reproducing itself. Hence if you lent 'food money', or monetary tokens of any kind, it was legitimate to charge interest. Food money in the shape of olives, dates, seeds or animals was lent out as early as c. 5000 BCE, if not earlier. Among the Mesopotamians, Hittites, Phoenicians and Egyptians, interest was legal and often fixed by the state.

Judaism[edit]

Main articles: Loans and interest in Judaism and Jewish views of poverty, wealth and charity

The Torah and later sections of the Hebrew Bible criticize interest-taking, but interpretations of the Biblical prohibition vary. One common understanding is that Jews are forbidden to charge interest upon loans made to other Jews, but obliged to charge interest on transactions with non-Jews, or Gentiles. However, the Hebrew Bible itself gives numerous examples where this provision was evaded.

Deuteronomy 23:19 Thou shalt not lend upon interest to thy brother: interest of money, interest of victuals, and interest of anything that is lent upon interest.

Deuteronomy 23:20 Unto a foreigner thou mayest lend upon interest; but unto thy brother thou shalt not lend upon interest; that the LORD thy God may bless thee in all that thou puttest thy hand unto, in the land whither thou goest in to possess it.

Christ drives the Usurers out of the Temple, a woodcut by Lucas Cranach the Elder in Passionary of Christ and Antichrist.
Israelites were forbidden to charge interest on loans made to other Israelites, but allowed to charge interest on transactions with non-Israelites, as the latter were often amongst the Israelites for the purpose of business anyway, but in general, it was seen as advantageous to avoid debt at all, to avoid being bound to someone else. Debt was to be avoided and not used to finance consumption, but only when in need. However, laws against usury were among many the prophets condemn the people for breaking.

It was the interpretation that interest could be charged to non-Israelites that would be used in the 14th century for Jews living within Christian societies in Europe to justify lending money for profit. As this conveniently side stepped the rules against usury in both Judaism and Christianity as the Jews could lend to the Christians as they are not Israelites and the Christians were not involved in the lending but were still free to take the loans.

Christianity
Main article: Usury
Originally, the charging of interest, known as usury, was banned by Christian churches. This included charging a fee for the use of money, such as at a bureau de change. However over time the charging of interest became acceptable due to the changing nature of money, the term came to be used for interest above the rate allowed by law.

The rise of Protestantism in the 16th century weakened Rome's influence, and its dictates against usury became irrelevant in some areas. That would free up the development of banking in Northern Europe.

Islam
Main article: Riba
In Islam it is strictly prohibited to take interest; the Quran strictly prohibits lending money on Interest. "O you who have believed, do

not consume usury, doubled and multiplied, but fear Allah that you may be successful" (3:130) "and Allah has permitted trade and has forbidden interest" (2:275).

Holy Quran states that taking of interest and making money through unethical means is not prohibited for Muslims only but were prohibited for earlier communities as well. Two verses (Al Quran – 4:160–161) clearly states that "Because of the wrongdoing of the Jews We forbade them good things which were (before) made lawful unto them, and because of their much hindering from Allah's way, And of their taking usury when they were forbidden it, and of their devouring people's wealth by false pretences, We have prepared for those of them who disbelieve a painful doom."

Riba is forbidden in Islamic economic jurisprudence (fiqh). Islamic jurists discuss two types of riba: an increase in capital with no services provided, which the Qur'an prohibits—and commodity exchanges in unequal quantities, which the Sunnah prohibits; trade in promissory notes (e.g. fiat money and derivatives) is forbidden.

Despite the prohibition of charging interest, during the 20th century a number of developments took place that would lead to an Islamic banking model where no interest is charged but banks would still operate for profit. This would be done through charging for loans in different ways such as through fees and using method of risk sharing and different ownership models such as leasing.

Goldsmiths of London

See also: History of Goldsmiths University, London and Goldsmith
Modern banking practice, including fractional reserve banking and the issue of banknotes, emerged in the 17th century. At the time, wealthy merchants began to store their gold with the goldsmiths of London, who possessed private vaults and charged a fee for their service. In exchange for each deposit of precious metal, the goldsmiths issued receipts certifying the quantity and purity of the metal they held as a bailee; these receipts could not be assigned; only the original depositor could collect the stored goods.

Gradually the goldsmiths began to lend the money out on behalf of the depositor, which led to the development of modern banking practices; promissory notes (which evolved into banknotes) were issued for money deposited as a loan to the goldsmith.

These practices created a new kind of "money" that was actually debt, that is, goldsmiths' debt rather than silver or gold coin, a commodity that had been regulated and controlled by the monarchy. This development required the acceptance in trade of the goldsmiths' promissory notes, payable on demand. Acceptance in turn required a general belief that coin would be available; and a fractional reserve normally served this purpose. Acceptance also required that the holders of debt be able legally to enforce an unconditional right to payment; it required that the notes (as well as drafts) be negotiable instruments. The concept of negotiability had emerged in fits and starts in European money markets, but it was well developed by the 17th century. Nevertheless, an act of Parliament was required in the early 18th century (1704) to overrule court decisions holding that the gold smiths notes, despite the "customs of merchants", were not negotiable.

The modern bank

The Louisiana Purchase of 1803 was handled by Francis Baring and Company of London.
The first bank to begin the permanent issue of banknotes was the Bank of England in 1695. Initially hand-written and issued on deposit or as a loan, they promised to pay the bearer the value of the note on demand. By 1745, standardized printed notes ranging from £20 to £1,000 were being printed. Fully printed notes that didn't require the name of the payee and the cashier's signature first appeared in 1855.

The rise of Protestantism freed many European Christians from Rome's dictates against usury. In the 18th century, services offered by banks increased. Clearing facilities, security investments, cheques and overdraft protections were introduced. Cheques were invented in the

1600s in England and banks settled payments by direct courier to the issuing bank. Around 1770, they began meeting in a central location, and by the 1800s a dedicated space was established, known as a bankers' clearing house. The London clearing house used a method where each bank paid cash to and then was paid cash by an inspector at the end of each day. The first overdraft facility was set up in 1728 by the Royal Bank of Scotland.

The Industrial Revolution and growing international trade increased the number of banks, especially in London. At the same time, new types of financial activities broadened the scope of banking far beyond its origins. The merchant-banking families dealt in everything from underwriting bonds to originating foreign loans. These new "merchant banks" facilitated trade growth, profiting from England's emerging dominance in seaborne shipping. Two immigrant families, Rothschild and Baring, established merchant banking firms in London in the late 18th century and came to dominate world banking in the next century.

A great impetus to country banking came in 1797 when, with England threatened by war, the Bank of England suspended cash payments. A handful of Frenchmen landed in Pembrokeshire, causing a panic. Shortly after this incident, Parliament authorised the Bank of England and country bankers to issue notes of low denomination.

The primary function of a central bank is to control the nation's money supply (monetary policy), through active duties such as managing interest rates, setting the reserve requirement, and acting as a lender of last resort to the banking sector during times of bank insolvency or financial crisis.

Primary duties for a Central Bank include: Implement a monetary policy that provides consistent growth and employment. Promote the stability of the country's financial system. Manage the production and distribution of the nation's currency.

Central banks are responsible for overseeing the monetary system for a nation (or group of nations), along with a wide range of other responsibilities, from overseeing monetary policy to implementing specific goals such as currency stability, low inflation and full employment.

A central bank, reserve bank, or monetary authority is an institution that manages a state's currency, money supply, and interest rates. Central banks also usually oversee the commercial banking system of their respective countries. In contrast to a commercial bank, a central bank possesses a monopoly on increasing the monetary base in the state, and usually also prints the national currency, which usually serves as the state's legal tender.

The primary function of a central bank is to control the nation's money supply (monetary policy), through active duties such as managing interest rates, setting the reserve requirement, and acting as a lender of last resort to the banking sector during times of bank insolvency or financial crisis. Central banks usually also have supervisory powers, intended to prevent bank runs and to reduce the risk that commercial banks and other financial institutions engage in reckless or fraudulent behavior. Central banks in most developed nations are institutionally designed to be independent from political interference. Still, limited control by the executive and legislative bodies usually exists.

Prior to the 17th century most money was commodity money, typically gold or silver. However, promises to pay were widely circulated and accepted as value at least five hundred years earlier in both Europe and Asia. The Song dynasty was the first to issue generally circulating paper currency, while the Yuan Dynasty was the first to use notes as the predominant circulating medium. In 1455, in an effort to control inflation, the succeeding Ming Dynasty ended the use of paper money and closed much of Chinese trade. The medieval European Knights Templar ran an early prototype of a central banking system, as their promises to pay were widely respected, and many regard their activities as having laid the basis for the modern banking system.

As the first public bank to "offer accounts not directly convertible to coin", the Bank of Amsterdam established in 1609 is considered to be the precursor to modern central banks. The central bank of Sweden ("Sveriges Riksbank" or simply "Riksbanken") was founded in Stockholm from the remains of the failed bank Stockholms Banco in 1664 and answered to the parliament ("Riksdag of the Estates"). One role of the Swedish central bank was lending money to the government.

Bank of England

The sealing of the Bank of England Charter (1694).
The establishment of the Bank of England, the model on which most modern central banks have been based, was devised by Charles Montagu, 1st Earl of Halifax, in 1694, following a proposal by the banker William Paterson three years earlier, which had not been acted upon. In the Kingdom of England in the 1690s, public funds were in short supply, and the credit of William III's government was so low in London that it was impossible for it to borrow the £1,200,000 (at 8 percent) needed to finance the ongoing Nine Years' War with France. In order to induce subscription to the loan, Montagu proposed that the subscribers were to be incorporated as The Governor and Company of the Bank of England with long-term banking privileges including the issue of notes. The lenders would give the government cash (bullion) and also issue notes against the government bonds, which could be lent again. A Royal Charter was granted on 27 July through the passage of the Tonnage Act 1694. The bank was given exclusive possession of the government's balances, and was the only limited-liability corporation allowed to issue banknotes. The £1.2M was raised in 12 days; half of this was used to rebuild the Navy.

The Bank of England, established in 1694.

Although this establishment of the Bank of England marks the origin of central banking, it did not have the functions of a modern central bank, namely, to regulate the value of the national currency, to finance the government, to be the sole authorised distributor of banknotes, and to function as a 'lender of last resort' to banks suffering a liquidity crisis. These modern central banking functions evolved slowly through the 18th and 19th centuries.

Although the Bank was originally a private institution, by the end of the 18th century it was increasingly being regarded as a public authority with civic responsibility toward the upkeep of a healthy financial system. The currency crisis of 1797, caused by panicked depositors withdrawing from the Bank led to the government suspending convertibility of notes into specie payment. The bank was soon accused by the bullionists of causing the exchange rate to fall from over issuing banknotes, a charge which the Bank denied. Nevertheless, it was clear that the Bank was being treated as an organ of the state.

Henry Thornton, a merchant banker and monetary theorist has been described as the father of the modern central bank. An opponent of the real bills doctrine, he was a defender of the bullionist position and a significant figure in monetary theory. Thornton's process of monetary expansion anticipated the theories of Knut Wicksell regarding the "cumulative process which restates the Quantity Theory in a theoretically coherent form". As a response to the 1797 currency crisis, Thornton wrote in 1802 An Enquiry into the Nature and Effects of the Paper Credit of Great Britain, in which he argued that the increase in paper credit did not cause the crisis. The book also gives a detailed account of the British monetary system as well as a detailed examination of the ways in which the Bank of England should act to counteract fluctuations in the value of the pound.

Walter Bagehot, an influential theorist on the economic role of the central bank.

Until the mid-nineteenth century, commercial banks were able to issue their own banknotes, and notes issued by provincial banking companies were commonly in circulation. Many consider the origins of the central bank to lie with the passage of the Bank Charter Act of 1844. Under this law, authorisation to issue new banknotes was restricted to the Bank of England. At the same time, the Bank of England was restricted to issue new banknotes only if they were 100% backed by gold or up to £14 million in government debt. The Act served to restrict the supply of new notes reaching circulation, and gave the Bank of England an effective monopoly on the printing of new notes.

The Bank accepted the role of 'lender of last resort' in the 1870s after criticism of its lacklustre response to the Overend-Gurney crisis. The journalist Walter Bagehot wrote on the subject in Lombard Street: A Description of the Money Market, in which he advocated for the Bank to officially become a lender of last resort during a credit crunch, sometimes referred to as "Bagehot's dictum". Paul Tucker phrased the dictum in 2009 as follows:

"to avert panic, central banks should lend early and freely (ie without limit), to solvent firms, against good collateral, and at 'high rates'".

Central banks were established in many European countries during the 19th century. The War of the Second Coalition led to the creation of the Banque de France in 1800, in an effort to improve the public financing of the war.

Although central banks today are generally associated with fiat money, the 19th and early 20th centuries central banks in most of Europe and Japan developed under the international gold standard, elsewhere[where?] free banking or currency boards were more usual at this time. Problems with collapses of banks during downturns, however, led to wider support for central banks in those nations which did not as yet possess them, most notably in Australia.

On 23 December 1913 the U.S. Congress created the US Federal Reserve through the passing of The Federal Reserve Act in the Senate and its signing by President Woodrow Wilson on the same day.

Australia established its first central bank in 1920, Colombia in 1923, Mexico and Chile in 1925 and Canada and New Zealand in the aftermath of the Great Depression in 1934. By 1935, the only significant independent nation that did not possess a central bank was Brazil, which subsequently developed a precursor thereto in 1945 and the present Central Bank of Brazil twenty years later. After gaining independence, African and Asian countries also established central banks or monetary unions.

The headquarters of the People's Bank of China in Beijing.
The People's Bank of China evolved its role as a central bank starting in about 1979 with the introduction of market reforms, which accelerated in 1989 when the country adopted a generally capitalist approach to its export economy. Evolving further partly in response to the European Central Bank, the People's Bank of China had by 2000 become a modern central bank. The most recent bank model was introduced together with the euro, and involves coordination of the European national banks, which continue to manage their respective economies separately in all respects other than currency exchange and base interest rates.

Naming of central banks
There is no standard terminology for the name of a central bank, but many countries use the "Bank of Country" form — for example: Bank of England (which, despite its name, is in fact the central bank of the United Kingdom as a whole. The name's lack of representation of the entire United Kingdom ('Bank of Britain', for example) can be owed to the fact that its establishment occurred when the Kingdoms of England, Scotland and Ireland were separate entities (at least in name), and therefore pre-dates the merger of the Kingdoms of England and Scotland, the Kingdom of Ireland's absorption into the Union and the formation of the present day United Kingdom), Bank of Canada, Bank of Mexico.

The word "Reserve" is also often included, such as the Reserve Bank of India, Reserve Bank of Australia, Reserve Bank of New Zealand, the South African Reserve Bank, and U.S. Federal Reserve System. Other central banks are known as monetary authorities such as the Monetary Authority of Singapore, Maldives Monetary Authority and Cayman Islands Monetary Authority. There is an instance where native language was used to name the central bank: in the Philippines the Filipino name Bangko Sentral ng Pilipinas is used even in English.

Some are styled "national" banks, such as the National Bank of Ukraine, although the term national bank is also used for private commercial banks in some countries. In other cases, central banks may incorporate the word "Central" (for example, European Central Bank, Central Bank of Ireland, Central Bank of Brazil). In some countries, particularly in formerly Communist ones, the term national bank may be used to indicate both the monetary authority and the leading banking entity, such as the Soviet Union's Gosbank (state bank).

Many countries have state-owned banks or other quasi-government entities that have entirely separate functions, such as financing imports and exports. In other countries, the term national bank may be used to indicate that the central bank's goals are broader than monetary stability, such as full employment, industrial development, or other goals. Some state-owned commercial banks have names suggestive of central banks, even if they are not: examples are the Bank of India and the Central Bank of India.

The chief executive of a central bank is usually known as the Governor, President or Chairman.

21st Century

After the financial crisis of 2007-2008 central banks led change, but as of 2015 their ability to boost economic growth has stalled. Central banks debate whether they should experiment with new measures like negative interest rates or direct financing of government, "lean even more on politicians to do more". Andrew Haldane from the Bank of England said "central bankers may need to accept that their good old days – of adjusting interest rates to boost employment or contain inflation – may be gone for good". The European Central Bank and The Bank of Japan whose economies are in or close to deflation, continue quantitative easing buying securities to encourage more lending.

Activities and responsibilities

The Eccles Federal Reserve Board Building in Washington, D.C. houses the main offices of the Board of Governors of the United States' Federal Reserve System
Functions of a central bank may include:

implementing monetary policies.
setting the official interest rate – used to manage both inflation and the country's exchange rate – and ensuring that this rate takes effect via a variety of policy mechanisms
controlling the nation's entire money supply
the Government's banker and the bankers' bank ("lender of last resort")
managing the country's foreign exchange and gold reserves and the Government's stock register
regulating and supervising the banking industry
Monetary policy
Central banks implement a country's chosen monetary policy.

Currency insurance
At the most basic level, monetary policy involves establishing what form of currency the country may have, whether a fiat currency, gold-backed currency (disallowed for countries in the International Monetary Fund), currency board or a currency union. When a country has its own national currency, this involves the issue of some form of standardized currency, which is essentially a form of promissory note: a promise to exchange the note for "money" under certain circumstances. Historically, this was often a promise to exchange the money for precious metals in some fixed amount. Now, when many

currencies are fiat money, the "promise to pay" consists of the promise to accept that currency to pay for taxes.

A central bank may use another country's currency either directly in a currency union, or indirectly on a currency board. In the latter case, exemplified by the Bulgarian National Bank, Hong Kong and Latvia, the local currency is backed at a fixed rate by the central bank's holdings of a foreign currency. Similar to commercial banks, central banks hold assets (government bonds, foreign exchange, gold, and other financial assets) and incur liabilities (currency outstanding). Central banks create money by issuing interest-free currency notes and selling them to the public (government) in exchange for interest-bearing assets such as government bonds. When a central bank wishes to purchase more bonds than their respective national governments make available, they may purchase private bonds or assets denominated in foreign currencies.

The European Central Bank remits its interest income to the central banks of the member countries of the European Union. The US Federal Reserve remits all its profits to the U.S. Treasury. This income, derived from the power to issue currency, is referred to as seigniorage, and usually belongs to the national government. The state-sanctioned power to create currency is called the Right of Issuance. Throughout history there have been disagreements over this power, since whoever controls the creation of currency controls the seigniorage income. The expression "monetary policy" may also refer more narrowly to the interest-rate targets and other active measures undertaken by the monetary authority.

Goals

High employment

Frictional unemployment is the time period between jobs when a worker is searching for, or transitioning from one job to another. Unemployment beyond frictional unemployment is classified as unintended unemployment.

For example, structural unemployment is a form of unemployment resulting from a mismatch between demand in the labour market and the skills and locations of the workers seeking employment. Macroeconomic policy generally aims to reduce unintended unemployment.

Keynes labeled any jobs that would be created by a rise in wage-goods (i.e., a decrease in real-wages) as involuntary unemployment:

Men are involuntarily unemployed if, in the event of a small rise in the price of wage-goods relatively to the money-wage, both the aggregate supply of labour willing to work for the current money-wage and the aggregate demand for it at that wage would be greater than the existing volume of employment.
—John Maynard Keynes, The General Theory of Employment, Interest and Money p11
Price stability
Inflation is defined either as the devaluation of a currency or equivalently the rise of prices relative to a currency.

Since inflation lowers real wages, Keynesians view inflation as the solution to involuntary unemployment. However, "unanticipated" inflation leads to lender losses as the real interest rate will be lower than expected. Thus, Keynesian monetary policy aims for a steady rate of inflation. A publication from the Austrian School, The Case Against the Fed, argues that the efforts of the central banks to control inflation have been counterproductive.

Economic growth
Economic growth can be enhanced by investment in capital, such as more or better machinery. A low interest rate implies that firms can loan money to invest in their capital stock and pay less interest for it. Lowering the interest is therefore considered to encourage economic growth and is often used to alleviate times of low economic growth. On the other hand, raising the interest rate is often used in times of high economic growth as a contra-cyclical device to keep the economy from overheating and avoid market bubbles.

The European Central Bank building in Frankfurt
Further goals of monetary policy are stability of interest rates, of the financial market, and of the foreign exchange market. Goals frequently cannot be separated from each other and often conflict. Costs must therefore be carefully weighed before policy implementation.

Policy instruments

The headquarters of the Bank for International Settlements, in Basel (Switzerland).

The Bank of Japan.

The BSP Complex, in the Philippines.

The Central Bank of Brazil in Brasília.
The main monetary policy instruments available to central banks are open market operation, bank reserve requirement, interest rate policy, re-lending and re-discount (including using the term repurchase market), and credit policy (often coordinated with trade policy). While capital adequacy is important, it is defined and regulated by the Bank for International Settlements, and central banks in practice generally do not apply stricter rules.

To enable open market operations, a central bank must hold foreign exchange reserves (usually in the form of government bonds) and official gold reserves. It will often have some influence over any official or mandated exchange rates: Some exchange rates are managed, some are market based (free float) and many are somewhere in between ("managed float" or "dirty float").

Interest rates
By far the most visible and obvious power of many modern central banks is to influence market interest rates; contrary to popular belief,

they rarely "set" rates to a fixed number. Although the mechanism differs from country to country, most use a similar mechanism based on a central bank's ability to create as much fiat money as required.

The mechanism to move the market towards a 'target rate' (whichever specific rate is used) is generally to lend money or borrow money in theoretically unlimited quantities, until the targeted market rate is sufficiently close to the target. Central banks may do so by lending money to and borrowing money from (taking deposits from) a limited number of qualified banks, or by purchasing and selling bonds. As an example of how this functions, the Bank of Canada sets a target overnight rate, and a band of plus or minus 0.25%. Qualified banks borrow from each other within this band, but never above or below, because the central bank will always lend to them at the top of the band, and take deposits at the bottom of the band; in principle, the capacity to borrow and lend at the extremes of the band are unlimited. Other central banks use similar mechanisms.

The target rates are generally short-term rates. The actual rate that borrowers and lenders receive on the market will depend on (perceived) credit risk, maturity and other factors. For example, a central bank might set a target rate for overnight lending of 4.5%, but rates for (equivalent risk) five-year bonds might be 5%, 4.75%, or, in cases of inverted yield curves, even below the short-term rate. Many central banks have one primary "headline" rate that is quoted as the "central bank rate". In practice, they will have other tools and rates that are used, but only one that is rigorously targeted and enforced.

"The rate at which the central bank lends money can indeed be chosen at will by the central bank; this is the rate that makes the financial headlines." – Henry C.K. Liu. Liu explains further that "the U.S. central-bank lending rate is known as the Fed funds rate. The Fed sets a target for the Fed funds rate, which its Open Market Committee tries to match by lending or borrowing in the money market ... a fiat money system set by command of the central bank. The Fed is the head of the central-bank because the U.S. dollar is the key reserve currency for international trade. The global money market is a USA dollar market. All other currencies markets revolve around the U.S. dollar market." Accordingly, the U.S. situation is not typical of central banks in general.

Typically a central bank controls certain types of short-term interest rates. These influence the stock- and bond markets as well as mortgage and other interest rates. The European Central Bank for example announces its interest rate at the meeting of its Governing Council; in the case of the U.S. Federal Reserve, the Federal Reserve Board of Governors. Both the Federal Reserve and the ECB are composed of one or more central bodies that are responsible for the main decisions about interest rates and the size and type of open market operations, and several branches to execute its policies. In the case of the Federal Reserve, they are the local Federal Reserve Banks; for the ECB they are the national central banks.

A typical central bank has several interest rates or monetary policy tools it can set to influence markets.

Marginal lending rate (currently 0.30% in the Eurozone) – a fixed rate for institutions to borrow money from the central bank. (In the USA this is called the discount rate).
Main refinancing rate (0.05% in the Eurozone) – the publicly visible interest rate the central bank announces. It is also known as minimum bid rate and serves as a bidding floor for refinancing loans. (In the USA this is called the federal funds rate).
Deposit rate, generally consisting of interest on reserves and sometimes also interest on excess reserves (-0.20% in the Eurozone) – the rates parties receive for deposits at the central bank.
These rates directly affect the rates in the money market, the market for short term loans.

Open market operations
Through open market operations, a central bank influences the money supply in an economy. Each time it buys securities (such as a government bond or treasury bill), it in effect creates money. The central bank exchanges money for the security, increasing the money

supply while lowering the supply of the specific security. Conversely, selling of securities by the central bank reduces the money supply.

Open market operations usually take the form of:

Buying or selling securities ("direct operations") to achieve an interest rate target in the interbank market .
Temporary lending of money for collateral securities ("Reverse Operations" or "repurchase operations", otherwise known as the "repo" market). These operations are carried out on a regular basis, where fixed maturity loans (of one week and one month for the ECB) are auctioned off.
Foreign exchange operations such as foreign exchange swaps.
All of these interventions can also influence the foreign exchange market and thus the exchange rate. For example, the People's Bank of China and the Bank of Japan have on occasion bought several hundred billions of U.S. Treasuries, presumably in order to stop the decline of the U.S. dollar versus the renminbi and the yen.

Capital requirements
All banks are required to hold a certain percentage of their assets as capital, a rate which may be established by the central bank or the banking supervisor. For international banks, including the 55 member central banks of the Bank for International Settlements, the threshold is 8% (see the Basel Capital Accords) of risk-adjusted assets, whereby certain assets (such as government bonds) are considered to have lower risk and are either partially or fully excluded from total assets for the purposes of calculating capital adequacy. Partly due to concerns about asset inflation and repurchase agreements, capital requirements may be considered more effective than reserve requirements in preventing indefinite lending: when at the threshold, a bank cannot extend another loan without acquiring further capital on its balance sheet.

Reserve requirements
Historically, bank reserves have formed only a small fraction of deposits, a system called fractional reserve banking. Banks would

hold only a small percentage of their assets in the form of cash reserves as insurance against bank runs. Over time this process has been regulated and insured by central banks. Such legal reserve requirements were introduced in the 19th century as an attempt to reduce the risk of banks overextending themselves and suffering from bank runs, as this could lead to knock-on effects on other overextended banks. See also money multiplier.

As the early 20th century gold standard was undermined by inflation and the late 20th century fiat dollar hegemony evolved, and as banks proliferated and engaged in more complex transactions and were able to profit from dealings globally on a moment's notice, these practices became mandatory, if only to ensure that there was some limit on the ballooning of money supply. Such limits have become harder to enforce. The People's Bank of China retains (and uses) more powers over reserves because the yuan that it manages is a non-convertible currency.

Loan activity by banks plays a fundamental role in determining the money supply. The central-bank money after aggregate settlement – "final money" – can take only one of two forms:

physical cash, which is rarely used in wholesale financial markets,
central-bank money which is rarely used by the people
The currency component of the money supply is far smaller than the deposit component. Currency, bank reserves and institutional loan agreements together make up the monetary base, called M1, M2 and M3. The Federal Reserve Bank stopped publishing M3 and counting it as part of the money supply in 2006.

Exchange requirements
To influence the money supply, some central banks may require that some or all foreign exchange receipts (generally from exports) be exchanged for the local currency. The rate that is used to purchase local currency may be market-based or arbitrarily set by the bank. This tool is generally used in countries with non-convertible currencies or partially convertible currencies. The recipient of the

local currency may be allowed to freely dispose of the funds, required to hold the funds with the central bank for some period of time, or allowed to use the funds subject to certain restrictions. In other cases, the ability to hold or use the foreign exchange may be otherwise limited.

In this method, money supply is increased by the central bank when it purchases the foreign currency by issuing (selling) the local currency. The central bank may subsequently reduce the money supply by various means, including selling bonds or foreign exchange interventions.

Margin requirements and other tools

In some countries, central banks may have other tools that work indirectly to limit lending practices and otherwise restrict or regulate capital markets. For example, a central bank may regulate margin lending, whereby individuals or companies may borrow against pledged securities. The margin requirement establishes a minimum ratio of the value of the securities to the amount borrowed.

Central banks often have requirements for the quality of assets that may be held by financial institutions; these requirements may act as a limit on the amount of risk and leverage created by the financial system. These requirements may be direct, such as requiring certain assets to bear certain minimum credit ratings, or indirect, by the central bank lending to counterparties only when security of a certain quality is pledged as collateral.

Limits on policy effects

Although the perception by the public may be that the "central bank" controls some or all interest rates and currency rates, economic theory (and substantial empirical evidence) shows that it is impossible to do both at once in an open economy. Robert Mundell's "impossible trinity" is the most famous formulation of these limited powers, and postulates that it is impossible to target monetary policy (broadly, interest rates), the exchange rate (through a fixed rate) and maintain free capital movement. Since most Western economies are now considered "open" with free capital movement, this essentially means that central banks may target interest rates or exchange rates with credibility, but not both at once.

In the most famous case of policy failure, Black Wednesday, George Soros arbitraged the pound sterling's relationship to the ECU and (after making $2 billion himself and forcing the UK to spend over $8bn defending the pound) forced it to abandon its policy. Since then he has been a harsh critic of clumsy bank policies and argued that no one should be able to do what he did.

The most complex relationships are those between the yuan and the US dollar, and between the euro and its neighbours. (The situation in Cuba is so exceptional as to require the Cuban peso to be dealt with simply as an exception, since the United States forbids direct trade with Cuba.)

Ambox current red.svg
This article needs to be updated. Please update this article to reflect recent events or newly available information. (June 2016)
US dollars were ubiquitous in Cuba's economy after its legalization in 1991, but were officially removed from circulation in 2004 and replaced by the convertible peso.

Banking supervision and other activities
Bank regulation and standards
Bank for International Settlements
Basel Accords Basel I Basel II Basel III
Background
Banking (Regulation)
Monetary policy Central bank
Risk Risk management
Regulatory capital Tier 1 Tier 2
Pillar 1: Regulatory capital
Credit risk
Standardized IRB Approach
F-IRB A-IRB PD LGD EAD

Operational risk Basic Standardized AMA
Market risk Duration Value at risk
Pillar 2: Supervisory review
Economic capital Liquidity risk Legal risk
Pillar 3: Market disclosure
Disclosure
Business and Economics Portal
v t e

In some countries a central bank, through its subsidiaries, controls and monitors the banking sector. In other countries banking supervision is carried out by a government department such as the UK Treasury, or by an independent government agency, for example, UK's Financial Conduct Authority. It examines the banks' balance sheets and behaviour and policies toward consumers. Apart from refinancing, it also provides banks with services such as transfer of funds, bank notes and coins or foreign currency. Thus it is often described as the "bank of banks".

Many countries will monitor and control the banking sector through several different agencies and for different purposes. the Bank regulation in the United States for example is highly fragmented with 3 federal agencies, the Federal Deposit Insurance Corporation, the Federal Reserve Board, or Office of the Comptroller of the Currency and numerous others on the state and the private level. There is usually significant cooperation between the agencies. For example, money center banks, deposit-taking institutions, and other types of financial institutions may be subject to different (and occasionally overlapping) regulation. Some types of banking regulation may be delegated to other levels of government, such as state or provincial governments.

Any cartel of banks is particularly closely watched and controlled. Most countries control bank mergers and are wary of concentration in this industry due to the danger of groupthink and runaway lending bubbles based on a single point of failure, the credit culture of the few large banks.

Independence

Governments generally have some degree of influence over even "independent" central banks; the aim of independence is primarily to prevent short-term interference. For example, the Board of Governors of the U.S. Federal Reserve are nominated by the President of the U.S. and confirmed by the Senate, publishes verbatim transcripts, and balance sheets are audited by the Government Accountability Office.

In the 2000s there has been a trend towards increasing the independence of central banks as a way of improving long-term economic performance. While a large volume of economic research has been done to define the relationship between central bank independence and economic performance, the results are ambiguous.

Advocates of central bank independence argue that a central bank which is too susceptible to political direction or pressure may encourage economic cycles ("boom and bust"), as politicians may be tempted to boost economic activity in advance of an election, to the detriment of the long-term health of the economy and the country. In this context, independence is usually defined as the central bank's operational and management independence from the government.

The literature on central bank independence has defined a number of types of independence.

Legal independence

The independence of the central bank is enshrined in law. This type of independence is limited in a democratic state; in almost all cases the central bank is accountable at some level to government officials, either through a government minister or directly to a legislature. Even defining degrees of legal independence has proven to be a challenge since legislation typically provides only a framework within which the government and the central bank work out their relationship.

Goal independence

The central bank has the right to set its own policy goals, whether inflation targeting, control of the money supply, or maintaining a fixed exchange rate. While this type of independence is more common, many central banks prefer to announce their policy goals in partnership with the appropriate government departments. This increases the transparency of the policy setting process and thereby increases the credibility of the goals chosen by providing assurance that they will not be changed without notice. In addition, the setting of common goals by the central bank and the government helps to avoid situations where monetary and fiscal policy are in conflict; a policy combination that is clearly sub-optimal.

Operational independence

The central bank has the independence to determine the best way of achieving its policy goals, including the types of instruments used and the timing of their use. This is the most common form of central bank independence. The granting of independence to the Bank of England in 1997 was, in fact, the granting of operational independence; the inflation target continued to be announced in the Chancellor's annual budget speech to Parliament.

Management independence

The central bank has the authority to run its own operations (appointing staff, setting budgets, and so on.) without excessive involvement of the government. The other forms of independence are not possible unless the central bank has a significant degree of management independence. One of the most common statistical indicators used in the literature as a proxy for central bank independence is the "turn-over-rate" of central bank governors. If a government is in the habit of appointing and replacing the governor frequently, it clearly has the capacity to micro-manage the central bank through its choice of governors.

It is argued that an independent central bank can run a more credible monetary policy, making market expectations more responsive to signals from the central bank. Both the Bank of England (1997) and the European Central Bank have been made independent and follow a set of published inflation targets so that markets know what to expect. Even the People's Bank of China has been accorded great latitude, though in the People's Republic of China the official role of the bank remains that of a national bank rather than a central bank, underlined by the official refusal to "unpeg" the yuan or to revalue it "under pressure". The People's Bank of China's independence can thus be read more as independence from the USA, which rules the financial markets, rather than from the Communist Party of China which rules the country. The fact that the Communist Party is not elected also relieves the pressure to please people, increasing its independence.

International organizations such as the World Bank, the Bank for International Settlements (BIS) and the International Monetary Fund (IMF) strongly support central bank independence. This results, in part, from a belief in the intrinsic merits of increased independence. The support for independence from the international organizations also derives partly from the connection between increased independence for the central bank and increased transparency in the policy-making process. The IMF's Financial Services Action Plan (FSAP) review self-assessment, for example, includes a number of questions about central bank independence in the transparency section. An independent central bank will score higher in the review than one that is not independent.

Fractional-reserve banking
Free banking
Full-reserve banking
History of central banking in the United States
Interbank lending market
List of central banks
Money creation
National bank
Seigniorage
State bank
Payment system
Real-time gross settlement

Hon. CHARLES N. FOWLER

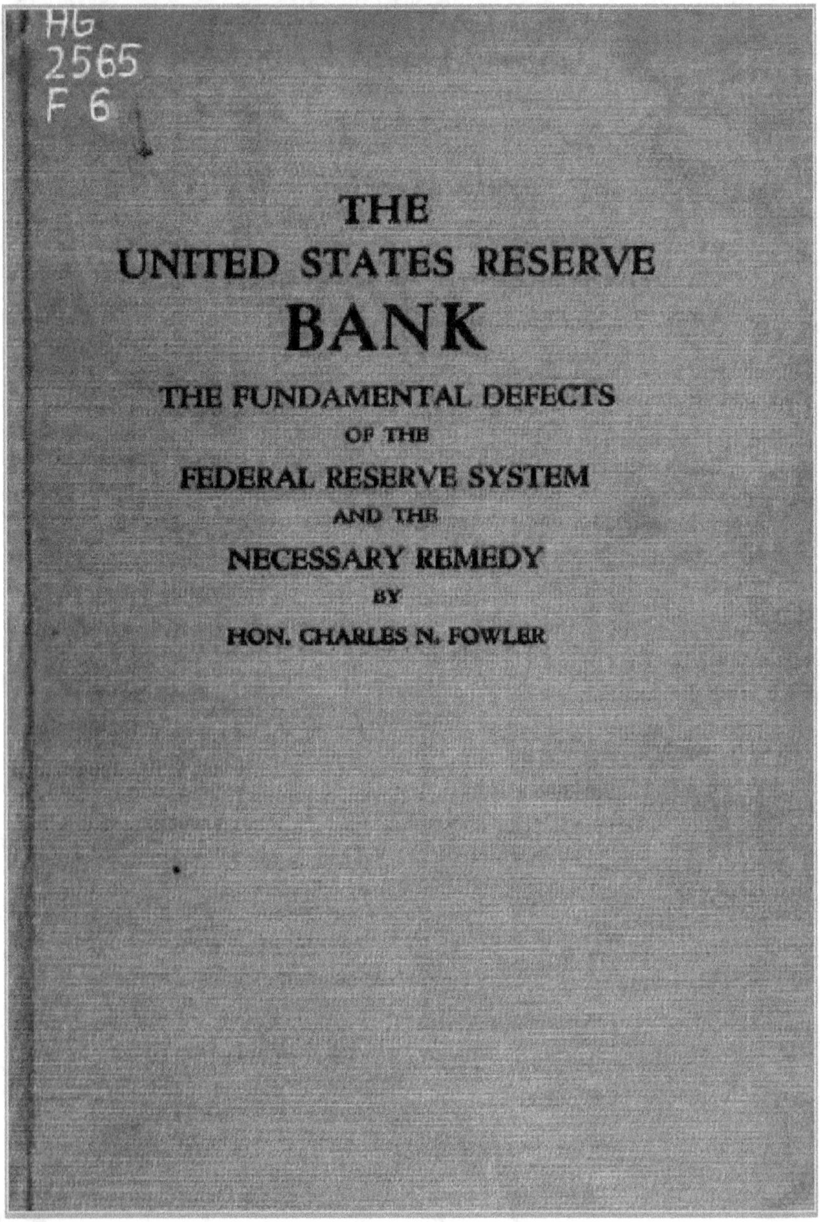

THE UNITED STATES RESERVE BANK

THE FUNDAMENTAL DEFECTS OF THE FEDERAL RESERVE SYSTEM EXPOSED AND THE NECESSARY REMEDY

BY

HON. CHARLES N. FOWLER

A. B., Yale University 1876. LL. B., Chicago University 1878. Engaged in business and banking, foreign and domestic, for fifteen years. Member of the Banking and Currency Committee of the House of Representatives fourteen years and Chairman of Committee eight years. Author "Seventeen Talks on the Banking Question" and "The National Issues of Nineteen Sixteen"

JANUARY FIRST, 1922

PUBLISHED BY

HAMILTON BOOK COMPANY

WASHINGTON

D. C.

PRICE TWO DOLLARS

THE ESSENTIAL PRINCIPLES AND IMPORTANT FEATURES OF A SIMPLE, SOUND, EFFICIENT & ECONOMICAL FINANCIAL & BANKING SYSTEM FOR THE UNITED STATES

CONTENTS

DEDICATED

TO

ALEXANDER HAMILTON

WITH profound reverence for and the sincerest gratitude to Alexander Hamilton, the greatest banking economist and greatest constructive statesman the world has ever produced—the architect and builder of this government—these pages are dedicated by

THE AUTHOR

Foreword

Origin and Passage of the Federal Reserve Act

THE first draft of the Federal Reserve Act was made by Mr. Fowler who introduced the bill on March 29, 1910, and made an extended speech on the measure and upon bank reform in general.

The Federal Reserve Act was drawn by Mr. Fowler for the express purpose of planting the United States irrevocably upon the gold standard, and of providing a currency as responsive to the demands of trade as bank credit itself, and currently redeemed in gold through our Clearing Houses precisely as checks and drafts are.

It was one of those strange freaks of fortune; it was the very irony of fate itself that under the dictation of the leading money fiatist of this half-century, the Federal Reserve Act was to become the vehicle of a practically unlimited issue of "Government Paper Money."

In 1913 the Democratic party came into power and took possession of every department of the Government. It was greatly to its credit that, in a patriotic and courageous way, it immediately set about the passage of a general financial and banking law.

Unfortunately, however, for true bank reform, Hon. William J. Bryan was then Secretary of State, and completely controlled the Democratic majorities in both houses of Congress. It is a matter of well-known history, that Mr. Bryan inspired, directed and dictated the fundamental or underlying principles of the Federal Reserve Act. Through his following he literally compelled Congress, in utter defiance of the objections and vigorous protests of the Gold Democrats, to make The Federal Reserve Notes primarily United States Notes, or Greenbacks, each note bearing these words: "The United States of America will pay to the bearer on demand..........................dollars." This is *one* of the fatal features or defects of The Federal Reserve Act.

Nearly every State in the Union has passed a law authorizing its State banks to hold Federal Reserve Notes as reserves. Indeed, all State Banks, more than 20,000 of them, do hold Federal Reserve Notes as reserves. And why not? The Federal Reserve Notes are United States Notes, with the guarantee of the Federal Reserve Banks; and the $346,000,000 of United States Notes that were outstanding at the time of the passage of the Federal Reserve Act have been lawful reserves for banks since 1862—legal tender.

The $150,000,000 gold reserve back of the $346, 000,000 Greenbacks or United States .Notes is a 43% reserve. The law requires only a 40% gold reserve back of the Federal Reserve Notes.

The $346,000,000 United States Notes or Greenbacks which are "legal tender" bear these words: "The United States will pay to bearer——dollars." These United States Notes are neither made payable "*on demand*" nor are they *guaranteed* by any strong financial institution, as the Federal Reserve Notes are.

By a parity of reasoning, therefore, can not any one show beyond a peradventure of doubt that the Federal Reserve Notes should be made lawful reserves for our banks—legal tender?

As late as 1916 the Federal Reserve Board did their utmost to get Congress to pass a law making the *Federal Reserve Notes lawful reserves for member banks. Of course, this is just what is going to happen. We can not escape it.*

Now, every intelligent man must know that, when the Banks of the country hold these Federal Reserve Notes as Bank Reserves, they *economically become legal tender* whether the National Government has made them so, by statute, or not. According to the circulation statement of United States Government on Jan. 1, 1921, there has been issued by the Government Federal Reserve Notes and Federal Reserve Bank Notes amounting to $3,978,000,000—paper promises to pay, merely I.O.U.'s—representing less than $1,600,000,000 in gold, the amount of the Reserves held; *and yet, the whole $4,000,000,000 Federal Reserve Notes are possible reservse of our banks.*

When normal conditions have again returned, how

long, under these circumstances, will it take Gresham's omnipotent law to work its way?

In 1896, Hon. William J. Bryan went before the country as a presidential candidate upon a platform declaring, " for the free and unlimited coinage of silver at the ratio of 16 to 1," and was overwhelmingly defeated upon that specific issue, as no other question was considered during that campaign. The silver dollar *was then worth fifty cents*. What Mr. Bryan failed to accomplish in 1896, however, he did accomplish 17 years afterward (in 1913) in the passage of the Federal Reserve Act, which provides " for the free and unlimited " printage of Government Paper Money —United States Notes or Greenbacks—of a pre-determined or fixed value of forty cents on the dollar *in gold, if used as a reserve, or as the basis of credit; for the remaining sixty cents is credit.* Certainly no one is so insane as to argue that any form of credit should be used as a reserve, or as a basis of another credit; for if one credit is good enough for a reserve, or as a basis of another credit, then all good credits are good enough for bank reserves or as a basis for other credits. Then Mr. Rockefeller's check, Mr. Armour's check—indeed every good check is good enough for a bank reserve, or a basis of other credits.

Therefore, the silver dollar of 1896 was twenty-five per cent more valuable as a reserve, or as a basis for other credits, than the Federal Reserve Notes are, which represent by the terms of the statute only forty cents in gold.

The danger differential in the silver dollar in 1893 was only fifty cents, because its actual, inherent or bullion value; its true reserve value was fifty cents. There was then only 540,000,000 silver dollars in the country; yet that amount was sufficient to precipitate the gold panic of 1893-4-5.

The danger differential in the Federal Reserve Note is sixty cents, because its actual or inherent value, its true reserve value is only forty cents.

Query: How long will it take four billion of these Federal Reserve Notes (and still more of them to come) to precipitate a gold panic?

If we but had the wisdom to comprehend and the courage to weigh accurately and impartially the folly and madness of many of our acts during the past few years, we would perceive that these very same Federal Reserve Notes were the chief, if not the only cause, of that wild expansion, that insane inflation, from whose dizzy heights of high prices and flush times we are now very slowly but very painfully descending; and the end is not yet!

On a memorable occasion Abraham Lincoln declared that this country could not endure half slave and half free; but that it would become one thing or the other.

With equal truth and certainty it may now be said that this country can not continue with gold money and a practically unlimited issue of Government Paper Money—United States Notes, or Greenbacks—but that we shall be compelled to decide sooner or later (and the sooner the better) whether we shall have gold money or government paper money.

That is the greatest and most serious question before the American people today. Shall we meet it intelligently and bravely now, or wait, and wait, until we have paid the full penalty of our ignorance and cowardice? And what a penalty that will be!

Two Facts to be Remembered

Fact one is, that while the price level of all commercial commodities rose between 1913 and 1920 from 100 to 250, the price of every ounce of gold was fixed by statute at $20.671834, and our unit of value—the gold dollar—was fixed by statute at 25.8 grains of gold, nine-tenths fine.

Fact two is, that if we are going back to the gold standard, and are going to maintain that standard, everything must be reduced to a gold level; that is, the interconvertibility of all commercial commodities and gold must be re-established.

When this condition, or price level is re-established then, but not till then, will the annual production of gold equal, and probably exceed, the quantity produced annually prior to the War. This result is very important, if indeed not essential to the commercial welfare of the world.

There is, however, always one variable factor that

must be recognized and reckoned with—that is, the differential in price, growing out of the law of supply and demand. For example, if the supply of some article is very great, and the demand very small, the tendency is to decrease the price of that article; and, on the other hand, where the supply of an article is very small, and the demand for it is very great, the tendency is to increase the price of that article.

Today, the price (wholesale price, as the retail prices have not yet been completely readjusted) of almost everything has been liquidated down to the gold standard, excepting coal, steel and wages. When these have reached the gold standard level, the business of the country will be resting upon a solid foundation from which it can confidently start to build up again; but, not until then. And the longer this complete liquidation and the re-establishment of the gold standard is delayed, the longer will universal and permanent prosperity be delayed.

Some Reflections

Napoleon carried on all his wars upon the gold standard, demonstrating that he was as great a banking economist as general.

When we entered the War we had about three billions of gold, and should have carried on the War upon the gold standard. But the unlimited facilities for expansion, the wide open invitation to inflation created by the Federal Reserve Act, and the apparent utter ignorance of the Federal Reserve Board of the laws of banking economics cost the American people from forty to fifty per cent of the total cost of the War; *or approximately twenty billions of dollars.*

Prof. O. M. W. Sprague of Harvard University used this language recently:

"That it is possible to finance without inflation expenditures as great even as those incurred by the United States government during the recent War I am fully convinced. That we could have financed that War without credit inflation I am equally convinced."

Willford I. King, a member of the Research Staff of the National Bureau of Economical Research, Inc.,

175 Ninth Avenue, New York, in the *American Economic Review* of December, 1920, used this language:

"The inflation of the currency and bank deposits continuing since 1914 has done much to drive laborers to look to radical and even revolutionary measures for relief. Increasing dollar efficiency has too often resulted in greatly diminished human efficiency. The need for a stable dollar can scarcely be over-emphasized, and this stability can be more easily attained if measures are taken to make the rate of increase of deposit currency correspond roughly to the growth in the physical volume of business." * * * * * * * * * * * * * * * * * * *

"The Federal Reserve Act was enacted chiefly as a safeguard against panics. Even its ardent supporters hardly contend that it will entirely prevent the periodical readjustments in business known as depressions. They do, however, insist that it renders a money panic practically impossible. But, granting that this contention is correct, it by no means follows that the new system is to be commended. The principal evil of a money panic is that it unjustly transfers much wealth from one person to another. It is, however, highly improbable that all the panics in the history of the nation have together caused the unwarranted transfer of more than a small fraction of the 60 billions of dollars' worth of goods, the ownership of which has been arbitrarily shifted by the workings of the Federal Reserve Act and its amendments." * * * * * * * * * * *

"The system as established, has proved to be merely a new model, producing results very similar to those yielded by its numerous predecessors in the past—the cheap money devices which have so often dominated the financial policies of the nations and always with untoward results." * * * * * * * * * *

"*While it will be impossible to repair most of the damage already wrought, steps should at least be taken to transform the Federal Reserve System from its present status as a mechanism for inflation into that beneficent regulator of credit which its originators sought to establish, thus preventing in the future an extension or repetition of the policy, which has upset the whole financial structure of the nation and has changed property rights from realities into phantoms."*

The author desires to call the attention of the reader to the fact that he has often used figures and graphs to illustrate principles without any reference whatever to any particular time, *e. g.*, the average amount of Federal Reserve Notes outstanding in 1920 was about $3,100,000,000. He has used $3,000,000,000 simply as illustrative. The same is true of the Canadian graph, page 46, 1902-1906, which illustrates the flexibility and marvelous adaptation of bank credit-currency in Canada in normal times to the needs of business. This is a discussion of principles.

Principles and Important Features

THE following statement of principles and important features must be studied and reread over and over again until they are perfectly comprehended and thoroughly understood, if the reader hopes to reap the greatest possible advantage from a study of this important—this vital question. These principles and features should literally fix and determine the mental attitude before one proceeds or undertakes to grapple with the details of this subject. For, if you once truly master the principles, the details will quite readily take care of themselves. Otherwise, you will become swamped with a multitude, a veritable morass of facts, as you get into the subject.

Gresham's Law*

Bad money will always drive good money out of circulation.

The cheaper metal will always drive out the dearer metal.

Paper money will always drive out metal money.

In 1857, H. D. Macleod summarized Gresham's Law in these words:

"The worst form of currency in circulation regulates the value of the whole currency and drives all other forms of currency out of circulation. Gresham's Law, when propounded, technically applied where there was underweight or debased coin of the same metal. But where there are two metals in circulation and one is undervalued, as compared with the other, or where inconvertible paper money is put into circulation, side by side with metal money, this law operates with the same deadly certainty."

"Whilst each of the two metals was equally a legal tender for debts of any amount, we were subject to a

* Sir Thomas Gresham 1519-1579 was a London merchant; founder of the Royal Exchange of London and Gresham's College.

constant change in the principal standard measure of value. It would sometimes be gold, sometimes silver, depending entirely on the variations in the relative value of the two metals; and at such times, the metal which was not the standard would be melted and withdrawn from circulation, as its value would be greater in bullion than in coin."—*Ricardo, 1772-1823.*

" Oftentimes we have reflected on a similar abuse
In the choice of men for office, and of coins for common use;
For your old and standard pieces, valued and approved and tried
Here among the Grecian nations, and in all the world beside,
Recognized in every realm for trusty stamp and pure assay*
Are rejected and abandoned for the trash** of yesterday;
For a vile, adulterate issue, drossy, counterfeit and base
Which the traffic of the city passes current in their place."

—*Aristophanes, "Frogs," 405 B. C.; 891-898; Frere's Translation.*

Gold Reserves

" The issuers of paper money (currency), regulate their issues solely by the price of bullion and never by the quantity of their paper in circulation. The quantity can never be too great nor too little while it preserves the same value as the standard."—*Ricardo.*

" Every loan which a bank makes is in its first shape, a credit given to the borrower on its books, the amount of which it stands ready to pay either in its own notes or in gold and silver at his option. (When this was written both gold and silver were legal tender at the ratio of 15 to 1)"—*Hamilton.*

* Gold Coin.

** Federal Reserve Notes.

"The interconvertibility of bank book credits (deposits), bank note credits (currency) and the standard of value (gold) is absolutely essential to a sound financial and banking system."—*Fowler*.

The bank reserves of every country should be related solely to and be determined by the *total amount* of bank liabilities of that country, and not be related to and be limited by the amount of currency in circulation in that country; because the amount of currency in circulation in any country at any given time will vary in character and quantity according to the habits of the people precisely to the degree or to the extent to which they use checks or currency in the daily transaction of their business.

Prior to the war approximately nine-tenths of the daily transactions in England were settled by check while approximately nine-tenths of the daily transactions in France were settled with bank currency. England had no currency except gold, silver and gold certificates,—(Bank of England notes which were fully covered by gold)—therefore the gold reserve held by the Bank of England was not to cover the Bank of England notes.

The International or Ultimate Gold Reserve

The international or ultimate gold reserve is held or controlled by that country which is the financial centre of the world, where all international balances are settled or adjusted. *It is the Clearing House of the world.*

The pre-requisite or condition precedent to the establishment and maintenance of the financial centre of the world is a *Free Gold Market.*

The essentials of a free gold market are:

(a) The constant interconvertibility of all bank credit and gold.

(b) The constant exchangeability of commercial and monetary gold.

(c) The free import and export of gold.

What a National or Central Gold Reserve Is For

First: it is to keep control of or direct the movement of gold to and from a country through the operations of international commerce by an economic rate of interest.

Second: it is to meet the extraordinary demands for credit during crop moving periods and other great seasonal productions.

Third: it is to conserve and control credit and keep the country in a sound commercial condition.

There should always be a real reserve.

The central reserve should consist of about one-half of all the required gold reserves, the balance being held by the banks throughout the Country for the purpose of testing current credit by daily redemption over the counters of the banks and through the clearing houses *in gold.*

Our central banking system should not itself be the source of over-expansion and lead the way to wild inflation, as the Federal Reserve Banks have, but should be a conserving, regulating power, checking the tendencies to excess beyond the safe boundaries fixed by the law of demand and supply of credit; and, the gold reserves held by our banks should be adequate and so distributed as to guarantee the soundness of all commercial credits passing through them and all currency credits created by them.

The Economic Rate of Interest

Under normal conditions the movement of gold to and from any country, under a rightly constituted financial and banking system, is influenced and controlled solely by what is paid for the use of gold expressed in a rate of interest, provided always that such country maintains a free market for gold; therefore, its supply of gold is wholly dependent upon the state of its international trade through which it obtains or purchases gold at such a rate of interest as to create a demand for gold.

In a rightly constituted financial and banking

system such a rate of interest is the *economic rate of interest* and, will be both by principle and practice uniformly, if not invariably, higher than the *commercial rate of interest.*

To insure ample gold reserves for any country the economic rate should always rise and fall with the state of international trade and therefore necessarily must be fixed by the institution holding the central gold reserve of that country.

The Commercial Rate of Interest

The supply of the currency of any country should be related solely to the state of the domestic trade of that country and should spring into being precisely as checks do in connection with some transaction in the production, transportation or distribution of commodities, and, having served its purpose, should be promptly returned to its creator for redemption precisely as checks are. The rate of interest by which the supply of such a currency is influenced or affected is the *commercial rate of interest,* which in precisely the same way and identically to the same degree, influences and affects bank credit.

In a rightly constituted financial and banking system such a rate of interest is the *commercial rate of interest* and will be both by principle and practice uniformly, if not invariably, lower than the *economic rate of interest.*

To insure sound business conditions in any country the commercial rate of interest should rise and fall with the demand and supply of *domestic credit* and therefore must necessarily be fixed by the commercial banks through which the business of that country is carried on.

The Functions of the Economic and Commercial Rates of Interest Further Differentiated

In a rightly constituted financial and banking system, the economic and commercial rates of interest are actuated and controlled by entirely different forces, and from entirely different points of view, and are raised or lowered for entirely different purposes or reasons; and, they are often diametrically opposed to each other; therefore it is a fatal mistake to bring them both under one single actuating and controlling force, as has been done in the Federal Reserve Act.

The separation of the economic and commercial rates of interest is vital to the untrammeled and most efficient use of the economic rate, either to influence the movement of gold; or to relieve the pressure growing out of an extraordinary demand for credit; or to check over expansion in trade. Their combination is fatal to such uses.

The separation of the economic and commercial rates of interest is of such vital importance to the current basic cost of production, expressed in the interest charge, that if there were no other reasons for the repeal of the Federal Reserve Act, this one *alone* would be of sufficient importance to compel its repeal.

Their separation is vital both to our highest international and also to our greatest domestic commercial success. Their combination is fatal to both. To observe this distinction between the economic rate and the commercial rate of interest is essential because the difference between the two is profound, indeed is fundamental; and, unless recognized and our bank practices made to conform to this principle we shall continue to fly in the very face of fate.

Wisely and properly actuated and controlled the economic rate of interest starting at a high point might be raised to a still much higher point, while the commercial rate—the current, basic cost of production—might be very low, and still falling to the great advantage of our commercial interests.

For the express purpose of keeping the commercial rate low the economic rate might be raised. To illustrate, it might be raised to maintain or even to increase the gold reserves of the country, and thereby insure that public confidence which is always essential to guarantee reasonable commercial rates.

In "Money Changing," Hartley Withers says:

"No country can afford to leave its exchange unregulated. We shall see later that the Bank of England is always watching the foreign exchanges, and when it sees fit, takes control of the money markets in order to regulate them. Among the countries that are prominent in international trade and finance, the only one that leaves its exchange to its own devices is America, and the results of its neglect rouse astonishment rather than envy among other nations, and make the American business world clamor continually for a regulating body."

Can any one who has any appreciation whatever of the operation of economic law doubt the certainty of our predestined fate, if the Federal Reserve Act should remain on our statute books?

Psychology in Finance and Banking

In the whole realm of thought in the whole field of human action, psychology is nowhere so potential and far-reaching in its influence and nowhere plays so significant a part as right in the world of finance and banking.

The North and South poles are no farther removed from each other on the earth's surface than confidence and suspicion of the public mind in the banking system of its country—*in its money.* The Federal Reserve Act, which when fully understood and appreciated *from an economic point of view* (the mechanics and science of banking are two very distinct, two very different things). is nothing more than a succe. of accumulated blunders, and the very limit of hu. folly was reached when the authors of the Act removed from the human touch and from the eyes of the masses of the people all our gold coin and its substitute, all gold certificates, and put forth an almost unlimited amount of make-believe money—stage money—just I.O.U.'s that derive the only virtue they have from the fact that they are temporarily redeemed in gold until the day of reckoning comes, when public confidence being disturbed, disappears before we are conscious of what has actually taken place.

If the people never touch any gold money; if they can never get any gold money; if they can never see any gold money; how long are they going to think in terms of gold money? As soon as the impression gets abroad that possibly the burden is too heavy for the gold fund, as it did in 1893-4-5, or that possibly the gold fund is a myth, doubt instantly impregnates the public mind from ocean to ocean; suspicion follows hot on the heels of doubt, and gold hoarding begins—a gold panic is on. Its consequences can be read in the story of 1893, 1894 and 1895, when the price level fell to sixty-eight—twenty points lower than it has been at any time within 100 years. Wise statesmanship will preclude the probability of such a disaster if it is at all possible.

The great strength of the British monetary system, always has been due largely to the fact that gold was always in current, daily use, and therefore presumably there was any quantity of it for any purpose whatever; and the fact is, there was; because England had a free gold market.

The universal presence of gold is such a source of confidence, the universal absence of gold is such a source of suspicion, that it is next to insanity to ignore this all powerful human element.

Like Caesar's wife, our money must be above suspicion, for money is the concrete expression of wealth, the symbol of property, the counterpart of goods. It stands for everything that we work for to provide against want, the ravages of age, and to protect those we love against the misfortunes of life.

The slightest suspicion that this symbol—this thing that we call money—is not absolutely genuine, that it is false to even the slightest degree, will send a withering blast across the whole country in the twinkling of an eye and will paralyze, if it does not actually destroy, the greater part of our liquid wealth.

If our money is gold and all the people are conscious of its presence in ample quantity for all our requirements, our banking system will be protected, safeguarded and buttressed by the first line of defense—the absolute confidence of the people.

Freedom from Politics Essential to Sound Banking

Our central banking system should be organized solely for the purpose of aiding and serving the commerce of the Country, and therefore should be entirely free from the dictation or influence, even, of the Executive Department of the Government, precisely as our Supreme Court now is, which was organized to aid and serve the ends of justice, free, unafraid and uninfluenced by the Executive Department of the Government.

The Outline of a Financial and Banking System Based Upon Established Principles and Centuries of Experience

An adequate central or national gold reserve should be created to control the movement of gold to and from the Country through the operations of international commerce; to meet the extraordinary demands growing out of seasonal trade and periods of unusual stress; and to conserve and control credit and keep the Country in a sound commercial condition.

All bank reserves should consist of gold and gold alone and adequate gold reserves should be held by the commercial banks of the Country to guarantee the current daily redemption of all bank credit in gold.

All currency created in any way out of bank credit (and there should be no other kind of currency except our subsidiary coin) should spring into being precisely as checks do in connection with the production, transportation, and distribution of commodities and should be redeemed daily precisely as checks are and therefore the currency of a Country should not, indeed can not, in the very nature of things, be created by or be identified with the central or national reserve.

To insure the greatest economy, efficiency and safety in our banking system and secure the greatest possible degree of protection and justice to all, all bank examinations should be made by organizations created by the bank clearing houses themselves and clearing house credit bureaus should be established in the interest of the whole system and for the public good.

To effect the speediest possible redemption of all bank credit the bank clearing houses located at all the natural, important economic centres should be coordinated and unified into one harmonious national system.

Clearing House Bank Examinations

Clearing House bank examinations have proved most efficient and satisfactory. The system should be extended.

Because—

1. They cover *all banks*, both State and National, within a specified district, and therefore, protect all banks included within that district.
2. They are more efficient, because under the inspiration and direction of a Clearing House Committee, and not under the direction of a *political official, State or National.*
3. There are now twenty cities which have Clearing House bank examinations, most of them having been in operation from 12 to 15 years with ever growing approval and satisfaction.
4. If Clearing House examinations are adopted as a uniform principle they would be in substitution of all other forms of examination—National, State, Federal Reserve Board and the twelve Federal Reserve Bank examinations.
5. If adopted and extended to cover the whole United States, the expense to the Banks of the Country (or the cost to commerce) would not be over one-half of what it is today.
6. It would be a matter of very little, if any, additional expense to establish a complete Credit Bureau of all business houses within each Clearing House district.
7. The Clearing House district should be identical with the commercial zone—that is, include all Banks naturally tributary to each economic centre, of which there are about fifty in the United States.

8. Fifty such commercial zones, fifty such credit bureaus, all coordinated and working in harmony, would make it possible for any bank to inform itself of the condition of any business house in the United States within twenty-four hours.

Departmental Banking Established

National Banks can now do all kinds of banking:

(a) Commercial Banking
(b) Savings Banking
(c) Trust Banking
(d) Note issuing

The Powers of State and National Banks are now the same (except note issuing).

Capital and Reserve requirements of all Banks, State and National, should be uniform, under like conditions.

All Banks, both State and National, should be coordinated and unified into one homogeneous and harmonious system.

How Unity, Homogeneity and Harmony of Our Banking System will be Attained

For every conceivable reason every bank in the United States will naturally desire to become a member of such a National System.

But should any bank because of any reason peculiar to itself — such as an unsound condition or bad practices—fail, voluntarily, to become a member of the National Clearing House system, nevertheless, such a bank, if it desires to continue in the banking business, must either become a member of the National Clearing House System or clear through some other bank that is a member. In either event, such a bank will become subject to all the rules and regulations of the National Clearing House System, but without enjoying many of its great advantages; and, therefore, as a matter of self-interest or protection, will soon join the system to avail itself of those great advantages.

From these facts, it becomes perfectly clear and

obvious that there can never arise any conflict between National and State banking laws such as is constantly occurring now; for, either voluntarily or involuntarily, every bank in the United States will become a member of the National Clearing House System.

Geographical Districts Within the Zone

Let there be established seven geographical districts in each commercial zone, each district containing the same number of banks. Let the bankers of each district select representatives to these two bodies of men:

First, the Bankers' Council, to which each district shall elect one banker and one business man, or 14 in all.

The United States Reserve Bank should have a representative upon each Bankers' Council who should be the presiding officer.

Second, the Board of Control, to which each district shall elect one banker, or 7 in all.

To say that such a body of men would literally prevent a bank failure is not going too far, as they could always prevent any bank from getting into a position where it would be necessary to fail. These men could and would control the banks of the commercial zone just as completely as if they were branches of a large bank, and yet, the banks would be independently managed *so long as they were wisely and safely managed.*

A Court of Finance

Subject to the consent and approval of the Senate, the President should appoint a Court of Finance, consisting of seventeen members to administer the affairs of the United States Reserve Bank.

The appointments should be made to serve until the member is 72 years of age; provided however, that the Court of Finance by a vote of at least ten of its members, may extend the service of any member beyond that age.

Six members should come from the Atlantic Coast Region, three of whom should be business men and three bankers.

Six members should come from the Mississippi

Valley Region, three of whom should be business men and three bankers.

Four members should come from the Pacific Coast Region, two of whom should be business men and two bankers.

One should be appointed from at large who shall be the presiding member.

What Our Currency Now Is — Is Just Precisely What It Should Not Be

The currency of our country, outside of our gold coin, (and its substitute, the gold certificates) and all our subsidiary currency, which includes all denominations below five dollars, should not, by every conceivable legislative device, be made to partake of the nature of *essential money* (or gold, which is the only true money we have), and the American people be thereby deceived and led to believe that because a debt—a demand for gold (such as our Federal Reserve Notes are)—is redeemable in gold, it is therefore itself gold or as good as gold, or may be used instead of gold, and consequently is fit to be held as a reserve by our banks.

Reserves and Currency

The reserves of a country and the currency of a country when strictly performing their respective functions are diametrically the opposite of each other—the one is the reserve and the other is the demand against it to be liquidated by payment in it; the one is the redeemer and the other is the redeemed; and nothing whatever should be done to change their relative natures; for, by so doing, you interfere with the perfect performance or fulfillment of their natural functions.

An Irrevocable Truth Established by History

Let it be remembered as an eternal economic truth that every act, every paragraph, every sentence, every word, every syllable that is used to change or convert a true bank credit instrument into paper coin, or make it perform the function of coin, correspondingly and iden-

tically to the same degree, destroys its virtue and usefulness as a credit instrument and makes it to the same degree and directly in the same proportion, the deadly and destructive enemy of the very coin whose nature it is made by statute to approximate or assume.

There is No Possible Escape from a Gold Panic if the Present Situation Continues

According to the circulation statement of the Government on Jan. 1, 1921, there had been issued by the government Federal Reserve Notes and Federal Federal Reserve Bank Notes combined $3,978,000,000.

The States of New York, Massachusetts, Pennsylvania, and probably all the rest of the States, have passed statutes authorizing their State Banks to carry these Federal Reserve Notes as reserve. Certainly this is true, of more than forty of the States. *But you must remember that when these Notes are made lawful reserves they, economically, become Legal Tender, whether they have been made so by National statute or not.*

We are actually in a far weaker, much worse and more dangerous position today than we were in 1893, 1894 and 1895. We are simply living in a fool's paradise; that is all.

The country must not only *liquidate*, but must *deflate* its currency circulation. For every intelligent man must realize that there can be no genuine and permanent deflation so long as the Federal Reserve Notes continue in circulation, with the absolute certainty of *their increasing upon the return of normal times and expanding credits.*

There is no possible escape from a gold panic except to make this overwhelming mass of paper legal tender, and that would be commercial suicide. That would be the end.

It is abject ignorance not to know this, and it is cowardice and treason to the government and to the people not to say it.

The Way Out or Way of Escape

Incorporate and establish under national law

THE UNITED STATES RESERVE BANK

The United States Reserve Bank will hold the central gold reserve, its object is three-fold, as already stated.

First, to keep control or direct the movement of gold to and from the Country through the operations of international commerce.

Second, to meet the extraordinary demands for credit during crop moving periods, and meet times of stress.

Third, to conserve and control credit and keep the Country in a sound commercial condition.

There should always be a real reserve.

The central reserve should consist of about one-half of all the required gold reserves, the balance being held by the Banks for the test of current credit by daily redemption through our fifty Commercial Zone Clearing Houses.

Bank Credit Currency

Gold is the only money, *true or basic money,* we have. All other forms of *so-called* money are only demands for gold. The $346,000,000 of United States Notes, the $723,000,000 of National Bank Notes, the $270,000,000 Standard Silver Dollars and the $3,978, 000,000 Federal Reserve Notes are *all alike*—demands for gold. All are, economically, mere debts—I.O.U.s. They must all be maintained upon a parity with gold by current redemption in gold. And, since they can be used as reserves they are several times, possibly ten times, more burdensome upon the gold fund than a corresponding amount of Bank deposits would be.

Bank Credit Currency is no more burdensome upon the gold fund than a corresponding amount of deposits would be. Indeed it is identical with Bank deposits, being distinguished from bank deposits only by being made current credit as distinguished from order credit.

The only kind of currency we should have in this country is Bank Credit Currency, such as they have had in Scotland for over 200 years; such as they have had in Canada for 100 years; such as the currency of the two United States Banks of 1791 and 1816 was, the principle upon which it was issued being laid down by Alexander Hamilton in these words;

> " *Every loan which a bank makes is, in its first shape, a credit given to the borrower on its books, the amount of which it stands ready to pay, either in its own notes or in gold and silver at his option.*"

This principle was in successful operation with most gratifying results in the States of Indiana, Missouri, Iowa, Ohio, Kentucky, Virginia, Louisiana and under the Suffolk System in the six New England States at the outbreak of the Civil War; but were all destroyed by the 10 per cent tax imposed upon bank note issues for the purpose of making a place for the bond secured National Bank Notes.

Method of Accomplishment

Establish fifty commercial zones, which shall include all Banks, both State and National.

The capital of all banks, both State and National, is now $2,568,000,000 and the surplus and profits are $3,000,000,000. Make such a readjustment of capital, and at the same time establish the principle of uniformity, between capital and other bank liabilities, as to make the capital of all banks amount to $3,000,000,000 in the aggregate, as this amount will be approximately the same as the present amount of Federal Reserve Notes in actual circulation.

Then provide that any Bank, State or National, may issue an amount of Bank Credit Currency equal to 25 per cent of its capital, upon its first having surrendered to the Government a like amount of Federal Reserve Notes; and, provide, at the same time, that thereafter the amount of Federal Reserve Notes outstanding shall not be increased.

Concurrently with this issuance of Bank Credit Currency equal to 25 per cent of the capital of the banks, the Federal Reserve Banks shall return or pay back to all member banks 25 per cent of the capital paid in by them and 25 per cent of the reserves carried by them, and also pay over to The United States Reserve Bank 25 per cent of the profits made by them and then standing on their books to the credit of the profit's account. Thereupon and concurrently the respective member banks shall transfer and pay over to The United States Reserve Bank all the money so paid to them by the Federal Reserve Banks. All other banks shall at the same time pay to The United States Reserve Bank identically the same proportionate amount to be credited to each of said accounts; to wit—the capital account and the reserve account.

At the end of the first, second and third succeeding years permit a corresponding increase of Bank Credit Currency upon identically the same conditions, including the repayment of capital, and reserves and distribution of profits.

The act creating *The United States Reserve Bank* will provide that all the powers now exercised by the Federal Reserve Banks except those covering the organization and note issues shall be extended to *The United States Reserve Bank;* and, further, that, should any conflict arise in the exercise of the powers that have been granted to both the Federal Reserve Banks and The United States Reserve Bank, The United States Reserve Bank shall have the prior right or authority to exercise all such powers to the exclusion of the Federal Reserve Banks; and, it shall be sufficient for The United States Reserve Bank to notify the Federal Reserve Board of its decision to exercise all such powers to the exclusion of the Federal Reserve Banks, to entitle it to such exclusive right or privilege.

At the end of four years we will have substituted Bank Credit Currency for all of the Federal Reserve Notes, and so gradually that the process will have been unobserved, and the effects can only be most salutary, as the Credit Currency will from the very start have been sent to the Clearing Houses for redemption, and thereby the amount in circulation always kept down to the very minimum of necessity—*never being too great, never being too small,* but *always just equal to the actual requirements of trade in strict accordance with the habits of the people.*

An American vs. A Foreign Institution

More than fifty branches of the United States Reserve Bank, one being located at every natural economic centre, would make the facilities for rediscounting far more convenient, and the relations between each individual bank and the United States Reserve Bank would be far more intimate, intelligent, sympathetic and helpful under the organization proposed for the United States Reserve Bank than they ever can possibly be with the twelve Federal Reserve Banks under their strange, complicated and foreign organization.

Federal Reserve Notes Limit to Their Full Amount the Economically Legitimate Rediscounts

Let it be observed and noted that, inasmuch as the total amount of the earning assets of the twelve Federal Reserve Banks have always been equaled, or completely covered by outstanding Federal Reserve Notes, the power or facilities for rediscounting *for economically legitimate purposes* must necessarily be restricted, or limited by exactly the amount of the Federal Reserve Notes outstanding at any given time; for, in a rightly constituted banking system all currency requirements are immediately and directly met with Bank Credit Currency, and not indirectly by the banks rediscounting their paper with some other institution like the Federal Reserve Banks which issue the currency.

The Total Cost of Creating the Federal Reserve Notes is All Wasted

In this age of economy and efficiency, the astonishing, the amazing, the unfortunate and deplorable thing about it is, that every single cent that has been expended in rent, in management, in clerk hire, and in express and postage, in keeping these $3,000,000,000 of Federal Reserve Notes in circulation has been thrown away—it has been literally wasted. Because, if Bank Credit Currency were substituted for the Federal Reserve Notes, note issuing would become a mere matter of bookkeeping by each individual bank. *However, we would indeed be fortunate if this waste were to be our only loss; but the worst is still to come, as already pointed out.*

Increased Bank Capital is a Gain to Commerce

During the year of 1920, the Banks of the United States paid the Federal Reserve Banks seven per cent for the use of more than $3,000,000,000 Federal Reserve Notes; or a total interest charge of $210,000,000. This was a tax upon production, because a burden upon the facilities of trade. It has indentically the same effect upon business as the excess profit tax has.

Amount of Profit to the Banks

If a tax of 2 per cent should be imposed by the Government on the Bank Credit Currency, the profit would be identically the same as upon the same amount of deposits. Let it be remembered that deposits and credit note issues are identical in principle and therefore that each bank would be able to increase its deposits to the amount of its capital.

A Gain to the Government

At the same time, the 2 per cent tax upon the Bank Credit Currency will net the government $60,000,000 annually, or a sum greater by $38,858,182 than the government has received upon the *average* from the Federal Reserve Banks during the past three years.

Therefore the government income will be greatly increased by substituting Bank Credit Currency for the Federal Reserve Notes, to say nothing of the other incomparable advantages.

The total amount received by the United States Government from the Federal Reserve System, since the Federal Reserve Banks were organized, is only $64,562,870.

If an annual tax of 2 per cent. had been paid the Government upon Bank Credit Currency equal in amount to the Federal Reserve Notes outstanding, the Government would have received about $225,000,000.

The United States Government Furnishes a Perfect Model for the Proposed Organization of The United States Reserve Bank

A government usually reflects the genius of its people and the character or wisdom of its laws, and the fidelity with which they are executed constitute the truest index of its stage of civilization.

Under our constitution we have within the borders of forty-eight states independent local self-governments, and the independence of the respective states in all local matters is the best possible guarantee of advancement throughout the whole nation by the sure and ever-safeguarding processes of evolution. And yet, while these forty-eight states are independent within their respective borders, they are all united and bound together for the common interest and the common protection of all in one indissoluble union, and each state is thereby made as strong individually as all are combined, united and bound together under the constitution of the United States.

In perfect harmony with this organic life of the nation, the fifty or more commercial zones will be absolutely independent of each other and yet economically and organically will be united and bound together for their common interest and their common protection in The United States Reserve Bank.

A more perfect counterpart to our national government could not be imagined. Nor can any national institution be in more perfect accord and complete harmony with the genius and spirit of our people. This is the very first principle to be observed in all social, political, and economic legislation, if it is wise.

Experience and Demonstration the Only True Test

There is not a single proposal made in The Commercial Zone Plan that is not in strict accordance with, and in perfect keeping with the laws of banking economics, and that has not been proved and demonstrated over and over again by long experience and under almost every conceivable kind of circumstances or conditions. Every step proposed bears the stamp of approval earned or acquired by trial and is justified by the test of time.

Conclusion

Every intelligent and thoughtful man, who will give this subject the attention and consideration its importance demands, must be convinced that if the principles of banking economics laid down in The Commercial Zone Plan are recognized and followed, and the bank practices therein proposed are adopted and put into execution, *the United States will have the simplest, the soundest, the most efficient and at the same time the most economical banking system in the world.*

To this conclusion I challenge the attention of all my countrymen, everywhere, and of all classes—the farmers, the manufacturers, the transportation interests, and the laboring men in all lines of work. For let it be remembered that the cost of our financial and banking system, which lies at the very foundation of all production, in the last analysis, must always be paid by labor. Therefore, there is no subject or question, excepting only our political liberty, in which every individual citizen of the United States is so deeply interested as the financial and banking system of his country.

A Supplement

IN order that I may illustrate the immutability of those laws of banking economics to which I have called attention, and of demonstrating, with mathematical certainty, how those bank practices referred to have worked wherever tried, I am introducing three charts or diagrams, which to any intelligent and candid mind must preclude the necessity of any further discussion or thought even about what this government should do at the earliest possible moment, if it would escape consequences that are more dire than any that have yet visited us.

First, I wish to call your attention to a chart or diagram prepared by the statistical department of the New York Federal Reserve Bank, and published by that institution in its sixth annual report. This chart covers the combined operations of the twelve Federal Reserve Banks from January 1, 1915, to January 1, 1921, or for a period of six years, and gives (a) their total earning assets, (b) the relation of the notes of the twelve banks outstanding to their total earning assets, and (c) the amount of the deposits of those banks.

Second, I wish to call your attention to a chart or diagram that I had prepared several years ago covering the movement of currency from and to the Canadian banks during the crop moving period for five successive years—from 1902 to 1906 inclusive.

Third, I wish to call your attention to a chart or diagram covering ten years—from 1852 to 1862—of the operations of the Suffolk Banking System, which completely covered all of the New England States, from 1819 to 1865 a period of forty-six years and included upwards of 500 banks with capital varying from a few thousand dollars—several of them less than $25,000—up to $500,000.

Concurrent Opinions of Students

A short time ago, when visiting the statistical department of one of the Federal Reserve Banks, I remarked, "It is my deliberate judgment that the Federal Reserve Act, together with the utter ignorance of the Federal Reserve Board of the laws of banking economics, have cost this government from forty to fifty per cent of its entire war debt, or approximately $20,000,000,000." To my utter amazement the statistician in charge replied, "You are about right."

As a result of that conversation I discovered that four different students of prominence had arrived at exactly the same conclusion, and entirely independent of each other,—a fact of profound significance.

The chart upon the opposite page, which was prepared by the New York Federal Reserve Bank, demonstrates one fact beyond all peradventure of a doubt, and that is, that the notes of the twelve Federal Reserve Banks, with the slightest possible variation have, from the first day of January, 1915, down to January 1, 1921, been always just equal to, and identical with, the total earning assets of the twelve Federal Reserve Banks.

From the establishment of this fact all must conclude that upon the return of normal times, and the coming of a period of expanding credits, the notes of the twelve banks will continue to equal the ever increasing assets of the twelve Federal Reserve Banks; *for it was equally true before the War, through the War, and has been true ever since the War.*

As the earning assets of the Federal Reserve Banks increase from $3,000,000,000, to $4,000,000,000, to $5,000,000,000, to $6,000,000,000, their notes will also increase to $4,000,000,000, to $5,000,000,000, to $6,000,000,000; but, what do you think will happen to the country before these notes reach the $6,000,000,000, mark.

1. Will any one say that the assets of the Federal Reserve Banks will not go on increasing?

Federal reserve notes, earning assets and member bank reserve deposits of all federal reserve banks.

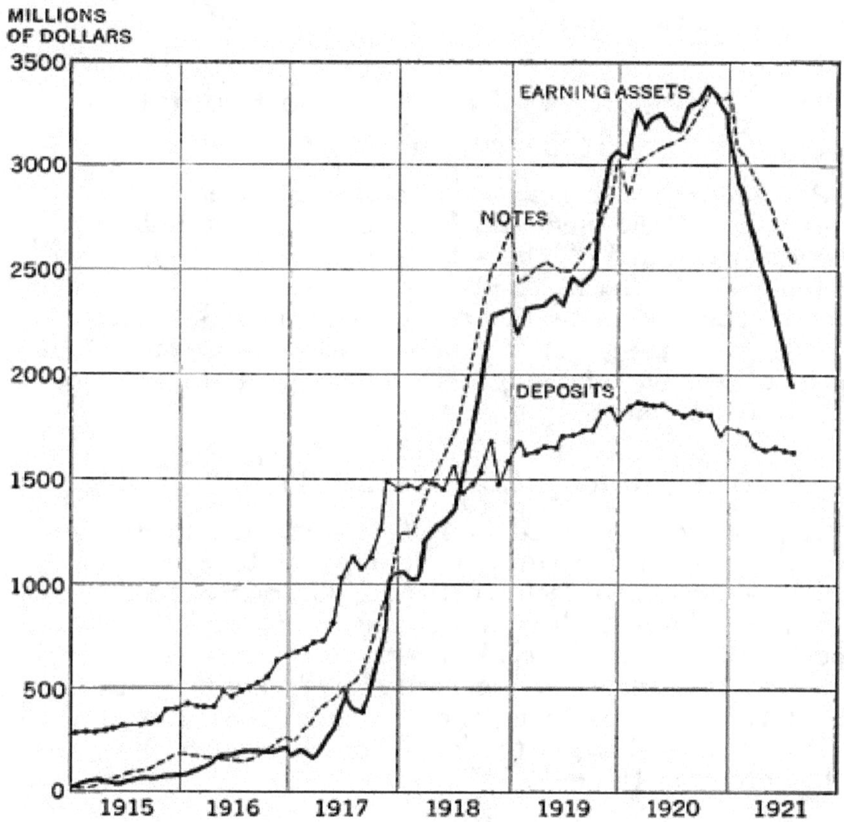

The above diagram or chart was prepared by the statistical department of the federal reserve bank of New York.

2. Will any one say that the notes will not go on increasing, *pari passu?*

3. Can any intelligent person doubt what the result will be?

Let every student of banking economics, yes, let every simple, clear minded, sane man ask himself what he thinks will happen if we continue as we are going, with mathematical certainty, to that fatal goal.

Some Prophetic Opinions of the Federal Reserve Act

An eminent banker, and distinguished citizen, upon the passage of the Federal Reserve Act, in a public interview, remarked, " The act is ninety per cent good, and ten per cent bad." Asked to express my opinion, he having called my attention to what this eminent banker had said, I replied, "It is just the other way round, ninety per cent bad and only ten per cent good, if indeed it is even that much."

A Prophecy that Came True

In a speech delivered in 1901 I pointed out the utter unfitness of the German banking system to our conditions, and then declared that, if Germany should continue as she was then going, she must declare the Imperial Bank Notes, legal tender. It took just ten years—a short time in the life, or affairs of a nation—but in 1911 Germany was compelled to make the notes of the Imperial Bank legal tender. That, of course, was the beginning of the end.

It may not be generally known, but it is a fact, that the system of note issue of the Imperial Bank of Germany was imported and incorporated bodily, almost word for word, in the Federal Reserve Act; and, we are now travelling over identically the same road that Germany was travelling when I made that prophecy in 1901, and, the result must inevitably be identically the same. *Are we ready and willing to take the plunge? That is the question.*

Shortly after the passage of the Federal Reserve Act, I wrote these words,—

First:

" The Federal Reserve Act is the most stupendous economic blunder ever committed in the life of this nation because, while it lays groundwork for practically unlimited expansion of credit, it also sets in motion forces which will ultimately drive gold out of the those country by the gradual substitution of paper credit, in the form of United States Federal Reserve Notes, for gold coin. No better device could possibly have been contrived and constructed to put Gresham's Law into operation."

That paragraph was written seven years ago, and in the light of seven years' experience with the Federal Reserve Act, I would not now change a single word of it even if I could.

Second:

" Willford I. King, a member of the Research Staff of the National Bureau of Economical Research, Inc., 175 Ninth Avenue, New York, in the *American Economic Review* of December, 1920, used this language,— " The Federal Reserve Act was enacted chiefly as a safeguard against panics. Even its ardent supporters hardly contend that it will entirely prevent the periodical readjustment in business known as depressions. They do, however, insist that it renders a money panic practically impossible. But, granting that this contention is correct, it by no means follows that the new system is to be commended. The principal evil of a money panic is that it unjustly transfers much wealth from one person to another.

" It is, however, highly improbable that all the panics in the history of the nation have together caused the unwarranted transfer of more than a small fraction of the 60 billions of dollars' worth of goods, the ownership of which has been arbitrarily shifted by the workings of the Federal Reserve Act and its Amendments.

" The system as established has proved to be merely a new model, producing results very similar to those yielded by its numerous predecessors of the past—the cheap money devices which have so often dominated the financial policies of the nations and always with untoward results." * * * * * * * * * * * * * * * * * *

"While it will be impossible to repair most of the damage already wrought, steps should at least be taken to transform the Federal Reserve system from its present status as a mechanism for inflation into that beneficent regulator of credit which its originators sought to establish, thus preventing in the future an extension or repetition of the policy, which has upset the whole financial structure of the nation, and has changed property rights from reality into phantoms."

A Striking Contrast

Occasionally you hear some one exclaim "But how could we have carried on the war without the Federal Reserve Act?" If as a matter of fact through its perfectly marvelous facilities for unlimited inflation the War actually cost us twice as much as it should, or 20 billions more than it should, we had much better have gotten along, in some way, without it. We would have muddled through somehow." All the other countries did.

The Nature of the Beast Exposed and Revealed

Seven years ago I also wrote this paragraph:

"Second: It is the most gigantic, complete and potential political machine ever constructed. A legislative enactment that makes it possible for the President to subject, dominate or even influence the commercial interests of the country by removing every member of the Federal Reserve Board, at any time, without cause and by empowering the Federal Reserve Board, in turn, to remove at any time without cause [amended afterward to read upon cause stated] all the directors of the twelve Federal Reserve Banks should not be tolerated."

In support of this allegation I will submit only two bits of evidence:

First, a letter written by one of the leading citizens of one of our great States and a man prominent even in the whole United States.

July 12, 1920

"Dear Mr. .. ..

"Your letter of June 29th, commenting on the Federal Reserve Bank management, at hand and noted.

" I was a Director of the .. .. District ( ) Federal Reserve Bank at the start of the system for I think three years. I withdrew from my connection with the bank because the Directors were merely 'rubber stamps' for the administration of affairs by the Federal Reserve Board in Washington, which in its turn was dominated by the administration through the ex-officio members of the Federal Reserve Board as was perfectly obvious. In other words, the Federal Reserve Board in Washington was itself not free-handed to apply sound banking principles to co-ordinate the banking system of the country under the Federal Reserve System along wise lines but it was politically, governmentally administered central bank, the very thing above all things that the Democrats ranted against in attacking the banking plan started by the very distinguished Rhode Island Senator who spent the last years of his life in digesting the banking systems of the leading countries of the world.

" My feeling is that the Federal Reserve Board in Washington should be freed from the 'collar' of the administration and that it should be composed of men of conspicuous banking and business ability. It will be difficult enough for the best of men to keep the Federal Reserve system, which in its essence is good, and which in its essence is the plan of the monetary commission gone wild and run for political ends.

"Very truly yours,

"Signature( )"

Since this letter was written by a man who is obviously a Republican I will now give some evidence from the lips of a Democrat who is one of the leading bankers in the United States.

I submitted all there is in this book preceding the supplement to this Democrat whom I regard as one of the very best economic scholars in the United States as well as the president of one of our largest banks, outside of the cities of New York and Chicago and asked him to give it his best consideration and severest criticism.

After studying and considering it for more than three months, reading and rereading it several times, once, with me, paragraph by paragraph and line by line he said:

" I can not find a flaw in this thing from beginning to end and I would like to find some one who can. I would like to have the judgment or opinion of some good business men who have analytical minds."

I then asked him, whose judgment or opinion he would like to have and he named three men, conspicuous in the business world. But no one of them, upon my solicitation, could, then, find time to consider it.

I then asked this leading banker and Democrat to write me a letter of approval and join me in this great reform. Surprising and appalling as it may seem this was his reply:

" I am president of this bank and we owe the Federal Reserve Bank........................millions and if I should become identified with this movement in a public way *that gang* would ruin this bank. Under the circumstances, you can not expect me to take a hand in it."

Here is one of the leading economic minds (a very rare talent and one greatly needed just now) in this country and standing at the head of one of our great banks literally blackmailed into abject silence through fear of " the most gigantic, complete and potential political machine ever constructed." And, as a consequence the Government of the United States and the American people are alike deprived of this man's great ability and vast experience just at the time when and where they are both most needed. What a deplorable situation this is.

The Fight to Enforce the Par Clearance of Checks a Most Reprehensible Conspiracy

The story of the campaign of the Federal Reserve System to force the banks of the country, in various sections, both national and state, to adopt the par clearance of checks discloses the most shameful and shameless, the most tyrannical and the most brutal as well as morally the most disreputable and damnable acts that have ever been committed in the history of American banking, including all the so-called devilish tricks and wicked practices of Wall Street.

If the reader wants the evidence, the indubitable proof, write either to Hon. Philip P. Campbell, Washington, D. C. for the hearings of the Committee of which he was Chairman upon that investigation. Or, write to "*The National and State Bankers Protective Association*," Atlanta, Ga.

It would seem, from the proof submitted as though the Federal Reserve System was quite as well worthy in its practices as in the principles of its progenitor—*The Imperial Bank of Germany*.

Need anything further be added to unearth and disclose the nature of the beast and the peril of the situation?

Do we really want it in this country?

To illustrate one principle of finance differing widely from that followed in the United States, by a single fact, *but a major fact*; the banks of Canada did not buy a single government obligation when Canada was financing the war, although Canada sold as large an amount of her obligations to her people, per capita, as the United States did.

Bank Credit Currency in Canada

The chart upon the following page illustrates the marvelous facility with which bank credit currency moves from and to the Canadian banks during the crop handling season; how bank book credits are converted into bank note credits to move the crops every fall; and, how these bank note credits are in turn, converted into bank book credits, as the crops are disposed of, the bank credit in its various forms adapting and adjusting itself to the current and ever-changing needs of the people. The amount of currency the people use upon the average, it will be observed, is 33 per cent greater every November than during the average of the year. The notes of the

CANADA.

Diagram exhibiting fluctuations of Canadian bank currency, by months, 1902 to 1906, inclusive, compiled from the monthly returns of the chartered banks of the Dominion of Canada, also indicating increase of United States national bank circulation from circulation statements for first of each month, same period.

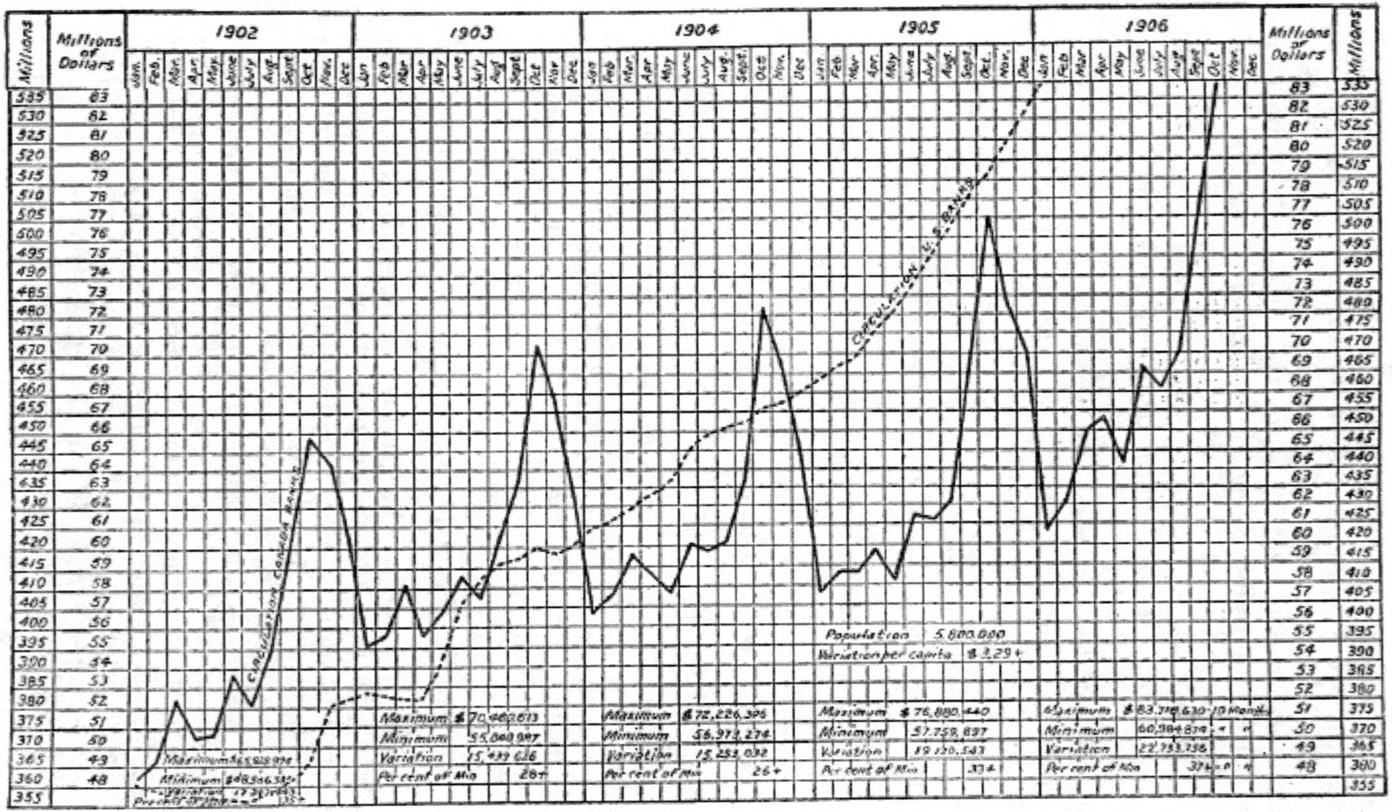

Canadian banks go to the clearing houses to be redeemed precisely as checks and drafts do, and it is by this daily current redemption through the clearing houses that the readjustment takes place, and it could take place in no other way. Otherwise the notes would become a fixed, sodden mass of circulation precisely as the Federal Reserve Notes have.

How did Canada come by this bank credit currency System? A prominent Canadian banker stated in a public address that Canada got it from the United States, following the charter of the Second United States Bank.

Second United States Bank

The charter for the Second United States Bank was granted in 1816, and was practically indentical with the charter of the first United States bank with the single exception that the capital was increased from $10,000,000 to $35,000,000.

It is interesting, and all important, to note that while the charter of the Second United States Bank provided that the bank could issue an amount of bank credit currency, or bank notes, equal to its capital—$35,000,000—the highest amount of bank notes ever outstanding at any one time was $23,076,422 or about 60% of the permissive issue. There were 25 branches literally covering the whole union and James Parton, the historian, says, "Its bank notes were as good as gold in every part of the country. From Maine to Georgia, from Georgia to Astoria, a man could travel and pass these notes at every point without discount. Nay, in Sweden, Paris, Rome, Cairo, Calcutta, St. Petersburg, the notes of the Bank of the United States were worth a fraction more or less than their value at home according to the current rate of exchange." *The reason was that they were currently redeemed in gold.*

In 1823, seven years after the charter of the Second United States Bank was granted, the people of Canada, observing its operation, adopted the same principle, and there it has been in operation for almost 100 years.

The principle laid down by Hamilton is simple, but

fundamental, and absolutely essential to sound, efficient and economic banking operations—*the current redemption of all bank credit in gold. There is no such redemption of the Federal Reserve Notes. The redemption, so called, of the Federal Reserve Notes is precisely and identically the same as that of the National Bank Notes. Economically speaking, there is no redemption of either of them. There is no redemption, payment and liquidation of them as checks and drafts are redeemed, paid and liquidated.*

Hamilton's Law

"*Every loan which a bank makes is, in its first shape, a credit given to the borrower on its books, the amount of which it stands ready to pay, either in its own notes or in gold or silver at his option.*"

Following the Hamiltonian principle through to its logical conclusion, in practice, three distinct facts or truths are to be noted, which involve sound economics and are essential to sound banking.

First, it is the office or function of the government to establish a standard value; to fix a unit of value; to compel the banks which are quasi-public institutions, to furnish the people that form of bank credit that will best serve their purposes, and to compel the banks to keep all bank credit as good as the standard of value by current redemption in that standard of value.

Second, it is the right and privilege of the people, farmers, manufacturers and all producers of wealth, to convert their products, *and their credit, also, whenever they have been granted credit by the banks*, into that form of bank credit which will best serve their purposes in the processes of production, transportation and the distribution of commercial commodities of whatsoever kind—from an ounce of radium to a pound of cotton, a bushel of wheat or a ton of iron, or a physician's fee.

Third, it is the duty of the banks to give to their customers that form of credit that will best serve their purposes—a draft upon a distant point, a book credit subject to check, or a current credit in the form of its own notes (since this is the cheapest, most economical and best form of currency), and to keep all these various forms of credit—the draft, the book credit, and the note credit—as good as our standard of value by their daily current redemption in that standard of value.

A Most Marvelous Development and Most Successful Achievement in the Evolution and Operation of the Hamiltonian Principle Without the Aid or Intervention of any Statute

In the early days of New England banking, the circulation or note issues were established by the State Legislature in the case of each individual bank and varied widely, not only from state to state, but also the different charters in the same state. The note issues generally exceeded the deposits and constituted the major part of the medium of exchange. This has always been true of the Bank of France.

The Suffolk Banking System

In 1819, without any statutory authority for that purpose, the Suffolk Bank was organized at Boston to compel the New England banks to redeem their notes at Boston in gold. The operation of the Suffolk Bank extended and covered all the New England states and was universally acquiesced in over all that territory now included in the First Federal Reserve Bank District, and more.

I hereby assert that the Suffolk Banking System was the most perfect banking system that has ever existed in the world and that it demonstrated more economic truths, that are of practical value to us today, if we will only take advantage of them, than any banking system that has ever existed.

In the light of all the banking experience of the world the Suffolk System lacked only three requisites to make it as perfect as is humanly possible.

First, It lacked uniform supervision over the entire territory covered by its operations.

Second, It lacked a uniform system of currency, such as our national bank notes are. Each New England bank then designed and printed its own notes, and it has been stated, upon good authority, that some of them were printed by the banks themselves in their own offices.

Third, It lacked the establishment of a guarantee fund for the protection of the note holder, although he had almost perfect protection through the daily redemption of the notes through the Suffolk Bank at Boston in *gold*.

Slight Cost of Guarantee Fund

Indeed, the protection of the note holder was so nearly perfect, through this daily redemption of the notes in gold, that from 1840 to 1860, a period of 20 years, a tax of only ⅛ of 1 per cent upon the whole note issue would have been sufficient to pay the notes of the failed banks, *including the panic of 1857*, without any reference whatever to their participation in the distribution of the assets of the banks.
A guarantee fund of 5%, such as Canada has would have lasted 40 years, or covered their losses for 40 years.

Compared with the National Bank Note System

How much better the notes of the 500 banks under the Suffolk Bank System were, *inherently* and without any reference to the Government Bonds deposited to secure their payment, is demonstrated by the fact that commencing with the National Banking System, in 1864, down to 1901—a period of 36 years—it would have taken a tax of *one-fifth* of one per cent each year upon all the National Bank Notes outstanding to pay the notes of the failed banks (omitting, of course, the Government Bonds deposited to secure them); or a Guarantee fund of 5%would have lasted only 25 years, under the National Bank Note System, while under the Suffolk Bank Note System, it would have lasted nearly twice as long or over 40 years.

The Actual Never Exceeded 40 Per Cent of the Permissive Issue

To demonstrate beyond any peradventure of doubt that the bank credit currency of New England, under the Suffolk System, never exceeded the demands of trade, was never too great, was never too small, but always just equal to its requirements, I want to call attention to the following facts:

First, in 1840 the permissive or possible issue was $70,323,000; but the actual issue of notes outstanding was only $16,570,893, or only 23% of the possible issue.

Second, in 1850 the permissive or possible note issue was $75,533,000; but the actual note issue outstanding was only $31,799,031, or only 40% of the possible issue.

Third, in 1860 the permissive or possible note issue was $131,310,000; but the actual note issue outstanding was only $47,539,877, or only 36% of its possible issue.

A Mathematical Demonstration

Here is a mathematical demonstration through the actual operation of a complete banking system,

(a) Including over 500 individual independent banks.

(b) Covering all of the six New England States (considerably more territory than is now covered by the First Federal Reserve Bank District).

(c) *During a period of 46 years, which proves beyond all question of a doubt that Bank Credit Currency contracts just as quickly and just as much or completely as it expands.*

The same fact is illustrated and demonstrated up in Canada every fall, during the crop moving season (see the Canadian Diagram).

In normal times, prior to the War, the Bank Credit Currency of France, which averaged something more than $1,000,000,000, often contracted or expanded more than 10%, or more than $100,000,000, in a single week. Indeed at times, this occurred in a single day.

By a parity of reasoning if the Federal Reserve Notes were directly related to current business, as Bank Credit Currency always is, the contraction as well as expansion of Federal Reserve Notes, at times, ought, *pari passu*, to be 10% or from 300 to 350 million a week; but it will be observed and remembered that the Federal Reserve Notes are always practically equal to and identical with the total amount of the earning assets of the twelve Federal Reserve Banks, a fact that proves conclusively that they are as utterly unfit for the purpose of currency, as the National Bank Notes and the Greenbacks, or United States Notes proved themselves to be; *and a thousand fold more dangerous because of the certainty of a practically unlimited expansion, without any contraction, except through financial disturbances and commercial disasters when the earning assets of the Federal Reserve Banks will necessarily be reduced.*

Should the Federal Reserve Act remain upon the statute books, it must be conclusively clear, therefore, to every student of economics that we shall have far more frequent commercial disturbances, reactions, panics or crises in the future than we ever have had in the past (until the final complete smashup comes) because of the very nature, character, expansibility and permanency of the Federal Reserve Notes.

Of this, there can be no possible doubt. The question then is, are these disturbances, reactions, panics or crises to be desired? Or should we adopt such a financial and banking system as to prevent them so far as humanly possible?

With this mathematical demonstration, this unquestioned, unqualified proof before him, let the reader return to the chart which demonstrates the fact that the Federal Reserve Notes are always just equal to and identical with the assets of the twelve Federal Reserve Banks, a fact that must lead to certain and overwhelming disaster as already pointed out.

Life of Bank Credit Currency

The average life of a bank credit currency is in bold contrast with that of our National Bank Notes or the Federal Reserve Notes.

The note of the Scotch Banking System remains out (short distances, good railroad facilities) 15 days.

The note of the Canadian Banking System remains out (distances are great, railroad facilities fair) 30 days.

The note of the New England Suffolk Banking System remained out (no railroads then) 45 days.

The note of the National Banking System remains out (the best of railroad facilities) 730 days, or more than two years, which is about the time the paper itself lasts, when it must be returned of necessity for renewal.

It will be found upon investigation that the life of the Federal Reserve Note is also the life of the paper upon which it is printed. The frequent redemptions of the Bank Credit Currency reflect its relation to business transactions, while the return of the National Bank Notes, and the Federal Reserve Notes as well, reflect little more than the life of the paper upon which both are printed.

National Bank Notes and Federal Reserve Notes Are Identical

I assert that there is no such thing as an economic redemption either of National Bank Notes, nor of Federal Reserve Notes; but, that they are identical in principle and character—a combination of government and bank credit—and that, *either directly or indirectly*, both are the absolute obligations of the government, plus or with bank credit added. They are both government debts guaranteed by banks.

All the true credit character or nature of both has been, literally and utterly destroyed, and both have been made the deadly enemies of gold. Both are hybrids; both are nondescripts; and, neither of them is fit to find a place, nor will find a place, in a rightly constituted banking system. Both of them in the same way, and to the same degree, are an ever-increasing, practically permanent sodden mass of credit, by which the peril of our financial and banking system, in a broad economic sense, is now growing weaker by the hour; for from several points of view, *we are far weaker today than we have been at any time since the passage of the Federal Reserve Act.*

And, should it remain on the statute book, we must inevitably continue to grow gradually, but certainly, weaker and weaker until the whole structure of our credit system goes down in overwhelming and indescribable disaster.

The Suffolk System Recognized Everywhere

The Suffolk Banking System was known and recognized all over the United States. The bank notes of the New England banks redeemed through the Suffolk Bank, *without any reference whatever to the size of the capital of the bank issuing them, whether $10,000, or $25,000, or $250,000, or $500,000, were at a premium at Buffalo, Chicago, Milwaukee and all other western centres, simply and only because they were redeemed through the Suffolk Bank at Boston in gold.*

Fundamental Principles Do Not Change

Economic principles do not change. They are as immutable as the law of gravitation, and the penalties for their violation will always be exacted by nature as certainly, and as relentlessly as any violation of the law of gravitation.

Permissive or Possible and Actual Issues of Bank Credit Currency

Need any further evidence be adduced to demonstrate the fact that bank credit currency always adjusts itself to the current demands of trade?

The assumption that a system of bank credit currency means only expansion and not a corresponding contraction as in the case with National Bank Notes and Federal Reserve Notes is completely refuted by the operation of the Suffolk Bank System, the annual expansion and contraction of Bank Credit Currency in Canada, and by the following table comparing the permissive and possible with the actual note issues wherever Bank Credit Currency has been in use, or is in use today:

		Permissive Issue	Actual Issue
France (1 bank)	1908	$1,160,000,000	$929,000,000
Canada (25 banks)	"	94,000,000	83,000,000
Scotland (10 banks)	"	148,000,000	40,000,0000
1st U.S.Bank (1 bank)	1811	10,000,000	5,000,000
2ndU.S.Bank (1 bank)	1836	35,000,000	23,000,000
Bank of Indiana (1 bank)	1862	6,600,000	4,900,000
Bank of Iowa (1 bank)	1865	2,096,000	1,400,000
New England Suffolk System (506 banks)	1860	$131,310,000	$47,539,877

From this comparison of the permissible and possible issues of Bank Credit Currency with the actual issues in every instance, every intelligent and fair minded man must conclude that a natural and perfect relation must necessarily exist between a true Bank Credit Currency and the work it is called upon to perform.

Please note that it is wholly immaterial whether Bank Credit Currency is issued by one bank as in France, or ten banks as in Scotland, or twenty-five banks as in Canada, or one bank as in Indiana or Iowa or one bank in the whole United States, or by more than five hundred banks covering all the New England States, the result has always been identically the same; and, always must be identically the same, *because it is issued and redeemed in accordance with a fundamental principle of economic law.*

Why Bank Credit Currency Always Contracts As Well As Expands and Is Always Just Equal to the Demands of Trade.

A Bank Credit Note is a cashier's check. It is the direct obligation of the bank issuing it, without the deposit of government bonds or any other collateral to secure its payment; but like a National Bank Note and also a Canadian Bank Note it should be a first lien upon all the assets of the bank issuing it. Public policy demands this.

A 5% guarantee fund, such as they have in Canada should be established, to meet the *immediate* payment of notes of any failed banks. But, with the organization and supervision herein proposed, it is very doubtful whether a single penny of it would ever be needed, as there never has been a bank failure where clearing house bank examinations were in force.

If a bank had the right to issue Bank Credit Notes to the amount of its capital, it would be interested in sending home the notes of every other bank for redemption and keeping its own notes out or in circulation; for (a) *Upon a 6% rate of interest, after paying a tax of 2% upon its bank notes outstanding, a bank would make 4%.* (b) *By sending the notes of all other banks home a bank would get gold for them or reserve money which would be worth ten times as much to the bank as the notes of the other banks were.*

Business Based on Selfishness

All business is based on selfishness and banking is the very refinement of business. Banking is the quintessence of trade. Whenever profit, or advantage, which is the equivalent to profit, disappears from human effort, business or trade will disappear. Business will die. Human effort will cease, as so strikingly illustrated, so conclusively demonstrated, in Russia at this very moment.

Why Federal Reserve Notes Will Not Contract But Always Expand, Except In Disturbances, Reactions, Panics, or Crises, Which They Themselves Will Inevitably Breed

There is no selfish motive such as there is in the case of checks and drafts, no reason whatever, measured in terms of profit or advantage, why any State Bank (all National Banks are practically, though not theoretically, in identically the same position) should send home for redemption and payment a Federal Reserve Note or a National Bank Note or a United States Note or Greenback. All three of these obligations—mere promises to pay, debts, just I.O.U.'s—are identical in nature and character. All are Government paper, differing only slightly in form. And, it will be found upon an exhaustive examination that all three are treated precisely alike by all banks—treated as reserves. And this is true, notwithstanding the fact that not one of them would find a place, either as a reserve or as currency, in a rightly constituted financial and banking system.

There are $346,000,000 Greenbacks, $730,000,000 National Bank Notes and $3,000,000,000 Federal Reserve Notes or $4,076,000,000 of this *Government Paper Money*; which, under present conditions is bound to constantly increase, when as a matter of economy, wisdom and prudence, Bank Credit Currency should be gradually substituted for every dollar of it.

It is the dual nature or character of this $4,076,000,000 of *Government Paper Money*, this double use of it for both reserves and currency, *when all reserves should be 100% gold and all currency should be 100% bank credit instead of this mongrel mess of 40% gold and 60% government bank credit combined;* that will, sooner or later, lead to the complete collapse of our financial and banking system; and, at a time of seemingly very great, but in fact, false prosperity. We have just had one of these illusive delusions; and are now headed for a still greater one.

Number of Banks in the Suffolk System

In 1857 there were 510 banks. In 1858 there were 499. In 1860 there were 504 banks. The capital ranged from only a few thousands—several having less than 25 thousand—up to 500 thousand.

The Diagram of the Suffolk Bank Note System Analyzed

The diagram upon the following page, covering the operations of the Suffolk Banking System for a period of 10 years demonstrates that in a rightly constituted banking system, bank book credits and bank note credits are identical in principle, *and that the life of each is determined wholly by the function it performs in trade and commerce.*

Let the reader note the movement or increase and

Dep. & Notes issued Even	Dep. & Notes combined Mins.	

Bank book credits and bank note credits are identical in principle, the one being order credit and the other current credit and therefore both should be subject to gold redemption through our Clearing Houses. This diagram shows the operation of the

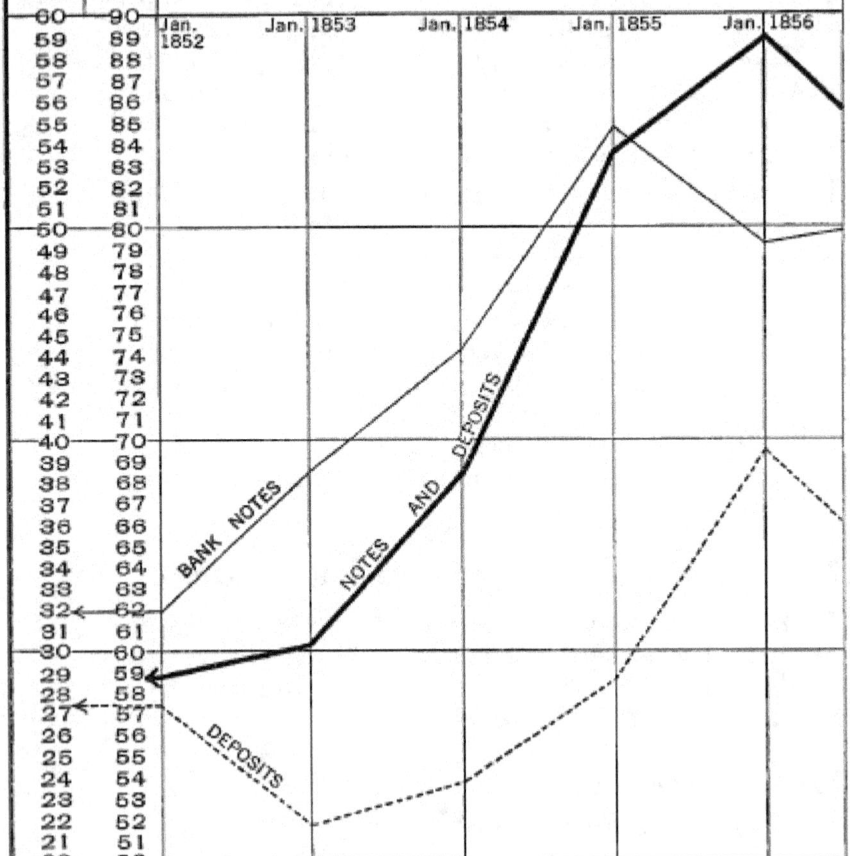

Circulation 31,700,000	38,500,000	44,300,000	54,800,000	49,400,000
Deposits 27,200,000	21,900,000	23,800,000	28,700,000	39,400,000
Total of both 58,900,000	60,400,000	68,100,000	83,500,000	88,800,000

Suffolk System of New England from 1851 to 1861, and demonstrates the perfect interplay of bank book credits and bank note credits, or deposits and bank notes, both having been redeemed daily at the Suffolk Bank in Boston. *in gold.*

Dep. & Notes combined — Even | Dep. & Notes issued — Mins.

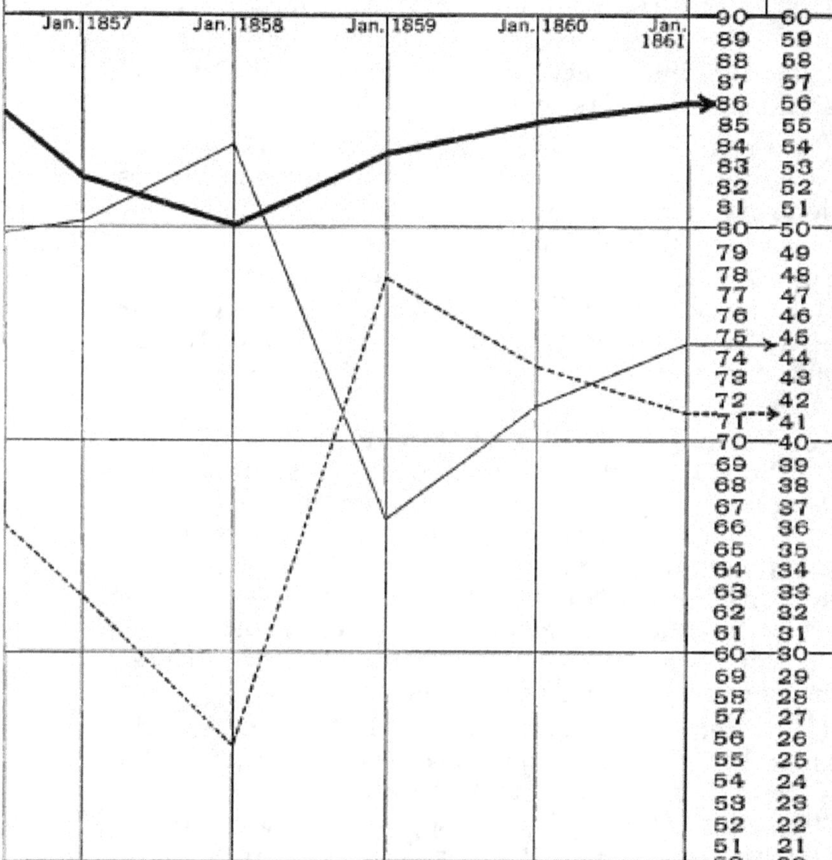

50,000,000	54,900,000	36,200,000	41,700,000	44,700,000
32,200,000	25,100,000	47,600,000	43,300,000	41,200,000
82,200,000	80,000,000	83,800,000	85,000,000	85,900,000

decrease of the deposits and notes during the ten years covered by the diagram upon the preceding page.

(a) At the outset there was a difference between the bank notes and bank deposits of only $4,000,000; the notes amounting, on Jan. 1, 1852, to $32,000,000, and the deposits to $28,000,000.

(b) During the next year, the deposits fell $7,000, 000, while the notes increased $7,000,000, and on Jan.1, 1853, the difference between the amount of the bank notes and the deposits was $18,000,000.

(c) From Jan. 1, 1853 there was a gradual and almost equal increase in both deposits and bank notes; the deposits standing on Jan. 1, 1855, at $28,000000, and the notes at $54,000,000.

(d) During the following year, ending with Jan. 1, 1856, the bank notes fell $5,000,000, or to $49,000,000, while the deposits increased from $28,000,000, to $39, 000,000, and the difference between the two was then only $10,000,000.

(e) From Jan. 1, 1856 to Jan. 1, 1858, the movement of both deposits and notes becomes most interesting, *because this period covered the paralyzing panic of 1857*. The notes constantly increased reaching the highest point they ever attained—$55,000,000, while the deposits fell to $25,000,000, showing that cash was necessary for the liquidation of accounts. Bank book credits were converted into bank note credits to meet the emergency growing out of the panic.

(f) From Jan. 1, 1858 to Jan. 1, 1859, occurred a correspondingly interesting episode of the panic. The notes fell from $55,000,000, to $35,000,000, or $20, 000,000, while the deposits rose from $25,000,000, to $47,000,000, or $22,000,000. Bank note credits to the extent of more than $20,000,000, were converted into bank book credits, showing that when cash had done its part of the liquidation, the bank notes became or took the form of bank deposits.

(g) It will be noted that the bank note and bank deposit lines again crossed each other a second time in the spring of 1860, the amount of each being then the same, or $43,000,000. And finally, that at the end of ten years the bank note credits and bank book credits were relatively exactly where they were ten years before, or only $4,000,000 apart; the notes now standing at $45,000,000 and the deposits at $41,000,000.

(h) The heavy black line which includes both the bank notes and bank deposits combined shows an increase in bank assets of $28,000,000, during the ten years.

Let it be noted and remembered that the currency of a country, outside of that coined out of its standard of value or its representative, such as Gold Certificates, should be subjected daily to redemption in that standard of value. Our standard of value is Gold; therefore the touchstone of all our currency or bank credit is daily redemption in Gold.

There is no such redemption and payment of the Federal Reserve Notes any more than there is of the National Bank Notes, or of the Greenbacks—United States Notes. They are all reserves and are all treated as such. But these, aside from the silver, constitute our currency system.

Neither the United States Notes, nor the National Bank Notes, nor the Federal Reserve Notes are ever returned to their makers unless, either the paper is too rotten or too filthy to be used; or, being in excess of their needs, the bank must get rid of them in some way. What a fine Currency System this is!

Not a Theory But a Complete, Well-Nigh Perfect, Tried and Approved Banking System

Let it be noted and remembered that I am not now discussing a mere theory but a principle proved and justified wherever tried and here more particularly, a complete, nearly perfect, tried and approved Banking System, that covered all of the six New England States, including more territory than the First Federal Reserve Bank District now does, was composed of more than 500 individual, independent banks, and was in successful operation from 1819 to 1865, or for a period of 46

All bank notes will be redeemed by numbers; so that identification will be instantaneous. The zone number will point the way home. The bank number will designate the account to which the note is to be charged.

To secure a perfectly uniform bank note, both in quality and character the United States goverment will provide the bank notes for all banks precisely as it now furnishes all National banks with their bank notes.

years; and, until it was destroyed by the 10% tax imposed on Bank Note issues; and, that it was marvelled at and appreciated all over the United States and was approved and commended without any qualification whatever by the Bank Commissioners of every New England State of that time.

Contemporary Comments of Official Reports on the System

" The currency of this State is of the first order and can not be improved, being equal to gold and silver. This is strong language, we admit, yet perfectly true, for every bill holder can on demand convert his bills into coin." (Connecticut Bank Commissioner's Report, 1841.)

" If there was no check upon circulation there might be some danger, but the frequent redemptions at the Suffolk Bank and the rapid communications between different parts of the country will prevent any greater circulation than the natural business wants of the country will sustain. * * * Indeed, this system of par redemption seems to be a most perfect regulator upon all the New England banks. It would seem somewhat surprising that something has not been adopted in other parts of the country that should produce the same beneficial results." (Connecticut Bank Commissioner's Report, 1848.)

" We believe there is not a more sound and safe currency in existence than that furnished by the banks in this State. We know of no better system of banking than ours." (Connecticut Bank Commissioner's Report 1849.)

" The bills of any country bank, redeemed at par in any commercial city, will always be current throughout the extent of region whose business channels flow to that city. Hence, New England money is worth more in the cities of New York and Philadelphia than the bills of their own country banks. Vermont bills have uniformly borne a premium in the eastern cities without loss, while bills of their own States are at a heavy discount." (Vermont Bank Commission's Report, 1852.)

"The 'Suffolk System,' though not recognized in our banking law, has proved to be the great safeguard to the public. Whatever objections may exist to this 'system' in theory, its practical operation is to keep the circulation of our banks within the bounds of safety. No sound bank can have any well-founded reason for refusing to redeem its bills in Boston, and a bank that is not sound can not long do business under that system and ceases to be in good credit when it is 'thrown out at the Suffolk.'" (Maine Commissioner's Report, December 31, 1857.)

"It is by no means wonderful that a system which has stood the test of time and struck its roots so deep as to have become incorporated with and formed a part of our banking system should be abandoned with hesitation for one which is new and untried." (Maine Bank Commissioner's Report, 1865.)

"The charters of the banks have been renewed. If the laws by which they are constituted the agents of the people to provide a currency, and by which their faithfulness in the discharge of such agency is secured, remained unchanged, there is every reason to believe that the currency of Massachusetts will be for the next twenty years what it has been for the twenty years past—as perfect as any in existence, as perfect as in the nature of things it can be. No reasonable man, no practical man, no man who is not bound hand and foot in the fetters of mere theory, can desire for the people a currency better adapted to meet all the circumstances of a business community than that which has been furnished by the banks of Massachusetts for the last quarter of a century." (James B. Congdon, cashier Merchant's Bank, New Bedford, in memorial to governor of Massachusetts, 1851.)

"The anomalous feature of the case is that the well-secured bond-protected bank issues of New York are at a greater discount at this point than the apparently unsecured circulation of New England, including places hundreds of miles off, and inaccessible, in a measure, for compulsory redemption. * * * * * * * * *

"We said that the Massachusetts currency was

apparently unsecured. In reality their bank paper is well secured. The experience of the last fifteen years has demonstrated that the losses from bank issues in the State of New York are four or five times greater than in Massachusetts. The system of the latter is better than our own." (New York Courier and Enquirer, 1854.)

" The State parts with these objects of her care and solicitude with many regrets, but with a just pride in their career, inspired by the belief that their capital has been highly instrumental in promoting the prosperity of the State, and that they have furnished as good a paper currency, based on individual credit, as any part of the country has ever enjoyed." (Massachusetts Banking Report, 1865.)

Appendix

What Does the Gold Standard of Prices Mean?

It Means the Exchange of Work or the Products of Work for Gold or for Gold Values.

IF, upon the average, a man, by working ten days, produces an ounce of gold the price of which the United States Government has fixed by law at $20.67, (and, therefore must remain invariable) and another man, *of equal skill*, by working ten days, produces an amount of coal which sells for $20.67; then these two men can *exchange their work*, expressed in gold and coal, upon equal terms, or upon the gold price level which has been established by the Government.

But, if the man mining coal, produces, *in five days, or only one-half the time*, coal which sells for $20.67, then the work that produces the ounce of gold and the work that produces the coal can not be exchanged on equal terms, or upon the gold price level which has been established by the government; because the cost of the two commodities expressed in work is not the same; for the man mining the coal is getting twice the wages of the man mining gold, and as a result, the man mining gold is paying twice as much as he should pay *or a double price*, for his coal.

The Gold Standard for Wages and Prices of Merchandise

" If the same profits are made producing all commodities as in producing gold, the value of all commodities in terms of gold (that is, prices) must be related through wages to the gold standard; for it is self-evident that otherwise gold would not be produced in exactly the required amount. This means that the wages of labor producing gold and wages of the same kind of labor producing any other commodity, on an average, must depend relatively on the amount of gold that can be produced by labor in a day. The more gold that can be produced by a day's labor, the more gold or money, labor of this class will receive for a day's work, and the higher the wage scale will be in terms of money. Gold is thus the medium by which the value of a day's work is measured, and after wages are thus set in terms of gold, the prices of commodities produced by labor are automatically controlled by the same standard."

Why All the Commercial Nations of the World Have Chosen the Gold Standard

"Gold is still used as the world's basis of all permanent values because (a) no better substitute has been found; (b) all permanent wealth is now founded upon it and measured by it; (c) it has an intrinsic value in the arts aside from its value as a basis of credits; (d) it does not oxidize and is thus almost permanent; (e) a large value can be represented in a small weight and bulk; (f) it is widely scattered and no one country has an abnormal advantage in its cheap production; (g) it is not susceptible of quick over production."

Prices and Gold for One Hundred Years

The graph upon the opposite page should be studied carefully, because the variations from the price level of 100 are, except as a result of the Civil War, from 1861-1879 and the World War, from 1915 to date have been comparatively slight; and it can be reasonably inferred, that, if we had had a central bank, like the United States Reserve Bank, under the control of an intelligent body of independent men, much of the speculation of 1837 and 1857 and the consequent misfortunes, as well as the trouble of 1893 would certainly have been greatly modified, if indeed, not entirely eliminated.

To control expansion and to prevent inflation is the peculiar function of the economic rate of interest.

Our price of gold is fixed at $20.67+ per ounce. Our unit of value – the gold dollar – is fixed at 25.8 grains of gold .9 fine. Allowing for those variations in individual cases growing out of the law of demand and supply, all commercial commodities should become interchangeable or interconvertible with gold at the average gold price level of the last one hundred years, if we hope to compete successfully in the markets of the world and hope to lay the foundation of a sound and continuing prosperity. Every intelligent and patriotic citizen of every walk of life – laborer as well as capitalist – will strive for this and do his part. When this gold price level is approximated, the gold production of the world will again reach the $480,000,000.00 mark of 1915; but not until then. In 1920 the gold production amounted to only $350,000,000.00; because, while the price of gold was fixed, the price of labor was not upon the same level but was much inflated, and therefore many gold mines could not be worked except at a loss.

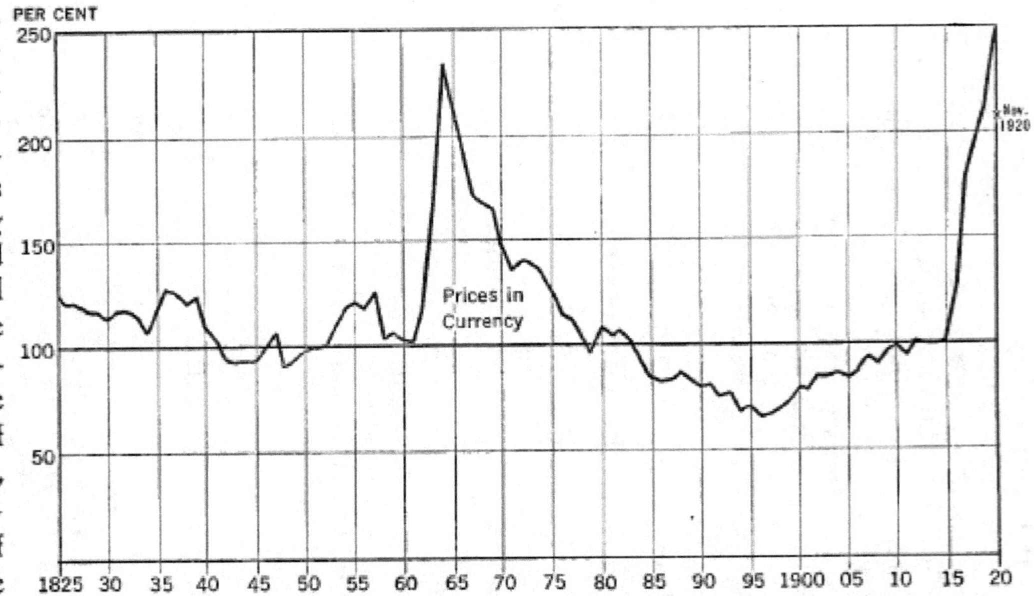

Average Wholesale Commodity Prices in the United States each Year from 1825 to 1920 in Percentages of the Figures for 1913

Present Prices and Wages Compared

The following data were furnished by the Bureau of Labor Statistics of the United States Department of Labor, Washington, D. C.

The combined retail prices of : sirloin steak; round steak; rib roast; chuck roast; plate beef; pork chops; bacon; ham; lard; hens; butter; cheese; eggs; milk; bread; flour; cornmeal; rice; potatoes; sugar; coffee; tea; rose from the price level of 100 in 1913 to 203 in September, 1920, or 103%.

In August, 1921, these combined retail prices had fallen to 155 or a total of 48 points, leaving a reduction of 55 per cent, based on the price level of 1913, to be made when all these commodities will again be upon the gold price level of 1913, which is the gold price level of the last one hundred years.

In other words, the total inflation of 103% will then have been eliminated.

The combined wholesale prices of; farm products; food, etc.; cloths and clothing; fuel and lighting; metals and metal products; building materials; chemicals and drugs; house furnishing goods; miscellaneous, rose from the price level of 100 in 1913 to 272 in May, 1920, or 172%.

In August, 1921, these combined wholesale prices had fallen to 152, or a total of 120 points, leaving a reduction of only 52 per cent based on the price level of 1913, to be made when all these commodities will again be upon the gold price level of 1913, which remember is the gold price level of the last one hundred years.

In other words, the total inflation of 172%, will then have been eliminated.

The wholesale prices of all the following commodities except anthracite coal alone have been greatly reduced; coal, bituminous; iron ore; steel billets; structural steel; copper ingots and wire; tin, pig and plate; lead; cement; brick; lumber; cotton; print cloth; wool; silk; cattle; beef, mess; hogs; pork, salt mess;

sheep; lambs; wheat; flour; corn; oats; coffee; tea; butter.

Fifteen or just one half of all these staple commodities are now at or below the price level of 1913.

Professor George F. Warren of the Department of Agriculture, formerly of the faculty of the New York College of Agriculture, in a recent study of prices published by the Department, makes the following statement relative to conditions touching the great body of our farming population:

"Compared with a five-year average before the war as 100, the purchasing power of some farm products at prices paid to farmers in June, 1921, were as follows: corn, 61; oats, 60; barley, 53; wheat, 93; rye, 101; buckwheat, 101; flaxseed, 55; beans, 81; corn, 56; cotton, 51; cotton seed, 52; hay, 68; cabbage, 111; onions, 73; potatoes, 64; sweet potatoes, 89; peanuts, 48; apples, 91; chickens,116; eggs, 77; butter,83; milch cows, 80; beef cattle, 69; veal calves, 73; sheep, 66; lambs, 79; wool, 58; hogs, 67; horses, 45.

"Practically nothing the farmer sells can be exchanged for the usual quantity of other things. It is physically impossible for farmers to absorb the products of factories. Farm prices have dropped much more than wholesale or retail prices of farm products."

Wages

In the face of all these impressive facts the attention is called to the following wage statistics as a quite full explanation of the reason why practically all of the wholesale and retail prices, more particularly, are not now upon the same price level of 1913. This does not include, of course, farm labor, because that has been practically liquidated or deflated as evidenced by the very important fact that nearly all farm products are already down to the price level of 1913, and would be completely so, *but for the war wage cost in transportation.* Certainly no one will claim that farm work is an easy job. Indeed, it will be admitted by any one who knows that it is one of the most toilsome of all kinds of work. Then why this present great inequality of compensation or wages?

Wages of Railroad Employees

In 1915 the section men on the railroads received 15 cents per hour. In the third quarter of 1920 they received 48 cents per hour. On May 1, 1921, they received 37 cents per hour.

In 1915 the passenger engineers received 82 cents per hour. In the fourth quarter of 1920 they received $1.34 per hour. On May 1, 1921, they received $1.24 per hour.

Average Union Rate of Wages Per Hour in the United States as of May Each Year

Bricklayers received in May, 1913, 69 cents per hour. In May, 1920, $1.20 per hour. In May, 1921, $1.19 per hour.

Carpenters received in May, 1913, 53 cents per hour. In May, 1920, $1.03 per hour. In May, 1921, $1.05 per hour.

Painters received in May, 1913, 50 cents per hour. In May, 1920, $1.04 per hour. In May, 1921, $1.09 per hour.

Plumbers received in May, 1913, 62 cents per hour. In May, 1920, $1.06 per hour. In May, 1921, $1.12 per hour.

Building laborers received in May, 1913, 23 cents per hour. In May, 1920, 75 cents per hour. In May, 1921, 75 cents per hour.

Anthracite Coal

The anthracite coal mine employees received in April, 1912, 42 cents per hour. In April, 1920, he received 99 cents per hour (no later data).

Anthracite coal laborers received in April, 1912, 23 cents per hour. In April, 1920, they received 60 cents per hour (no later data).

Anthracite coal, chestnut, per ton, at tidewater New York in 1913, was $5.31. In March, 1921, it cost $10.64. In August 1921, it cost $10.54.

The wages of the section men are two and one half times as high as they were in 1915. The wages of the passenger engineers are more than 50% higher than they were in 1915.

The wages of the bricklayers, carpenters, painters, plumbers, and building laborers are today just as high or higher than they have been at any time since we entered the war.

The anthracite coal miners are getting higher wages today than upon any prior wage scale. With the result that with the increased wage cost in transportation the anthracite coal now costs in New York at tidewater $10.54 as against $5.31 in 1913.

Is it fair that the millions of homes of fellow workers in the manufacturing industries should be warmed by coal costing war prices, while practically all of these workers are receiving greatly reduced wages? Indeed, many of them are receiving wages as low as they received in 1913 when they bought their coal for $5.31 per ton.

This difference is due, first, to war wages paid for mining, and second to war wages paid for transportation. Is there any justice or equity in this frightful inequality of compensation of wages of today as compared with those of 1913?

Cost of Building Determines Rent

Under these circumstances, is there any justice in the brick and cement manufacturers, the lumber dealers, the bricklayers, carpenters, painters and plumbers doubling the cost of houses and thereby necessarily doubling the rent of all their co-workers in America in all lines of agricultural and manufacturing industry?

These artisans of the building trades seem to think that their wages come out of capital, and that the capitalist is the sufferer. But capital demands a certain per cent of income to protect or maintain itself, whether loaned by our Building Loan Associations, our savings banks or our life insurance companies, all of which are mutual institutions; and, therefore, owned by the people. It is self-evident, therefore, that if a house costs $10,000 when it should of cost only $5,000 the rent will be doubled. The rent is paid by some co-worker almost universally. Of course, you can not have low rent unless you have low cost of house room.

I submit that these conditions should be equalized and that all should unite to bring about universal prosperity by an equalization of wages. As it is, one class of our laborers is greatly wronging all other classes of our laborers, not for a year but so long as the houses built at double cost stand; for the rent will run with the life of the houses unless this great inequality should be rectified. It can be rectified on the gold price level of the last one hundred years—the price level of 1913—and it can be rectified in no other way.

The Rent Payers' Fight

All rent payers everywhere are vitally interested in bringing rents down to the same level of all other commodities. And, if they are sensible and can possibly do so, they will not engage in any building operations until this level is reached; and this can only be done when the wages of those building houses are brought down approximately to the 1913 wage level, or the level of the gold standard of the last one hundred years.

If all classes everywhere should unite to achieve this all-important, this vital result, there would be no question about their getting reasonable rent rates *for no one class of American workers can make war upon all other classes of American workers and succeed in the long run.*

The time has come for a show down and a demand for equal justice so far as humanly possible between all classes of American workers. Now is the time and here is the place to apply the American principles of fair play and equal justice to all.

Business Abhors Uncertainty

Again, and every working man in the United States is vitally interested in this, all business abhors uncertainty and the sooner we get down squarely and fully upon the solid foundation of our standard of value, the sooner all commercial commodities will become interconvertible with gold and the sooner will a sound, continuing and permanent prosperity be ours to enjoy and all the people become equal participants in its great benefits.

Foreign Trade Essential to Our Prosperity

The wages paid throughout the country today to our industrial mechanics and workers in the manufacturing industries as well as those paid in our agricultural pursuits must be such as to make it possible to send American products into the markets of the world and successfully compete with other nations, if we hope for prosperity in this country. *Because a market for our excess production of both the farm and the factory is absolutely essential to our national prosperity.*

But the present wage cost of transportation will, whenever international competition is involved, destroy utterly all hope of any foreign trade which is, as just stated, absolutely essential to our national prosperity.

The question to be settled is, therefore: should the whole nation, more than one hundred millions of people, be made to suffer very greatly and indefinitely, possibly even overwhelming disaster, to the end that only one per cent or even two per cent of the people may receive the inordinate wages of war times and therefore *by comparison* get most inequitable compensation for the services they render? That is the question.

Duty of the United States Government—All State Governments—All Counties and All Municipalities

In the name and interest of justice, it is perfectly obvious that neither the United States Government, nor any State Government, nor any municipality should engage, at this time, in any undertaking of a public character which is to be paid for out of taxes wrung from the people for the purpose of relieving the unemployment situation, except upon the price level of 1913, which has already been reached by a very great part of our American producers—*the gold price level of the last one hundred years.*

Co-Operation is Patriotism

Primarily labor produces all wealth and, on the average, labor cost constitutes 95% of all our commercial commodities; therefore, generally speaking, wages must go down before prices can fall. But, in the complicated, intimately interrelated life of today, ready responsive and hearty co-operation on the part, both of price-makers and wage earners, is essential to a just relationship, the banishment of unemployment, the return of a sound and enduring prosperity and is, therefore, the highest, the finest and the most genuine expression of patriotism—a love of country through a love of countrymen.

Definition of Wealth and How Now Established

"Wealth has been described as 'canned' labor. The value of wealth is indicated by amounts of that 'canned' labor. All wealth, like gold in the bank, or the cost of the bank building, represents a certain amount of labor equivalent, translated in terms of the gold standard of measurement. Now that this wealth, made by labor, is translated in terms of gold produced by labor, it certainly is not fair or possible to give up the gold standard measure of that 'canned' labor, and use another standard which would represent a different amount of labor. Because we have just now gotten part of our always fluctuating values under an unusual strain of conditions, entirely out of this proper relation, by an artificial use of credits *instead of gold*, we are not in any way justified in changing the fundamental measure of our permanent values. This is unthinkable. Nor could we change from the gold standard unless all the world changed at the same time. Royalties on mines and lands, rent on properties, ninety-nine year leases, bonds and preferred stocks, insurance, bank deposits, notes and even the debt that Europe owes us, all amounting to tens of billions of dollars, are fixed on the gold standard, and any abandonment of it in order to save temporary wages and prices from reaching their true natural level, would be an inconceivable act of injustice and would destroy the confidence of the work in fairness of man and in the stability of values."

The Gold Standard and Our Banking System

The United States Government, having fixed, by law, the price of an ounce of gold at $20.67 and having declared that 25.8 grains of gold .9 fine shall constitute a dollar and be our unit of value, it follows, necessarily, that all credit—bank credit, commercial credit, and long time loans—should be based upon the gold standard.

Purposes of Our Banking System

The purposes of our banking system should be:

(a) To keep all credits within the limits or sphere of gold values.

(b) To give the greatest possible mobility and the highest degree of facility to all forms of bank credit that will aid in the exchange of commodities upon a gold basis, by expanding credits wherever necessary and by converting bank-book credits into bank notes and order credit into current credit; *providing always that all forms of bank credit are kept interchangeable or interconvertible with gold.*

(c) The effect of achieving these two objects will be to bring both wages and prices into a consistent, just, and harmonious relation with the gold standard; and, therefore, except in a few extreme instances, to bring wages and prices into a consistent, just and harmonious relation with each other.

Expansion and Inflation

In banking economics there is a fundamental, a profound difference between expansion and inflation.

Expansion is the extension of something within itself; and in banking economics, since gold is our standard of value, it is the extension of the use of gold by basing credit upon it—a sound principle so long as the credit so based maintains the same value as the gold.

Inflation is "*to swell or distend with air or gas;*" and, in banking economics, it is to base one credit upon another credit—an unsound principle because it starts with wind and ends in a whirlwind—a wind storm—a hurricane of destruction.

An Illustration of Inflation

Today, if a State bank takes a certain amount of

its customers' paper to its correspondent bank, which is a member of the Federal Reserve Bank, it can get $100,000 of Federal Reserve notes, which, in accordance with the laws of the State where located, it can put into its reserves and proceed to loan at the ratio of ten to one, or a million dollars, based upon these Federal Reserve Notes as a reserve—only 40% of which represents gold, while the other 60% represents credit—inflated credit.

Having finished this exploit, the same bank can then take some of this newly acquired customers' paper, based on these Federal Reserve Notes, and get another $100,000 of like reserves in the form of Federal Reserve Notes and so on, ad infinitum.

This is just precisely what has been going on for the past seven years—credit upon credit—wind upon wind—the wildest kind of inflation.

Federal Reserve Banks Are Doing the Same Thing

Now, let the reader observe and note that there is no difference whatever in principle, only in degree, between what the State banks are doing and what the Federal Reserve banks are doing when they absorb all the required reserves of the member banks and then in turn use them up to complete exhaustion by accepting deposits or issuing Federal Reserve Notes against them to the maximum limit.

This is inflation. True, it is subtle inflation, but the more serious and more dangerous because so subtle. Have we ever had any pyramiding of credit in this country that would compare with this for dilution, especially when you consider the slender reserve requirements of the member banks?

Now, note and remember that these Federal Reserve Notes, based upon reserves twice exhausted, twice used to the maximum limit, are the self same Federal Reserve Notes that the State banks are authorized by practically every state in the union to use as reserves.

The Federal Reserve Act was designed by its

authors to pyramid credits; indeed that was its chief aim. But they built far better than they knew; for we have discovered that the sky is the limit of inflation under the act.

We have just had a full feast of this inflation carried to the nth power, and the fit of indigestion is still with us in the form of frozen credits, every dollar of which must be thawed out, and, in the last analysis, must be paid in gold or repudiated through bankruptcy proceedings and therefore lost by the creditors, which is economically the same thing.

Banking Economics

Banking economics is a science, and a highly specialized one, and nowhere in the realm of business is the expert so essential to wise action and successful operation.

We do not ask great surgeons to build bridges across the North River; nor great engineers to amputate the arms and legs of victims of serious accidents; nor do we ask in the blacksmith to administer to our children when they are stricken with typhoid. Experts are demanded everywhere today in critical cases. Certainly no one will deny that the economic situation in the United States is a critical one and therefore in need of expert guidance.

Read the opinions of only two—one English and one American—of the many recognized economists who have condemned the Federal Reserve Act.

Sir E. Mackey Edgar a leading English economist under the topic " The American Halt," wrote as follows in Sperling's Journal, August, 1921:

Defects of the Banking System

" There is no country today anything like so wealthy as the United States, and also there is none in which capital has been so effectively gagged and handcuffed by a stupid fiscal system. It has ceased to circulate and to function with anything like the freedom that the situation demands. It is manacled and tied down. The new banking system has turned out to be neither a preventive nor a remedy for the state of useless immobility in which capital has been immured. It worked well enough in the early days of the war, when everything was going America's way, and before its defects were apparent through the haze of prosperity."

Willford I. King, a member of the Research Staff of the National Bureau of Economical Research, says:

"The system as established has proved to be merely a new model, producing results very similar to those yielded by its numerous predecessors of the past—the cheap money devices which have so often dominated the financial policies of the nations and always with untoward results."

Our Financial System and Our Banking System Should be the Counterparts of Each Other

Our financial system is based upon the gold standard.

Our banking system should tie all of our production and all the factors of transportation, trade and commerce, expressed in wages and prices, to the gold standard, and keep them there, if we hope to escape the injustice and suffering that invariably follow in the wake of periods of inflation and the corresponding periods of deflation.

We do not want a banking system so organized that its very structure and practices develop and induce inflation and breed speculation through which incalculable injustice and suffering are brought upon the people.

The United States Reserve Bank

The United States Reserve Bank is organized to provide the fullest possible expansion of credit consistent with sound business conditions, and at the same time keep all bank credit liquid by subjecting it to daily redemption in gold.

The United States Reserve Bank organization stands for the highest degree of efficiency, the greatest possible economy, and the most certain and the most enduring business conditions possible because of its principle of credit expansion and its mobility of bank credit, and its facility in the adaptation of bank credit to the needs of trade and commerce—always subject, however, to current redemption in gold.

The Federal Reserve Banks

The Federal Reserve banking system, contrary to the intention of its framers, is organized for practically unlimited inflation as already pointed out. As the inflation proceeds, there is transferred unjustly, millions and probably billions of property or property rights from one class of our citizens to another; and, after the disturbance comes, as it must, the destruction of paper values sets in and when depression settles down upon the country, through the deflation that must follow, millions, yes, probably billions, of property or property rights unjustly, and to all intents and purposes forcibly are transferred from one class of our people to another —usually, if not invariably, from weaker to stronger hands.

Mr. King asserts that at least sixty billions have been so unjustly transferred as a result of the operations of the Federal Reserve Banks.

The Federal Reserve Banking System, by comparison with the United States Reserve Banking System, is astoundingly inefficient; wastefully extravagant; and, as has already been demonstrated, fundamentally unsound.

Conditions of American Banking under the United States Reserve Bank Compared with the Present Conditions Under the Federal Reserve Act.

Organization and Administration of American Banking Under the United States Reserve Bank

(a) One Central Reserve Bank and approximately fifty branches.

(b) A court of Finance to administer the affairs of

The United States Reserve Bank, consisting of seventeen members who shall be fairly representative of all sections of the United States.

They shall be appointed by the President for life, subject to the approval of the United States Senate.

(c) At each natural, important, economic commercial center, there shall be organized a Clearing House covering all the territory naturally tributary to that center for the clearance of all bank credit—checks, drafts and bank notes—and the establishment also of a Credit Bureau covering identically the same territory.

This Clearing House organization shall constitute and be a branch of *The United States Reserve Bank*, and the territory covered by this Clearing House shall be known as a " Commercial Zone."

(d) There shall be in each Commercial Zone a *Bankers Council* consisting of fifteen members, whose duty will be to manage the branch bank of that Zone. There will also be a Board of Control consisting of seven members whose duty will be to examine and supervise all the banks in that Commercial Zone subject, however, to the Bankers Council.

The members of the " Bankers Council " and the Board of Control will be selected as follows: Each Commercial Zone will be divided into seven geographical districts, each district consisting as nearly as possible of identically the same number of banks.

The banks of each district will appoint one business man and one banker upon the Bankers Council, making fourteen, and *The United States Reserve Bank* shall appoint a representative upon each Bankers Council, making fifteen in all.

The banks of each district shall appoint a representative upon the Board of Control, making seven in all.

Sound in principle and practice, and natural, simple and direct, yet complete, indeed practically perfect so far as human experience points the way, *The United States Reserve Bank* with its fifty branches provides the most intelligent, convenient and best possible machinery for rediscounting, while the Clearing

House examinations will be the most efficient and most economical supervision of American banking that can possibly be devised.

This constitutes the entire system. It stands for simplicity, efficiency, economy, the stability of credit and therefore sound business conditions.

Organization and Administration of American Banking Under the Federal Reserve Act

(a) Twelve central Reserve Banks, each with power to establish branches.

(b) The Federal Reserve Board—a politically controlled umbilical cord—connecting the twelve central Reserve Banks and subjecting them to the political ambitions and purposes of the party in power.

(c) A system of National Bank examinations covering the whole Unites States.

(d) A system of State Bank examinations covering the whole United States.

(e) A system of Federal Reserve Bank examinations covering the whole United States.

(f) A system of Federal Reserve Board examinations covering the whole United States and all the rest of the world.

(g) A system of Clearing House Bank examinations in upwards of twenty cities.

(h) Under the name of " Federal Reserve Notes " a practically unlimited issue of Government paper money of predetermined reserve value of only forty cents on the dollar which nearly every state in the Union has declared by statute to be a lawful reserve for all their state banks.

Basing one credit on another credit is a certain and the most prolific and most dangerous source of inflation, and yet, during the year 1920, approximately $50,000,000 was wasted, yes, literally thrown away by the Federal Reserve Banks in keeping over $3,000,000,000 of this false reserve—these I. O. U.'s, these debts, these demands for gold—in circulation.

(i) The situation is such a conglomerate one and has

been so complicated by the Federal Reserve Act that it can not be unravelled and perfected by evolutionary processes; because the act is fundamentally unsound, both in principle and practice, and therefore the situation must be righted by substitution and succession.

(j) While many of the changes introduced by the Federal Reserve Act suggested things wholly right in themselves as a matter of principle or practice, nevertheless they have been *invariably* applied either only in part or altogether wrongly applied; so that, it may be asserted, without any fear whatever of successful contradiction, that there is not a single important feature of the Federal Reserve Act that can be declared to be wholly, unreservedly and unqualifiedly right either from the standpoint of principle or practice.

(k) The double, possibly triple, cost of bank examinations under present conditions in no way protects either State banks or National banks against duplicate borrowing, from which much if not most business troubles arise; and therefore necessitates the organization of a staff of credit investigators by every large bank or the employment, at great expense, of firms of accountants, all of which could be obviated by a properly organized system of Credit Bureaus covering the whole United States which would be at the service of all banks both State and National.

This constitutes the present condition under the Federal Reserve Act. The situation is almost unfathomably complicated; but obviously, most inefficient, most expensive, and the Federal Reserve Act is an ever existing peril to the stability of credit, and therefore the very foundation of business conditions is always threatened.

INDEX

A

B

C

D

E

F

G

G

S

T

U

W

Z

Bitcoin Blockchain Inspirations

MIT - Cryptography and everything related to bitcoin and the blockchain

Eric Young - Bitcoin Digital wallet

Satoshi Nakamoto - Bitcoin blockchain creator

Nick Szabo - E Gold

Naval Ravikant – Very knowledgeable in the crypto currency space

J.R. Willett – Founder of the ICO's

Don & Alex Tapscott CEO The Tapscott Group Authors blockchain revolution

Tim Lea - CEO Veredictum.io - Author Down the rabbit hole

Matt Elton - CEO at Finnolux

Ivan J - Sunshine Coast Innovation Center D Health

Bill Field – V2Pay

Perianne Boring - Founder and President of the Chamber of Digital Commerce.

Blyth Masters – Digital Asset Holdings (yet to meet her she seems pretty cool in her YouTube videos)

James Rickards – The Road to Ruin

Juan Carlos – Bankcoin Global

Carlos Slim – Mobile phones for the people

There are so many incredible people in this blockchain space if you believe you can play a part in what we are doing reach out to us we are open to all send to me directly support@bankcoinreserve.com

www.ingramcontent.com/pod-product-compliance
Lightning Source LLC
LaVergne TN
LVHW052301200926
848481LV00002B/434

* 9 7 8 0 6 4 8 1 7 3 7 0 0 *